MAXIMUM BRAINPOWER

**PREVENTION'S LIBRARY
OF MEDICAL CARE AND NATURAL HEALING**™

MAXIMUM BRAINPOWER

by the Editors of Prevention®
Magazine Health Books

Rodale Press, Emmaus, Pennsylvania

If you have any questions or comments concerning this book, please write:

> Rodale Press
> Book Reader Service
> 33 East Minor Street
> Emmaus, PA 18098

Library of Congress Cataloging-in-Publication Data

Maximum brainpower / by the editors of Prevention magazine health books.

p.   cm. — (Prevention's library of medical care and natural healing)
Bibliography: p.
Includes index.
ISBN 0-87857-833-1   hardcover
1. Brain.   2. Neurophysiology.   3. Mental health.
4. Intellect.   I. Prevention (Emmaus, Pa.)   II. Series.
QP376.M44   1989
612.8'2—dc20   89-10090
                                                         CIP

2   4   6   8   10   9   7   5   3   1   hardcover

NOTICE

This book is intended as a reference volume only, not as a medical manual or a guide to self-treatment. If you suspect that you have a medical problem, we urge you to seek competent medical help. Keep in mind that nutritional and health needs vary from person to person, depending on age, sex, health status, and total diet. The information here is intended to help you make informed decisions about your health, not as a substitute for any treatment that may have been prescribed by your doctor.

PREVENTION'S LIBRARY OF MEDICAL CARE AND NATURAL HEALING™

Editor in Chief: William Gottlieb
Group Vice President, Health: Mark Bricklin
Series Editor: Carol Keough
***Maximum Brainpower* Editor:** John Feltman

Writing Contributions

Don Barone
    Artificial Intelligence; Decision Making; Exercise and Your Brain; Genius; Intelligence; Left Brain, Right Brain; The Neurologist

Lance Jacobs
    Concentration, Creativity, How Your Brain Works

William LeGro
    Diseases of the Brain, Gender and Your Brain, Your Senses and Your Brain

Judith Lin
    Aging and Your Brain, Alertness, A Course in Power Thinking, Endorphins, Hypnosis, Psychic Powers, Sleep

Claudia Allen Lowe
    Memory

Ellen Michaud
    Imagination, Learning, Meditation, Nutrition and Your Brain

Don Wade
    Intuition, Music, Neurotransmitters, Personality

Russell Wild
    The Animal Brain, The Healing Brain, Medications and Your Brain, Reasoning, Wisdom

Research Editor: Holly Clemson
Research Chief: Ann Gossy
Research Associates: Christine Dreisbach,
Staci Hadeed, Dawn Horvath, Karen Lombardi

Editorial/Production Coordinator: Jane Sherman

Copy Editor: Lisa D. Andruscavage

Series Art Director: Jane C. Knutila
Designers: Julie Burris, Lisa Gatti, Debbi Sfetsios
Illustrators: Jean-François Allaux, Karen Barbour,
Laura Cornell, Mellisa Edmonds, Leslie Flis,
Carol Gillot, Narda Lebo, George Masi,
Susan Rosenberger, Kurt Vargö, Wallop

Director of Photography: T. L. Gettings
Photo Editor: Margaret Skrovanek
Photo Stylists: Renee R. Keith, Troy Schnyder,
Pamela Simpson
Photo Researcher: Donna Greenwood
Staff Photographers: Angelo Caggiano, John P.
Hamel, Mitchell T. Mandel, Sally Shenk Ullman

Production Manager: Carolyn Gavett
Composition Manager: Gloria Kline
Senior Production Coordinator: Eileen F. Bauder
Production Coordinator: Helen Clogston

Office Personnel: Roberta Mulliner, Karen
Earl-Braymer, Connie Young

RODALE BOOKS, INC.

Publisher: Pat Corpora
Editor in Chief: William Gottlieb
Senior Managing Editor: Carol Keough
Managing Editor: Ann Snyder
Managing Editor, Health and Fitness: Debora Tkac
Managing Editor, Home and Garden: Margaret
Lydic Balitas
Art Director: Anita G. Patterson
Marketing Director, Trade Sales: Ellen J. Greene
Marketing Services Manager: Thomas Rocco
Continuity Marketing Manager: Mark Strasburg
Marketing Manager, Mail Order: Brian Carnahan
Senior Promotion Manager: Kathy Fry-Ramsdell
Business Manager: Robert Sayre
Book Club Manager: Janine Slaughter

CONTENTS

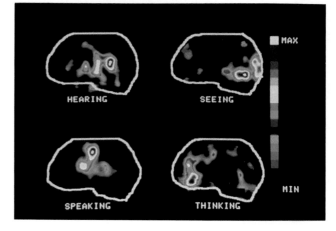

Glimpsing the brain in action, see p. 79.

How to raise a "Superkid," see p. 89.

Software to make you smarter, see p. 21.

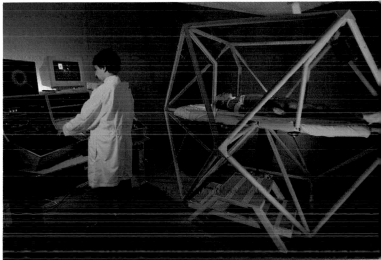

Machines that turn off tension, see p. 67.

Intelligence on the wing, see pp. 18-19.

PREFACE THE FUTURE OF YOUR MIND

Some men are woodworkers. Some collect stamps. My hobby is the brain.

Every day for the past 15 years I've delighted in altering its electronic wave patterns, those measurable pulses of mental power that flicker and flash with each thought, emotion, and sensation. Now don't get me wrong: Dr. Frankenstein is not my mentor, and there is no laboratory with sizzling electrodes where I live. But there is a living room, and that's where I conduct my daily experiment. I sit on the sofa, close my eyes, and—by easily and repeatedly thinking a soothing phrase—slowly sink into mental serenity.

My brain loves it. The wave patterns that usually look as spiky and clipped as a punk hairdo are groomed to a *GQ* clean: smooth and full. And while in my normal state the patterns pop up randomly in my brain like bubbles in boiling water, these are spread evenly throughout, like a series of gentle ripples across a lake. But a scientist would describe my brain waves just a little bit differently:

"Rhythmic amplitude-modulated beta waves were present over the whole scalp. . . . The most striking topographical alteration was the synchronization of anterior and posterior channels."

That's a quote from an article in *Electroencephalography and Clinical Neurophysiology,* a research journal that reports new advances in measuring brain waves. The article is talking about the waves a person experiences while practicing meditation—my daily brain hobby. Which brings me, balanced brain waves and all, to the very important point of this preface:

The last frontier of science is not genetic engineering or space exploration. It is discovering the secret of you—your brain, your identity, your true and total potential. Scientists—for the first time—are measuring the brain waves of meditators to discover the mental equivalent of inner peace; they are analyzing newly discovered brain chemicals that create pleasure; they are learning how to balance nutrients in your diet for maximum alertness; they are uncovering neural pathways no one even knew existed five years ago, pathways to a stronger memory, increased alertness, and enhanced intelligence. They are, in short, discovering the inner workings of the brain and charting that previously unexplored territory for immediate and practical use. This book is your guide to that new realm of personal power—the future of your mind.

William Gottlieb

William Gottlieb
Editorial Director, Prevention® Magazine Health Books

AGING AND YOUR BRAIN

"Y ou're not getting older, you're getting better!" proclaims the ruby-lipped cartoon character in sassy birthday-card style. Easy for *her* to say, you mumble, far removed as she is from graying temples, muddled memory, and other flesh-and-blood realities of growing old in three-dimensional life. But what she says is true—or at least it is to a larger degree than previously believed. People can continue to lead productive, fulfilling lives long into their later years, say researchers in human aging, despite the inevitable changes that take place.

THE INCREDIBLE SHRINKING BRAIN

"As the years go by, the human brain appears to shrink in size," says Alexander Reeves, M.D., chairman of the neurology department of Dartmouth-Hitchcock Medical Center. "It loses up to 10 percent of its weight."

Alterations begin to occur at the age of 40, says brain scientist Michael Gazzaniga, Ph.D., author of *Mind Matters*. "The most noticeable changes are found in the cerebral cortex, the structure in the brain that supports our ability to think and serves as the repository for memories." In some parts of the brain, shrinking appears to result from a loss in the actual number of nerve cells, or neurons.

Neurotransmitters, chemicals produced by neurons to relay messages to their neighbors, also decrease. Neurons that produce dopamine, a neurotransmitter important in movement control, decline by as much as 40 percent in healthy aging people, says Dr. Gazzaniga. If all this weren't bad enough, tissue abnormalities called plaques begin to appear in the brain.

Memory problems, commonly associated with old age, may result. Then again, they may not. "No matter what our age, we're all benignly forgetful," observes Dr. Reeves. "When we get older, we may simply be recognizing the absentmindedness that we've always had."

But it's true that short-term memory—trying to recall where you went to lunch last Tuesday, for example—seems to short-circuit in many older people, says neurologist Norman Foster, M.D., director of

LIFE IN THE SLOW LANE

Mentally, we may slow down as we grow older. But does it really matter?

"Central reaction time slows down slightly, but not as much as we thought," says Alexander Reeves, M.D. "In studying how long it takes people of various ages to respond to a visual cue, we have found about a 1½ millisecond decrease in reaction time per year from age 20 to 70. It's not much at all."

In separate research conducted at the University of Colorado, elderly people were found to be slower than younger people in a test that required them to look at a series of paired pictures and decide whether they were the same or different. But when allowed to take all the time they needed, the older people were *just as accurate*. What's more, other studies have shown

that they can be trained to become faster, says Dr. Reeves.

Variables other than brain function might account for differences in speed, Dr. Reeves says. "Older folks are more deliberate when you test them. They tend to be more motivated to be right than younger people, and they take the time to make sure they are."

And an elderly person sometimes approaches an experimental test with a more dubious attitude than someone younger. "Young people are used to tests and just zip through them," notes Jan Sinnott, Ph.D. "An older person, though, may actually turn to the tester and ask, 'So tell me, why do you think this is worth doing?'"

James Michener

LIFELONG ACHIEVERS

Striving for accomplishment in the days of one's youth is one thing, embracing challenge throughout a long lifetime is quite another. Extraordinary examples of ageless achievement may inspire us all to approach our later years in anything but a retiring fashion.

American artist Georgia O'Keeffe, born in 1887, painted far into her nineties. Her innovative work became known in 1916 to photographer Alfred Stieglitz, who exhibited her paintings in New York. They were later married.

While in her forties, she visited New Mexico, where the landscape became the major focus of her life's work. In her seventies, she painted a 24-foot mural of the sky "paved with clouds." In her eighties, she discovered that her eyesight was no longer sharp and briefly threw her energies into pottery-making. But in her nineties she was painting again, saying that her new way of seeing gave her new painting ideas.

Novelist James Michener was born in 1907. He held a number of jobs in his youth, including that of leading man in a traveling show, sports columnist, and naval historian. His first novel, *Tales of the South Pacific*, published when he was 40, won a Pulitzer prize and was made into the popular Broadway musical *South Pacific*. Among his many best-sellers, *Hawaii* was published while he was in his sixties, and *Chesapeake* and *Texas* in his seventies. He traveled to all corners of the state of Alaska and lived in a log cabin while researching and writing his 868-page *Alaska*, published when he was in his eighties.

Georgia O'Keeffe

PUZZLE POWER

People who lead active lives, take advantage of educational opportunities, and have hobbies that are mentally stimulating have an advantage in later life, says K. Warner Schaie, Ph.D., professor of human development and psychology at Pennsylvania State University. In his studies, Dr. Schaie found no deterioration in various mental skills among those over 60 who kept mentally active. Stay sharp, he suggests, by reading, playing Scrabble, and doing crossword puzzles . . . like this one. (For solution, please turn to page 170.)

ACROSS

1 Legal guarantees: abbr.
4 Onetime Russian ruler
8 People who don't do this will age more slowly
13 People who eat less red _____ will age more slowly
14 Telegram
15 Kitchen tool
16 This kind of person will retain mental skills in later years: 2 words
19 Musical preface
20 Persuade
21 Summit
22 Right away
24 Deviate from a course
26 Cat's foot
29 Have a chat
32 Kind of exercise that will enhance intellectual skills
37 "_____'s Irish Rose"
39 One way to stay mentally sharp
41 Yogi of baseball
42 Mental ability that improves with age: 2 words
45 Ceramic repair person
46 Reach across
47 Most August babies, astrologically
48 Novel that Michener wrote in his eighties
50 Gets better, they say
52 Sign of Broadway success: abbr.
53 Letters after R
55 Remained inactive
57 Sphere
60 Largest continent
63 People who have more of this in their diets may age more slowly
67 This seems to short-circuit in older people: 2 words
70 Musical sounds
71 Not genuine: abbr.
72 Run in neutral
73 People who keep mentally active stay
74 Little bits
75 Recolor

13 1051 in Roman numerals
17 Ill-gotten gains
18 Final or midterm
23 Advise of danger
25 Jack of "Dragnet"
26 Italian food specialty
27 Seething
28 Author Cather
30 Table supports
31 Phi Beta _____
33 Singer/actress Carter
34 Joyce Kilmer poem
35 Knight wear
36 Cowboy's rope
38 December 24 and 31
40 Haul
43 Annoys
44 Unspecified people
49 Rat-_____ (rapping sound)
51 Place for valuables
54 "_____ or lose it": 2 words
56 Shy
57 Expression of dread: 2 words
58 Hollywood reporter Barrett
59 Rabbit or Fox of fiction
61 _____ La Douce
62 In the center of
64 Main part of a letter
65 Author _____ Stanley Gardner
66 Deli bread
67 Urban thoroughfares: abbr.
68 Recipe measure: abbr.
69 The Rockies, for instance: abbr.

DOWN

1 Jockey's strap
2 President before Wilson
3 Violinist Isaac _____
4 Bill that Jefferson is on
5 Mineral deficiency linked to senility
6 Jason's mythical ship
7 Kind of race
8 Fitness center
9 Shopping center
10 "Yes _____ — make up your mind!": 2 words
11 Hold onto
12 Make a mistake

the Cognitive Disorders Program at the University of Michigan Medical Center. Long-term memory—such as recalling events from your childhood—appears to be unaffected. "Past memories may simply have been rehearsed more often," Dr. Foster theorizes.

Certain other mental processes, studied by researchers through various psychological tests, appear to slow down with the years. (See the box "Life in the Slow Lane" on page 10.) But the subject matter of the test may make a difference. "Older people often do fine if you ask questions about real-life experiences, about things they need to do and care about

REVERSING SENILITY

Doctors once accepted senility as one of the irreversible penalties of old age, but some now say just the opposite is true. They say that the symptoms of senility can be prevented or even reversed in many cases.

That's because many of the factors behind these symptoms really aren't signs of *true* senility at all. Taking care of these factors can make the difference between giving up hope and getting a fresh start. Here are some of the things to be aware of.

Vitamin status. Researchers found that older people who were deficient in vitamins B_{12} and C, for example, scored worst on memory tests. And those with the lowest levels of B_{12}, C, folate, and riboflavin did poorly in problem solving. Mental confusion in the elderly, on the other hand, has been linked to thiamine deficiency.

Zinc intake. Senile elderly people and those just starting to show signs of senility have significantly lower levels of this mineral than the nonsenile, according to a British researcher who says there may be a strong case for zinc supplementation among those at risk.

Diseases in disguise. Poor concentration, disorientation, loss of interest, and other symptoms that mimic senility might be caused by undetected disorders such as depression, alcoholism, Parkinson's disease, Huntington's disease, and heart disease. Treating them may alleviate senile symptoms, says Norman Foster, M.D.

Side effects of prescription drugs. A number of medications can have side effects that masquerade as senility, says Dr. Foster. Sleeping pills and tranquilizers are common culprits, he says.

Sensory decline. Hearing loss (more than two-thirds of the population over 65 has it to some degree) and cataracts and other vision problems can dull the elderly person's interaction with his environment. Getting a hearing aid or having vision corrected can often restore this crucial link to reality, says Alexander Reeves, M.D.

rather than nonsense syllables," says Jan Sinnott, Ph.D., a Towson State University psychologist and researcher in human aging.

And good news: Despite brain changes, verbal IQ—the ability to define words and to learn from reading, among other skills—remains largely unchanged with age, notes Dr. Reeves.

USE IT OR LOSE IT

Better news yet is scientific evidence that a decline in brainpower as you age is not inevitable. In some cases, losses may even be reversed.

"People used to say that after age 40 or 50, things really go on a slide," he notes. "But there are too many exceptions, people who have maintained their mental capacities by continuing to do things."

Many factors are being linked to maintaining vigorous brain capacity, including overall health habits. "People who are eating pretty well—getting more fiber, less red meat—and who are exercising and not smoking or drinking will age more slowly," says Dr. Reeves. "And this will affect their brains." Aerobic exercise like swimming or bicycling can particularly help keep that portion of the brain involved with motor activity (movement) in shape, he says.

Mental exercise may be just as important. "Most people who have a long-term willingness to learn new things and to engage in new intellectual activities not only retain their intellectual skills but actually enhance them," says Ewald Busse, M.D., professor emeritus of psychiatry at Duke University Medical Center. Activities like reading, learning new languages and skills, increasing your vocabulary, and solving puzzles may be beneficial, says Dr. Reeves.

And now, the best news of all: An older mind in some ways is actually quite superior to a young one, according to Dr. Sinnott, who has extensively studied the positive mental developments that come with advancing age.

There are improvements in expertise. "The longer a person does something, the more aspects of the task become automatic," says Dr. Sinnott. "The older executive, for example, knows how to respond to a bad day without having to think his or her way through each part of it. The expert typist or the expert chess player doesn't need to sit there and ponder each piece of information. They've formed mental patterns and can focus on what's important."

ALERTNESS

ometimes it's a matter of life and death—if you're piloting an F-16 fighter jet at 800 miles an hour in precision drills above the glaring sands of the Mojave desert, for instance. Or more likely, when you're in your Chevy doing 55, merging into traffic on a six-lane beltway at rush hour. In situations like these, alertness is everything. Fortunately, the highways of life usually lead us through much more manageable territory, but still we need to exercise alertness throughout the day, whether it's to handle the details of a stressful job or to attentively listen to our kids' problems after school.

Alertness might be defined as that passive, open mental state in which you are aware of the myriad events all around you and are able to respond quickly and efficiently. Alertness can keep you safe from harm, improve your relationships, and contribute to a productive, satisfying life.

Your capacity for being mentally on the ball is actually built right into your biology. Thanks to your brain's efficient design, most of the work of alertness takes place without your even having to think about it.

The regulator of human alertness lies in a tiny part of your brain called the suprachiasmatic nucleus (SCN). Located between your optic nerves in the hypothalamus (a section in the base of the brain that exerts powerful control over a wide range of func-

tions), the SCN regulates circadian rhythms—daily biochemical patterns that hold you in harmony with the natural ebb and flow of your environment. "That's advantageous because when your environment requires you to be alert, you *will* be alert," explains Kenneth Groh, Ph.D., assistant biologist in the biological, environmental, and medical research division at Argonne National Laboratory.

YOUR BODY'S WAKE-UP CALL

One of your body's "master clocks," the SCN has the task of making sure the right biochemical pathways in your brain are activated at the right times of day, explains Dr. Groh. It receives its wake-up call each morning when your eyes begin to perceive daylight and relay this information back through your optic nerves. The SCN then stimulates something called the catecholamine pathway—your alert pathway.

"This pathway tells the adrenal glands to pump epinephrine (also known as adrenaline) out into the bloodstream so that you—like your primitive ancestors—can go out and kill your dinosaur," says Dr. Groh. Adrenaline and other natural wake-up chemicals speed up your heart rate and release stored sugars into your bloodstream to give you the steady supply of energy you'll need throughout the day. Other adjustments are made. Your body temperature, for instance, will rise by as much as 1½°F

Staying alert is one of the hardest parts of a pilot's job, says Richard Jensen, director of the Aviation Psychology Laboratory at Ohio State University. He trains pilots to squelch sleepiness by regularly checking the aircraft's status on the in-flight computer and visually scanning the scenery in all directions.

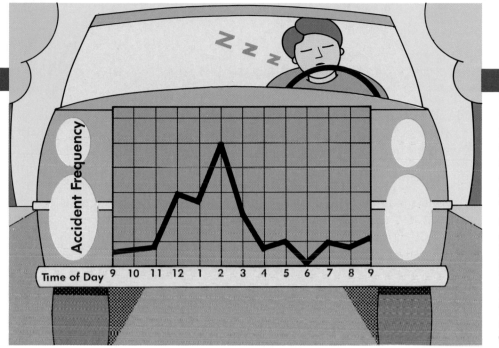

Research shows that more drivers fall asleep at the wheel and crash at 2:00 P.M. than at any other point during their active daytime cycles. To maximize alertness despite this naturally occurring biochemical low point, stay away from alcoholic drinks at lunchtime and eat high-protein foods like tuna or low-fat cottage cheese, plus salad or fruit.

during the day. It peaks at around noon, the most active part of your daytime phase and probably the hour when you feel most alert. Then, in early afternoon, your alertness suddenly sinks (see the illustration above). Contrary to the popular theory that lunch launches this dip, it is actually just part of your body's natural cycle, Dr. Groh says. In an hour or two, alertness perks up again. Finally, toward evening, an altogether different biochemical pathway begins to kick in, slowing you down for bedtime.

As remarkably efficient as this system usually is, it gets out of sync at one time or another for every one of us. Not getting enough sleep can do it, as can switching from the day shift to the night shift. So can jet lag, a disorder suffered by many people when they travel from one time zone to another.

"You can become very confused," says Dr. Groh. "Your ability to concentrate and solve problems goes down. It's not good, for instance, to get on a plane at 4:00 P.M., fly overseas, and be in a business meeting at 7:00 A.M. with your company's future on the line. This is a situation where you can make terrible mistakes."

STAYING IN SYNC

Fortunately, you can help keep your alertness system in top form by following a few guidelines.

● Eat three meals a day at your regular mealtimes, even if other events in your life are off schedule, recommends Jim Solomon, administrator of driver training programs for the National Safety Council. Wake up your alertness pathway, suggests Dr. Groh, with a high-protein breakfast. Yogurt, fresh fruit, and cereal are great, but sweet rolls are not. And don't stuff yourself at any meal, because too much of the blood your brain needs for business upstairs will end up downstairs in your digestive tract.

● Drink coffee with caution. Because it is a stimulant, coffee will certainly wake you up, but in the long run it can interfere with your alert system. "Caffeine has depressive side effects that actually turn off your brain's awakeness pathway," says Dr. Groh. Switch to decaf, he suggests. And don't prop your eyes open with coffee at night, especially during long drives, warns Solomon. You'd do better to take a break and a walk to stimulate your circulation, he says.

● Whenever possible, try to adjust to shift changes or air travel in advance, advises Dr. Groh. Take a day or two off between shift changes to change your schedule. Fend off jet lag by "putting yourself on destination time as soon as you get on the flight."

● Steer clear of "alertness products," says Solomon. "Don't expect a chemical to do something for your body that your body is incapable of doing because it's tired," he says. "Your body reaches a point where it says, 'Excuse me, I'm tired.' Give it a break."

15

THE ANIMAL BRAIN

Have you ever gazed into the eyes of a dog, cat, or goldfish and asked yourself "What in the world is this creature thinking?"—or wondered whether it's thinking anything at all?

Do animals think? Are they intelligent? Does Rover, lying by the fireplace looking so innocent, know all of your darkest secrets? Might he blackmail you someday into giving him extra dog biscuits?

"There really is no difference between human and animal intelligence, because humans *are* animals," says Francine Patterson, Ph.D., a California scientist whose success in teaching sign language to gorillas has become legendary. She says that humans may be smarter, but "it's only a matter of degree, rather than kind."

Not too long ago, such statements would have been considered (pardon the expression) bird-brained, but recent studies with rats, dolphins, big apes—and yes, even birds—are leading scientists to believe that nonhumans may have much more on their minds than humans generally give them credit for.

Consider for instance, Dr. Patterson's star gorilla, Koko. At age 17, Koko has a sign language vocabulary of over 600 words. In addition, she can recognize more than two dozen written words. Most impressively, she often forms *new* words out of her existing vocabulary. Do something to anger her, for instance, and you risk being called a "dirty bad toilet."

Veteran animal-behavior researcher Donald Griffin, Ph.D., professor emeritus at Rockefeller University in New York City, and author of *Animal Thinking,* says that not all thinking animals are higher primates, or even mammals. Birds, ants, even bees, he says, appear capable of thought.

Green herons, for instance, sometimes use bait for fishing. They drop a tad of food into the water and hang around until small fish come to feast.

Of course, any animal behavior is open to human interpretation.

SPEAK SOFTLY AND CARRY A BIG TRUNK

If you remember your old Tarzan movies, beware the elephant that raises its trunk and loudly trumpets—it's probably ready to attack. But loud trumpeting isn't the only sound elephants make. They also emit low-frequency rumbles. Although inaudible to the human ear, these sounds can be felt as a throbbing sensation in the air or seen as a vibration on the elephant's massive forehead.

Researchers from Cornell University suspect that the rumbles may be how elephants chat. It could explain, for example, some mysteries about elephant behavior, such as their very coordinated movements within herds—movements that to the human eye and ear seem to occur without signal.

A WHALE OF A MISTAKE?

What does it mean, for instance, when whales run themselves up onto beaches? Here, after all, is a supposedly highly intelligent animal that is seemingly doing something overtly irrational.

Alan Macnow asserts that this is clear evidence of their *lack* of intelligence. "If whales were so intelligent, you'd think they'd understand the nature of tides," says the U.S. public relations spokesman for the Japan Whaling Association.

But Lou Herman, Ph.D., director of the Kewalo Basin Marine Mammal Laboratory at the University of Hawaii, says that sick whales often seek shallow waters to be able to rest on the sand while keeping their blowholes above water. They also escape deep-water sharks at the same time. Sure, they risk getting whisked ashore, but swimming into shallow waters could still be deemed intelligent, not stupid, behavior.

Besides, says Dr. Herman, "if doing stupid things were a mark of lack of intelligence, then human beings would top the list."

John Staddon, Ph.D., a professor of psychology, zoology, and neurobiology at Duke University, says there's much more about animal intelligence that we still need to discover. For that matter, he says, we don't know a lot about human intelligence, either.

So what we learn about animal intelligence may tell us some surprising things about ourselves.

For the final word on the subject, we consulted two of the world's most renowned experts on animal thinking: Koko the gorilla and her 15-year-old boyfriend, Michael.

We first ask Michael if he is smart. "Gorilla smart," he replies in sign language.

"Can people learn from gorillas?" we ask. Michael signs "nice good."

We next question Koko about what gorillas are better at than people. "Gorilla canines [teeth] good," she says.

Then we ask Koko whether she thinks people are smart, but she refuses to comment.

"Aw, come on—are they or aren't they?" we ask. Koko signs: "Humans are 'nuts.'"

- Body sense
- Hearing
- Sight
- Smell

SPECIES SPECIALTIES

Humans are the only animals to drive cars, use deodorant, and play "Wheel of Fortune." But what really makes us humans different from all other animals is our brain, or more specifically, that part of the brain known as the cerebral cortex. This is where we store much of our intelligence. In the illustrations above, specialized areas that control senses are highlighted. Animals that depend on their sense of smell, like the cat, have highly developed olfactory regions. The monkey, on the other hand, relies much more on vision than smell. Notice that the human cerebral cortex has proportionately less of its total area devoted to the senses and more to advanced thinking processes.

HOW BIRDS NAVIGATE

One of the great marvels and mysteries of nature is how birds navigate their way across wide continents and oceans, often at night, seemingly without ever getting lost.

Actually, the marvel of bird migration involves not one but *two* big mysteries, says Charles Walcott, Ph.D., executive director of the ornithology lab and professor of neurobiology and behavior at Cornell University. The first mystery, he says, is how do birds know north from south and east from west? Dr. Walcott calls this the compass problem.

To understand the second problem, says Dr. Walcott, "Imagine I put you in a rubber raft far from land with a lovely little compass— that wouldn't be enough to get home. You still have to know where you are in relation to where you want to go." So do birds. He calls this the map problem.

For many years scientists tried to address the first problem, the compass problem, but they didn't get very far in their understanding because of one terribly wrong assumption, says Dr. Walcott. "We thought there was *one* cue that birds used to navigate. We didn't know what it was, but we thought we could find it."

By the 1970s, however, it became clear that birds use not one but a large number of cues, says Dr. Walcott. It's now known that birds use the sun, stars, wind currents, polarized light, magnetism, and possibly even smell to find their way. (Dr. Walcott jokingly calls this last one the "stink theory.")

In addition, scientists have learned that while an individual bird will typically use several cues, exactly which cues it uses depends on what kind of bird it is, what time of day it is, and what the weather is like.

Look to the Heavens

Day-traveling birds such as ducks, geese, and starlings often pay attention to the position of the sun. Twilight travelers, such as white-throated sparrows, savannah sparrows, and myrtle warblers use the glowing westward sky long after the sun has set.

But what about birds that fly in the dead of night, such as the indigo bunting? (The vast majority of migrating birds do fly at night.) Just like sailors, explains Dr. Walcott, they look to the stars. And just like sailors, they most often use the North Star and the star patterns surrounding the North Star. Different birds, however, are thought to prefer different stars.

So far, so good. But as any sailor can attest, the stars are not always visible—that's when a compass comes in handy. But birds, unlike sailors, don't need the hand-held kind—they have built-in compasses in their heads.

That is, they have in their little noggins deposits

of a substance called magnetite, which allows them to somehow sense which way it is to the North Pole. (Salmon, tuna, dolphins, and bees also have magnetite deposits in their heads.)

In addition, says Dr. Walcott, some birds are thought to be able to actually *see* the angle of the earth's magnetic field. (The planet's magnetic force runs vertically at the poles and parallel to the earth's surface at the equator.) Birds known to use magnetism to navigate include warblers, robins, and homing pigeons.

Wind currents are also used by certain birds to direct their journeys, although wind, says Dr. Walcott "is a real funny one." In some areas, such as Louisiana, there is a high correlation between wind patterns and the routes of migrating birds. But in other regions, such as upstate New York, there is absolutely no correlation, he says.

Another cue widely assumed to be used by our feathered friends is polarized light, a kind of light that humans can see only by looking through polarized lenses. Running at right angles to the sun, polarized light is also an essential navigational tool to many insects, such as honeybees.

These are the major cues birds use to determine north, south, east, and west. But what about that other problem, the map problem?

"We have to plead almost total ignorance about that," says Dr. Walcott. "We simply do not know."

As far as scientists know, birds don't read street signs, carry maps, or ask policemen for directions. So just how do they find their way across continents and oceans, never mind across town? Just like humans, they use a number of cues— although different ones, for sure. Instead of street signs and maps, birds use the following navigational tools: (1) The sun. As every boy scout—and any day-flying bird—surely knows, it rises in the east and sets in the west. (2) A sense of time. Necessary for using the sun as a guide. (3) The stars in the night. Night-flying birds (perhaps as many as 80 percent of all birds migrate at night) use the North Star or other stars to find their way. (4) The earth's magnetic field. Some birds may have the ability to actually see this field, which is invisible to humans, or they may somehow sense it in a way that we do not understand. (5) Wind currents.It makes sense for birds to follow prevailing wind currents—they pick up extra speed and largely have their navigation done for them. (6) Polarized light. Here again, some birds seem capable of seeing what is invisible to the human eye. (7) Landmarks. Helpful to older birds who already know the route, but not as necessary for birds as for humans. (Experiments with blindfolded homing pigeons show that they can find their way home regardless.) (8) Hearing. The sounds of such things as the distant surf are thought to be helpful to some birds for short trips, but probably not for long migrations. (9) A keen sense of smell? It has been suggested that some birds may use their sense of smell to judge their whereabouts, but this theory remains highly controversial.

ARTIFICIAL
INTELLIGENCE

I am putting myself to the fullest possible use, which is all I think that any conscious entity can do.

HAL 9000 COMPUTER—2001, A SPACE ODYSSEY

Artificial intelligence is what allows computers to talk about themselves in the first person. It's an IBM with an id, a MacIntosh with a mind, an Apple that grows on you.

If you're the type who thinks that a VDT is a banned pesticide or that a byte refers to what the purchase of a computer does to your wallet, you'll be surprised to hear how simply artificial intelligence can be explained.

"The only way to define artificial intelligence," says Nobel laureate Herbert A. Simon, Ph.D., professor of computer science and psychology at Carnegie-Mellon University, "is in two steps. If a computer program does something that would require human intelligence, then it's intelligent. If humans develop that program, then it's artificial."

Artificial intelligence is not mere word processing, unless of course your computer tells you it doesn't like the last sentence you wrote. Most computer programs, as we know them, are based on something called algorithms, or rigid mathematical formulas. Artificial intelligence, on the other hand, is based on something entirely different: heuristics.

THE ULTIMATE OPPONENT

Do you feel lucky? Well, do you? Igor Ivanoff felt lucky. He was, after all, an international chess master from Canada. What could a computer chess game called Deep Thought have over him?

So he pulled up a chair, turned the game on, and had a go at it. And he lost.

Imagine! A highly ranked chess master defeated in chess by a chip. A computer chip. "Computer chess games are getting closer and closer to beating most of the best chess players," says Vince McCambridge, associate director of the United States Chess Federation. "The top computers play well enough to rank them with the top 1 percent of our membership."

These plastic whizzes come in a variety of shapes and sizes, from handheld models that look like calculators to full-size electronic chess boards like Fidelity International's Phantom, shown here.

McCambridge calls these games, which range in price from $29.95 to hundreds of dollars, "the perfect practice partners. Computers are always ready for a game." The question is, are you?

"People can beat the computers," he says. "Every chess move has about 60 possibilities. Humans immediately toss out most of those, narrowing it down to 1 or 2. Computers, on the other hand, need to look at every single move, so if you're playing 2 moves ahead, the computer must sort through over 12 million possible moves. That may give you an edge."

"Computers are also good teachers," says McCambridge. "You can lose to one and it doesn't hurt your ego. It's not the same as having your friend beat you."

Wonder if Master Ivanoff agrees?

SOFTWARE FOR YOUR MIND

There's an old saying that originated with computer programmers: "Garbage in . . . garbage out." If that's the case, then the flip side of that—"Intelligence in . . . intelligence out"—should also be true. Listed below are a few of the available programs based on the latter principle, all designed to boost your brainpower.

Breakthrough, from Profit Technology. This program piggybacks on whatever software program you're using by allowing flash cards to appear in one or more areas of the screen. You can learn French (and other things) while writing letters to friends.

Mentor, from Heuristic Research. A rigorous workout for the mind, this program contains 58 "psychometric" exercises and tests to boost mental prowess.

Remember, from DesignWare. This is a powerful learning tool that uses personalized written, auditory, and pictorial hints to promote long-term retention of facts.

The Idea Generator, from Shamrock Press. You can use this program, described as "brainstorming software that helps you think," to turn on creativity, generate options, and solve problems.

"When people solve difficult problems, they don't do it by examining all the possibilities or crunching out answers the way computers typically do. We do it by searching very selectively," says Dr. Simon.

"We do a certain amount of trial-and-error seeking, but we constantly watch where we are, seeing clues and using them to steer the search. These sly tricks we use are called heuristics. And in artificial intelligence we program that experience, rather than just numbers, into the computer."

LEARNING FROM MACHINES

While the computers are learning from us, we are also learning from them. "By writing computer programs that do intelligent things—that try to mimic human cunning, for example—we can learn a great deal about how humans think." says Dr. Simon. "That translates into improvements in the ways we teach, solve problems, and train people to make decisions."

Some artificial intelligence programs are already in use, thinking about problems as diverse as approving credit card purchases or making medical diagnoses. Still other programs have moved right into the classroom. "A good computer tutorial is better than a book as a learning tool," says Tim Jay, Ph.D., a professor of cognitive psychology at North Adams State College in Massachusetts.

"When people go through a book, they go in a linear fashion. They turn the page and they don't usually go back. But a computer, if it tests you and you don't know the subject, won't let you get around it. It keeps you on the topic until you've mastered it," he says.

Some researchers believe that one day we may be able to profit from artificial intelligence in even more profound ways. "Would not high-quality music, poetry, and art enrich our society, even if the composer, poet, or artist were a computer program?" asks John Baer, a National Science Foundation Fellow studying cognitive psychology at Rutgers University. "Would a nuclear arms treaty or union contract that satisfied both sides be any less desirable if it were arranged by an artificial intelligence negotiator?

"Computer programs like these should be thought of as a new wave of immigrants, enriching and enhancing the civilization that they become a part of," says Baer.

CONCENTRATION

It's a magical time. Outside noises go unheard, body aches go unnoticed. Time stands still, or perhaps it races by. Your body and mind are relaxed but alert. Self-conscious feelings and anxiety drift away.

"Runner's high?" Meditation? Hypnosis? No, nothing so profound. It's just concentration. Pure, simple concentration.

There's nothing quite like it. Call it the very essence of thought—that single-minded dedication to purpose that produces results, puts you on top in whatever you're trying to accomplish, and feels good, too.

Can't concentrate? Don't be so hard on yourself. There's more to concentration than desire or ability. The subject you're concentrating on probably has as much control over your ability to concentrate as you do. Maybe more. In fact, concentration is so very dependent on subject matter that you can think of concentration as the ability to absorb the information that absorbs you.

But concentration is a balancing act, too. If a subject (an important final exam, for instance) excites you too much, information overflow is sure to destroy your concentration. If the subject bores you to tears, the brain never gets excited enough to register the drab information forced on it.

Somewhere between fear and boredom, however, lies a world in which concentration flourishes, where it becomes a natural, easy function somewhat akin to meditation or hypnosis—a world in which information is welcomed and flows effortlessly inside, soaked up by your eager, waiting brain.

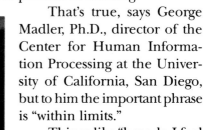

Maybe National Spelling Bee champion Rageshree Ramachandran, 13, has a built-in edge: her name. More likely, hard work and concentration are "Raga's" keys. "I had to give it my all," she says of her championship performance.

THE UNCLUTTERED WINDOW

"Concentration is little more than an interaction between the task and the observer," says John N. Flowers, Ph.D., a specialist in human attention mechanisms at the University of Nebraska at Lincoln. "Things that are important or enjoyable tend to sustain our interest, while things we don't like tend to bore us.

"Even so, we are not slaves to the material in front of us," Dr. Flowers maintains. "We do have the ability, within limits, to decide how much effort or attention we want to put into something."

That's true, says George Madler, Ph.D., director of the Center for Human Information Processing at the University of California, San Diego, but to him the important phrase is "within limits."

Things like "how do I feel about this task" or "what's my competitor going to do today" destroy the ability to concentrate, Dr. Madler says. But how can we clear the decks of emotional clutter?

The experts offer several strategies. If boredom is the problem, bargaining with yourself may overcome it. Try saying, "I will concentrate on this boring subject, then do something nice for myself." "If you're feeling fearful or tense, you're probably thinking about irrelevant information," says Dr. Madler. His suggestion: Get rid of it.

Finally, tackle the problem one step at a time. "Research has shown that you're generally better off breaking up tasks into smaller increments punctuated with occasional breaks," says Dr. Flowers. "That helps you maintain a heightened state of arousal."

CONCENTRATION ON THE ROCKS

They call it a game of vertical chess played with your own body. Most of us wonder why anybody plays. The dangers of rock climbing are immense and immediately apparent, but what are the rewards? More than that, what's the motivation, and what does it take to reach the top?

The answer to all three questions can be found in a single word: concentration.

Notes John Harlin, 32, who has been a rock climber since age 6 and is the author of three climbing books, "One of the real beauties of climbing is that the level of concentration required empties your mind and makes everything else in the world seem unimportant. You use your mind and your body to the utmost of your abilities and tune out everything else in the world. It leaves you feeling incredibly relaxed when it's over."

Reaching such high levels of concentration means finding that magical place between fear and boredom. "You have to get in the right frame of mind first," Harlin says. "It's a matter of relaxing and telling yourself that you can do it and that fear and doubt will not stand in your way." Sounds like good advice for horizontal chess playing, too.

A COURSE IN POWER THINKING

You're logical and knowledgeable, clever and creative. You know what you like and what you don't, what will work and what won't. All in all, you think you're pretty smart, and no doubt you are. *But how smart is your thinking?*

Probably not as smart as it would be if you were to really put your mind to it, says Edward deBono, M.D., an international authority in the art of thinking. Intelligence aside, most of us approach problems with scrambled brains. "Suggestions, judgment, criticism, information, and plain emotion are all mixed up in a sort of thinking stew," he says.

To counteract such confusion, Dr. deBono developed a new approach to thinking and described it in his book *Six Thinking Hats*. Each colored hat represents a distinct thinking style—a separate brain setting, if you will. When "put on" one at a time, these symbolic thinking hats encourage fresher ideas, more accurate assessments, and better decisions, Dr. deBono says. So try them all on for size.

WHITE HAT: FACTS AND FIGURES

Scott, a brilliant straight-A student in high school, has his heart set on four years at an expensive private college. But you, his devoted parents, don't know how you can possibly afford it.

Another house on your block was broken into last night, the third unsolved burglary in the past two weeks. You and your neighbors are angry with the police and meet to discuss a course of action.

You're staring at a restaurant dessert menu. For two weeks you've been an absolute saint on your strict diet, but a piece of chocolate cream pie seems sinfully tempting.

Large and small, momentous and mundane, problems challenge us every day. We deal with them in a variety of ways. We may respond by rote. We may react emotionally. We may even try to avoid them. But the best approach, says Dr. deBono, is to put on your thinking hats one at a time to make a mental "map" in which all aspects of the problem and its potential solutions are clearly seen.

The white hat is a good place to start. Its lack of color, Dr. deBono explains, indicates its "just-the-facts-ma'am" neutrality. When you and your fellow thinkers put on your white hats, you agree to try to put forth the most objective information you can about the situation. You refrain entirely from emotion (that comes under the red hat) as well as from seeking a quick fix.

The facts may be clear-cut: *Scott's outstanding college entrance exam scores qualify him for a partial scholarship from at least one expensive college, he says. But additional expenses will still kill your budget, you and your spouse state.*

The facts may need checking: *Your next-door neighbor says he heard that the police have cut back on the number of neighborhood patrol squads.*

The facts may not be facts at all: *One slice of cream pie won't make any difference on your diet, you tell yourself.* Dr. deBono cautions that guesses, your own opinion, or wishful thinking are not permitted.

Try not to argue or push a particular point of view, Dr. deBono says, although this habit can be hard to break.

RED HAT:
EMOTIONS AND INTUITION

Now that you've faced the facts about the situation you're in, how do you *feel* about it? Many people mistakenly believe, says Dr. deBono, that emotions "muck up" thinking. They assume that a good thinker is supposed to be cool and detached, not influenced by emotion. To the contrary, he says, emotions interfere with thinking only when they are suppressed. When not given their voice, they "will lurk in the background and affect all the thinking in a hidden way."

When you and your fellow thinkers put on your red thinking caps, you state your feelings without regard for rationality. Love or hate, excitement or fear, pleasure or pain, all such emotions are real and valid, says Dr. deBono. You don't have to justify them, he says. What you feel is what you feel.

Scott says he feels resentful toward you and angry that all his hard work may not be enough to fulfill his dream of attending a top college.

Your neighbors say they're terrified that their houses are next on the burglar's hit list and are infuriated with the apparent lack of police protection.

You want, you desire, you crave a slice of that pie.

Intuition and hunches also find their places under red-hat thinking. Intuition, Dr. deBono explains, is a kind of immediate understanding of a situation, a complex judgment based on experience. Such a judgment "probably cannot be itemized or even expressed in words," he says, but it is nevertheless quite valid and useful. Yours may have such a definitive edge.

You tell Scott that given his obvious intelligence and competence, you feel he's going to end up at the kind of college he's interested in one way or another. These things, you say, have a tendency to work themselves out. You just don't know exactly how yet.

Or you may have a hunch. (But keep in mind, warns Dr. deBono, that both intuitions and hunches are not infallible. They are simply additional pieces of information).

You have a feeling, you say, that the burglars are going to strike again tonight, and it's going to be at your place.

Feelings inform thoughts, Dr. deBono says. Putting them on your mental map gives you the opportunity to explore or even change them.

Having acknowledged that you feel desperate for a piece of pie, you now remember that for a long time you've been feeling even more desperate to lose weight.

Collectively putting on your red hats when you're in a group helps take the glaring focus off one person and his particular feelings, says Dr. deBono. Everyone gets a chance to get his or her nonrational thinking out in the open. This can also help cut through group bickering, he says.

So put on your red hat and feel free to feel. And remember that you don't need to justify a single bit of it.

YELLOW HAT: POSITIVE THINKING

Golden and bright like sunshine, the yellow hat symbolizes optimism. "For a few people, being positive is a natural habit of mind," says Dr. deBono. For the rest of us, what seems to come more naturally is negative thinking (that's under the black hat). Most people, he says, will be positive only when putting forward an idea of their own or when they see something in it for themselves.

Yellow-hat thinking means making a delib-erate effort to make optimistic suggestions.

Scott says, he is willing to at least consider attending an inexpensive college for his first year or two, then transfer to a better school. Yes, you add, and maybe he could get a part-time job while he's at it and put some money in the bank toward that extra expense.

In some cases, putting on the yellow hat means changing your interpretation of a situation.

If nothing else, you and your neighbors acknowledge, the burglaries have brought you together for the first time as a cohesive community group.

Yellow-hat thinking is not necessarily practical nor need it be totally justifiable. But it isn't "Pollyanna foolishness" either, Dr. deBono points out. Even optimism can be carried too far.

Go ahead and have the pie, but make believe that you didn't, you tell yourself, and the calories won't count.

"Visions and dreams can become reality," says Dr. deBono. "It is those who expect to succeed who succeed." The point is to look at the action that might follow the optimism. If you expect Scott to save money toward college but he has no intention of getting a job, your optimism is unfounded.

Being positive can be surprisingly difficult, says Dr. deBono. Sometimes your deliberate circumvent that problem. In a group, the device of asking the negative person to put on and take off the black hat—or to simply point out that he seems to have been wearing the black hat during the entire discussion—establishes limits and encourages him to switch gears.

Getting together like this is dumb, an absolute waste of time, hollers one of your neighbors. Let's just file a complaint against the police, he says. (Avoid negative adjectives such as "childish" and "stupid," by the way.)

This is also a time to challenge facts that were presented under the white hat as well as to ask negative questions.

Are you setting yourself up to fail on your diet, you ask yourself, and do you really want to repeat that mistake?

search for something good about a situation may prove futile, at least temporarily.

BLACK HAT: LOGICAL/NEGATIVE

This six-hat thinking is too complicated and artificial and can't possibly work, you might be saying to yourself about now. Congratulations! You have just displayed your facility with black-hat thinking. This is your chance to give negativity full rein, Dr. deBono says, looking for errors of thinking or illogical conclusions.

No job would give him the kind of flexibility or pay him the kind of money he needs to save for two years at any private school, Scott says. This whole situation is beginning to sound hopeless, you think, and Scott better just get used to the idea of going to a less expensive college.

Some people are negative by nature, Dr. deBono says. Darkness is cast over all their thinking. "Destruction is always easier than construction," he points out. "Proving someone wrong provides immediate satisfaction."

Fortunately, orderly six-hat thinking can

Especially when you are considering new ideas, be sure to put on the yellow hat *before* the black hat, says Dr. deBono. Once the mind has been directed toward the negative, he says, it becomes very difficult to see the positive.

GREEN HAT:
CREATIVITY AND EXPLORATION

The color of things fertile and growing, the green of this hat represents new concepts and perceptions, an important yet often neglected part of problem solving. Putting on the green hat offers an opportunity to generate numerous alternatives.

You tell Scott that maybe he should forget about college and become an animal trainer with the circus. That reminds him, he says, of something he read about a guy who put himself through college running a business walking people's pets, taking them to the vet, and so on—something that he might try himself.

A neighbor suggests you could all be policemen and protect yourselves. (This suggestion, in fact, was the impetus for the Neighborhood Watch programs.)

The point is to "jerk thinking out of current patterns," Dr. deBono says. One approach he suggests is to try reversal: Spell out the way something usually happens, reverse it and see what kind of "movement" you can get out of that.

The more pie you eat, you propose to yourself, the more weight you'll lose. Which makes you wonder: Perhaps if you did allow the occasional treat, you'd be more likely to succeed in the long run.

Refrain from criticizing other's ideas, Dr. deBono warns. "New ideas are delicate seedlings that need the green hat to protect them from the instant frost of black-hat habits."

Creativity is not a special gift but a normal and necessary part of everyone's thinking, he says. And with practice, you will probably find your yield of new ideas increasing.

BLUE HAT:
DIRECTOR AND CRITIC

Envision a conductor leading a symphony orchestra through a beautiful piece of music, suggests Dr. deBono. The conductor's job is representative of blue-hat thinking. With the music score as his guide, he directs the perform-ance of each orchestra member (in this case, each of the other five hats).

Putting on the blue hat means thinking about thinking. One person can do it or everyone in a group can.

Before starting your discussions, you and Scott clarified that the issue to be addressed is not whether he'll go to college but how to finance it.

Blue-hat thinking means creating a plan and a strategy. The plan may change, because going through all six hats (which, by the way, needn't always follow a specific order) may take minutes or months, but it's important to have a plan nevertheless.

You and your neighbors decide to start with red-hat thinking to clear the air about the burglaries, then run through the other hats one by one.

Making a plan is especially important if you're thinking about something by yourse Otherwise, your thinking tends to drift.

Okay, you tell yourself, what I need to think about is not how yummy pie sounds or how fat I feel, but the relationship between eating pie and sticking to my diet.

The blue-hat thinker has a degree of ongoing authority. In a group, he informs other members when it's time to switch from one hat to another. He asks focusing questions. And he observes and comments.

All in all, the blue-hat thinker helps keep things sorted out. "The biggest enemy of think-ing is complexity, for that leads to confusion," concludes Dr. deBono. "When thinking is clear and simple, it becomes more enjoyable and effective."

CREATIVITY

Mention the word *creativity,* and most people think of writers, poets, musicians, and artists. After all, these are the occupations of creative greatness. It's assumed that the rest of us, untouched by the creative spirit, are destined to move about our 9-to-5 world in steady, dull-gray fashion, doing our job and collecting a check.

Do you believe that? Well, don't.

That traditional view of creativity is being challenged more and more today, as new findings change many outdated notions of what creativity is and who among us possesses it.

Scientific scrutiny is peeling back the layers of mystery that have surrounded the muse for ages. The results of this work are fascinating, forcing us to look at creativity not as the realm of a chosen few but as a world in which we all can and do participate on a daily basis.

WHAT IS CREATIVITY?

Let's exercise our own creativity at this point by asking three important questions, then let the answers take us where they will. First, what is creativity? Second, can we develop more of it? And third, will it gain us anything if we do?

Sidney X. Shore, editor of *Creativity in Action,* a monthly creative-enhancement publication, offers a creative response to the first query, telling us plenty about creativity while refusing to answer the question.

"I'd prefer not to define the term," he says. "Defining is for engineers, and creativity has to do with individuals and individual situations. It could be a flash of insight. It could be the ability to see and be aware and respond. Or it could be the absence of fear of failure, the absence of fearing what others will think of you. When you ask for a definition of creativity, you ask for an impossible answer."

Not necessarily, says Teresa Amabile, Ph.D., a psychologist at Brandeis University in Waltham, Massachusetts, and one of the best-known researchers studying creativity today. "Most people who work in the field define creativity as producing something that's both novel and appropriate," she says.

CREATIVE GAMES

Any potential human capacity, says Eugene Raudsepp, author of *Creative Growth Games,* can be increased by exercise—and this is especially true of creativity, which tends to thrive on a good challenge. Try out the games below and see how you do. (The answers are on page 170.)

1. This classic puzzle sounds easy, but don't be fooled— plenty of bright folks get left "up a tree" when trying to solve it. The challenge: draw four straight lines through these nine dots without retracing or lifting your pen from the paper.

2. Imagine you are the person shown standing in the room below. You must tie the two ends of the suspended strings together without removing them from the ceiling. The strings are located so that you cannot reach one while holding the other. The room is completely bare, but you have the resources available that you would normally carry in your pocket or purse.

"Novel means that it has to be different from something done before, and appropriate means that it can't be different just for the sake of being different. It has to work, to be meaningful and useful in some sense."

Dr. Amabile refutes those who believe that only a few select individuals are born to creativity. "Creativity is a matter of degree," she says. "Some people may not realize the creative potential inside themselves and may not be creative in their day-to-day lives, but that doesn't mean they can't be creative or don't have the ability."

Creativity expert Ruth Richards, M.D., Ph.D., a psychiatrist at Harvard Medical School and McLean Hospital in Belmont, Massachusetts, seconds Dr. Amabile's definition of creativity. She too believes that all people and fields hold creative potential.

"Originality and meaningfulness are the criteria of creative thinking," she says. "And you can apply that definition to anyone or anything," she adds, dismissing the notion of "absolute" creativity. "Some people have said certain individuals—Einstein, Bee-

thoven, and so on—were creative, but the rest of us aren't. Or else certain fields are creative, such as the fine arts or writing, but no others. Yet we've discovered that there's just about nothing you cannot do creatively."

CREATED EQUAL?

So the phrase "different and useful" helps us understand what creativity is. But before we discover if it's possible to increase creativity, we have to ask a related question: Why are some people naturally more creative than others? Searching for that answer has produced some fascinating findings. Why do some people seem better able to think thoughts that are unique and useful? Why is original thinking almost child's play for these people? Playfulness—surprisingly—proves to be part of the answer.

HOW CREATIVE ARE YOU?

Originally designed for corporate executives, this test can help you determine your creative business strengths and weaknesses. It's adapted from *Creating Excellence,* by Craig Hickman and Michael Silva. To take the test, circle the number in the appropriate column, then total the numbers. The higher your score, the higher your creative abilities.

	ALWAYS	OFTEN	SELDOM	NEVER
1. You are stimulated by problems that tax your thinking.	4	3	2	1
2. You ask many questions and don't worry if they reveal your ignorance.	4	3	2	1
3. You surround yourself with people who promote different points of view.	4	3	2	1
4. You encourage open discussion and disagreement among people.	4	3	2	1
5. You entertain new ideas with enthusiasm rather than skepticism.	4	3	2	1
6. You look at things from a variety of viewpoints before making a decision.	4	3	2	1
7. You read voraciously to expand your knowledge.	4	3	2	1

"Just watch a child at play, and you'll see creativity in action," says Shore. "But then watch Mom and Dad interact with the child—'Don't do that or you'll get hurt,' or 'Don't play with that dirty thing,' and so on. Creativity becomes inhibited at a very early age."

Most researchers agree, noting that circumstances tend to stamp out creativity as children "mature" into adulthood. Even so, why do some of us seem to maintain greater levels of that childlike creativity throughout adult life?

"Intrinsic motivation," says Dr. Amabile. "The motivation to do what you're doing simply because you enjoy it—that's the most important factor in creativity. Skills are important too, naturally. You have to have skill in the area you're applying creativity to."

Motivation may help explain why some of us

are naturally more creative than others, but there's a more disturbing aspect to the question as well. Researchers have now shown a strong, virtually undeniable link between mental illness and creativity.

Are the mentally ill *naturally* more creative than the general population? Is there something about mental illness that sparks creativity?

Dr. Richards and Harvard psychologist Dennis Kinney, Ph.D., developed a Lifetime Creativity Scale capable of measuring creativity in both leisure activity and work, then used it to determine the creative abilities of manic-depressive patients.

"We looked at people with severe manic depression, people with a mild form of manic depression, the normal relatives of people with severe manic depression, and control subjects who did not have a history of mood disorder problems in their families," Dr. Richards explains.

"We found that creativity was high in people with mild manic depression, but it was highest in the *normal relatives* of people with severe manic depression," she says.

Such findings force Dr. Richards to conclude that the relatives of manic depressives may not really be normal after all. Just how or what is making them different, though, isn't known. "It could be that manic depression is just the tip of an iceberg with a different and more positive meaning," she says. "Perhaps those who end up with manic depression simply have too much of whatever makes their 'normal' relatives creative."

CLAIMING YOUR SHARE

Now we can address the second question with more clarity (and caution), asking not only if creativity can be increased, but also whether it can be done without risk to mental health. "Yes," says Dr. Richards. "There are many routes to creativity. You don't have to have mental problems to be creative."

Sometimes just a shift in attitude will get you started, says Shore. "A creative person usually starts with a positive attitude, whereas the noncreative person starts with a negative attitude. The creative person looks at challenge eagerly and aims at a solution, whereas the noncreative individual looks at the challenge and knows only fear."

Shore believes the latter response is an acquired characteristic. "As a child you didn't think negatively, and what you need to do is capture the feelings of a child combined with the wisdom of an adult. You have to get rid of the 'automatic no' response."

Dr. Amabile also believes creativity can be increased. "And one way to do it is to raise your level of skill," she says. "Skills are very important, and there are courses and self-help books that I believe may, in fact, help improve creativity." Not surprisingly though, she places the greatest importance on improved motivation. "Concentrating on intrinsic values will better your creative performance. Even if you know the boss is looking over your shoulder at

Need a burst of creativity? Take a laugh break. Researchers found that students who first watched a comedy film were more likely to creatively solve a perplexing puzzle.

ACCIDENTAL CREATIVITY

One of the last places you'd probably go looking for creativity is in the claim files of our nation's insurance companies. Ah, but creativity seems to flourish on automobile accident forms. To wit:

"I pulled away from the side of the road, glanced at my mother-in-law, and headed over the embankment."

"In my attempt to kill a fly, I drove into a telephone pole."

"The pedestrian had no idea which direction to run, so I ran over him."

"I was thrown from my car as it left the road. I was later found in the ditch by some stray cow."

"An invisible car came out of nowhere, struck my vehicle, and vanished."

work, you need to play a trick on yourself and put that realization as far out of mind as possible while you're actually doing the work."

CREATIVE CLUSTERING

Behavioral changes, however, need not always accompany increased creativity. Perhaps one of the simplest and most effective creativity boosters yet devised comes from Gabriele Rico, Ph.D., a professor of English, creative arts, and humanities at San Jose State University in California and author of *Writing the Natural Way*. The technique she developed is called clustering, and it's so simple you can do it today. In fact, says Dr. Rico, "There's nobody who can't cluster."

She's right. To cluster, simply write a word on a blank piece of paper, then for the next minute or two radiate words and phrases inspired by that word all around the page. Keep going, circling back to the center word until an associative pattern emerges. When you feel the magical "Aha!!" of creative inspiration, start writing for 8 to 10 minutes or so without stopping, using as many of the cluster words and phrases as you like. The important thing is to keep writing and don't look back—worry about the details later.

While this little technique might sound great for writers and writing, its use is not limited to that craft alone. Dr. Rico says that by carefully choosing your center word, you can apply her clustering technique to any problem or topic under the sun. "Once you learn it, and there's nothing to it," she says, "you can use it for problem finding, problem solving, interpersonal relationships—anything. Clustering is a generic tool to tap basically nonverbal processes and make them visible and graspable."

WORTH THE EFFORT?

So, we've discovered that creativity is the ability to think in ways that are unique and useful and that all of us apparently possess this ability to a greater or lesser degree. Using devices such as the Lifetime Creativity Scale, researchers can even measure our

PRESERVING YOUR CHILD'S CREATIVITY

It's an age that marks the beginning of childhood's creative utopia, a time when everything is possible—even a pink-eyed sun smiling with ruby-red lips in the drawing at right.

It starts shortly after the second birthday. Regardless of what you say, your child inevitably responds with a single, one-word reply: "Why?"

Before long, you'll think you've explained the "whys" of everything under the sun—but you haven't. In fact, you've left so much unexplained that your child starts inventing his own, often profound explanations and pictures of why things work and behave as they do.

Those who retain even a fraction of that imagination into adulthood are lucky—the words *no, don't,* and *can't* make creative casualties of most.

If you wish to preserve that early creative magic in your child, be warned that it's not an easy task. "Creative kids can be more difficult." says Ruth Richards, M.D., Ph.D., "They're thinking for themselves a lot, and they may be underachievers or disruptive."

And, says Dr. Richards, creative children are seldom appreciated in school, where teachers prefer classrooms filled with neat, cooperative students—traits rarely associated with creativity. "School really doesn't prepare people for a creative life," she says. "There's too much emphasis on being correct, when making mistakes is part of the creative learning process."

Her advice? "Be a mentor. Help your child understand that creativity is a different way of being but that it's a good thing. And respect your child's ideas, no matter how wild they may be—always hear them out."

creative ability at work or play, and since we all possess it, the experts say we can improve it. We can do so either by adopting a creative attitude, remaining mindful of our intrinsic motives for doing things, or by using creativity boosters such as clustering to help jump-start the process. Creativity-building exercises and creativity courses may also help. Only one question remains: Is creativity worth the effort?

Dr. Richards, whose research reminds us that good things sometimes contain hidden costs, replies, "I think people who are creative enjoy it. I think that in both disturbed and healthy people, creativity serves a healthy end and that people are usually better off for making the effort to be creative.

"Nobody forces anyone to be creative," she adds. "In fact, to be creative often puts you at odds with others, so there must be something worthwhile behind being creative."

Dr. Amabile agrees. "I think people who are less creative than they could or should be feel dissatisfied with aspects of their work or leisure activities. They feel they are boring, that there's a certain sameness to them and their lives."

Any effort made on behalf of creativity, then, may simply be the price one pays for living a fuller life. Sounds like a bargain.

CREATIVITY SECRETS OF THE PROS

If creativity is the ability to produce things that are unique and useful, then few individuals participate in the creative process more than advertising copywriters, the men and women who conceive and write the hundreds of commercials we see every day.

It's a tough, competitive field that demands top creative performance on a constant basis. But when advertising works, new images and characters enter the nation's consciousness and remain there for decades. Remember the early Volkswagen ads? And who hasn't heard of Ronald McDonald? The Pillsbury Dough Boy? The Maidenform woman? The offspring of copywriters, every one.

Here is a trio of bright young minds from some of the nation's largest advertising agencies to tell how they keep their creative batteries charged and share some creativity tips the rest of us can use in our daily lives.

LARRY SIMON

Age 35. Twelve years in advertising. Also taught copywriting on college level.
Agency: Leo Burnett, Chicago.
Memorable campaigns: Bud Light, McDonald's.

His thoughts on the creative process: "I do a lot of blue-sky thinking, just letting ideas flow and writing them down. Sometimes I find myself writing the same thing different ways or coming back to one particular idea time and again. Generally, ideas come like a spark. Somebody has to come up with the germ, the seed. Then you nurture it and make it grow."

His advice to others: "First, approach things with a sense of humor. Not that everything has to be funny, but you need to maintain a feeling of wit, especially about yourself. Never be so serious that you can't laugh—that's the first stumbling block to creativity. The other thing is maintaining an ability to let yourself go. Don't be afraid to do something."

DAVID LEWIS

Age 34. Fifteen years in advertising. Started off in mailroom and worked up.
Agency: DDB Needham, Chicago.
Memorable campaign: Busch Gardens theme parks.

Strokes of black paint on white paper mean little until the camera pulls back, revealing first a pair of eyes and then the unmistakable head. As music plays, the creature takes on life and ambles offscreen. Five letters in oriental script confirm the TV viewer's vision, followed by the name Busch Gardens. No words are spoken, but none are needed. All in a day's work for commercial maker and "creative thinker" David Lewis.

His thoughts on the creative process: "Basically, my job is sitting down and thinking. The job of an advertising copywriter could be more aptly called 'creative thinker.' In my case, I turn creativity on when I come to work and turn it off when I go home. This is my job. Sometimes I'll get an idea at home or while shopping, but I try to leave creativity at the office. This is my environment for doing creative work. If I have to work on the weekend, I come in here to do it. If I keep work and home separate, then my aim stays true."

His advice to others: "People who say, 'Gee, I'm just not very creative,' never will be. Everybody has it in them; you just have to find a way to bring it out."

RICK KORZENIOWSKI
Age 37. Sixteen years in advertising.
Agency: Leo Burnett, Chicago.
Memorable campaign: Nut & Honey Crunch.

His thoughts on the creative process: "I get my creative inspiration in any number of ways and places. There's no 'usual' when it comes to that. My partner and I are the ones who came up with the play on words for Nut & Honey Crunch. At first we laughed about it. My partner said, 'This is called Nut & Honey Crunch.' I said, 'Yeah, like nothing, honey. Like, *nut'n honey.*' The client saw it pretty quickly as the right approach.

"There's a process you go through. You get all the information you can first, though you never feel like that's enough. After you gather information, you spend some time talking about it, then some time thinking about it. But then there's a time when you have to get away from it for a while. That may last 5 minutes or five days. It seems like you almost overload yourself with information, and then you have to get away from it. You have to let your subconscious mind play with it a little bit—putting the information together in different relationships that your organized, conscious mind would never think of."

His advice to others: "First, define the problem as best you can. To me, that's the most important thing. If you're having trouble solving the problem as you have it defined, see if it can be redefined. Reword it, look at it a different way, then go at it again. It's very difficult to come up with solutions unless you understand exactly what it is you're trying to solve. Keep restating the problem whenever you hit a dead end."

DECISION MAKING

Harvard or Yale? Republican or Democrat? To be or not to be?

Choices. You would think that after years of choosing one from column A and one from column B on life's "Chinese menu," we would have the decision-making process down pat. Ah, but this is real life we're talking about here—where, just as you're about to make your final decision, you find out that there's also been a column C all along.

"The problem for most people in making a decision is not what option to pick but their fear of losing the option they don't pick," says Miriam Ehrenberg, Ph.D., a decision theorist and psychologist in private practice in New York City.

Okay, so you can't have your cake and eat it, too. But if you don't choose, if you don't make a decision, all you may ever get is a few crumbs. "When you don't act, then things just happen and you have to go along with what others choose for you."

If you don't want that to happen, you have to become the decision maker. And the best way to make decisions, according to Dr. Ehrenberg, is to go out on a limb.

GROW A "DECISION TREE"

"One way to make decisions clearer is to make what's called a decision tree," says Dr. Ehrenberg. "Write down on a piece of paper all the advantages and disadvantages that apply to either choice. Give each consequence a numerical weight and then add them up and see which choice comes out ahead."

Give your decision tree some time to grow. "Sleeping on a decision has value because then you're not making a choice in haste," says Dr. Ehrenberg. "If you are in an emotional state, that's not the best time to make a rational decision. Your judgment can be clouded by your feelings. Sleeping on it helps make sure that when you do make a decision, you're in a good frame of mind for making it."

But what about those cases where you must think on your feet and respond quickly? Dr. Ehrenberg recommends making sure you have all the information you need to make a proper decision, and then "get out of the rut of looking at only the options that are given you. Come up with new proposals that can make for a more creative decision."

Timewise, *when* you think about that decision is important, too. "People usually think of themselves as night people or day people," Dr. Ehrenberg says. "In either case, it's important to make a decision when you're on your toes. Many people have very clear thinking in midmorning. Around 11:00 A.M. is probably a good time for them to make a decision."

Thinking about what to order from the menu is probably the only decision you should concern yourself with during lunch. "After eating, your body is busy processing food and less blood is available to the brain for high-energy thinking. So that's not a

The missiles were so close they almost had a south Florida ZIP code. In a hectic "blur of meetings and discussion," President John F. Kennedy first turned to his advisers, special counsel Theodore Sorensen recalled. But ultimately, the final blockade decision rested on the shoulders of this one man, who told the world, "It shall be the policy of this nation to regard any nuclear missile launched from Cuba against any nation in the Western Hemisphere as an attack by the Soviet Union on the United States, requiring a full retaliatory response upon the Soviet Union." Less than one week later, Soviet Premier Nikita Khrushchev gave the order to dismantle the missiles.

real good time to make a decision," warns Dr. Ehrenberg. No wonder waitresses complain about tips.

DESTROY DEADLOCK

It seems like you can never win. Or can you? When you just don't know which option to choose, try to see both as potentially "correct." Experts who apply game theory to decision making say we can view choices as win-win situations or win-lose situations. Try to approach your decisions in ways that are always win-win. Look for something in each option that is good.

Sometimes though, pride and perfectionism can make the decision-making process a lose-lose proposition. It's not as if you aren't trying. You've been agonizing over the problem for days, but something keeps getting in the way.

Perfectionists are especially prone to decision deadlock. "When they try to make a decision, they must realize that nobody is perfect and that it's okay to make decisions that aren't perfect," Dr. Ehrenberg says. "Usually there is something salvageable in whatever decision you make."

And when all else fails, "trust your gut feelings," Dr. Ehrenberg advises. "They probably reflect subconscious decision-making processes that we can't always articulate. Something in our psyche is telling us something, and it's good to be able to listen to that."

And if even that fails, you could always flip a coin.

DISEASES OF THE BRAIN

When disease strikes the soft, wet, 3-pound, 100-billion-cell universe encased in your skull, your entire reality can change. Short-circuits momentarily banish awareness; Alzheimer's disease, stroke, and trauma kill cells that create your world; schizophrenia shapes a jumbled, frightening reality that uses normalcy only as a starting point. Disorders like these illuminate in glaring harshness how dependent you are on your fragile brain and to just how great an extent you are your brain and your brain is you.

ALCOHOLISM

Alcoholism more than holds its own in the brain disruption department, matching any infection, defect, or injury. What makes it especially tragic is that it is extremely hard to treat.

"About 75 percent of alcoholics develop brain disease," says Ralph Tarter, Ph.D., professor of psychiatry at the University of Pittsburgh School of Medicine. "Alcohol changes the structure of the brain." It destroys both neurons (nerve cells) and glial cells. Glial cells have important duties, involving nutrition, energy storage, and certain neural functions.

By shrinking and killing neurons, alcohol weakens the brain. It also swells it with edema, an accumulation of fluid that further damages cells by creating excess pressure.

"There's also a higher prevalence of strokes in alcoholics," Dr. Tarter says, "because alcohol increases blood pressure and hypertension, and because alcoholics have very destructive lifestyles." This destructiveness includes smoking and poor nutrition. The thiamine (vitamin B_1) deficiencies many alcoholics get can cause memory loss, psychosis, and an unsteady gait.

Alcoholism can also bring about alcoholic dementia, a permanent loss of intellectual function.

Alcoholism reduces the amounts of at least three vital neurotransmitters—epinephrine, serotonin, and acetylcholine—biochemical messengers that carry impulses from one neuron to another in the brain and throughout the nervous system. "At the very least the brain is functionally compromised," Dr. Tarter says. "Very low serotonin levels are associated with impulsive and very often aggressive behavior. If you don't have enough acetylcholine, you'll have impaired memory, learning, and thinking. People with low epinephrine may not be able to mobilize their energies to sustain alertness."

Finally, withdrawal from alcohol can cause delirium tremens, the DT's. Although some can get through withdrawal with only increased irritability and insomnia, others suffer hallucinations, delu-

BOOZE BATTERS THE BRAIN

Alcohol can shrink and kill brain cells in alcoholics and heavy social drinkers, says Clive Harper, M.D., professor of neuropathology at the University of Sydney, Australia. The shrinkage is in both gray and white matter. Gray matter consists of the neurons and the network of short nerve fibers called dendrites that surround each neuron like a tangle of roots, sending and receiving information. Each neuron also has one axon, a long nerve fiber that sends out information; the axon is the white matter.

"The gray matter network seems to shrivel up and retract," Dr. Harper says. Without incoming impulses, the neuron itself also shrinks, and as it does, so does the axon, the white matter. "As the cell shrinks, it functions less," he says. "Once it reaches a point of no return, it can't repair itself, and it fades away and dies." The only good news is that if you stop drinking soon enough, some of the damage may be reversible.

sions, and seizures, all signs of brainstorms and malfunctions.

For many, alcohol's devastating effects add ten years of premature aging to their brains. A study of 40 alcoholics, ranging in age from the thirties to the sixties, showed that their performance on neuropsychological tests was closer to that of normal people ten years older than it was to their own age groups. Reporting on the somber findings, the researchers said, "In a manner of speaking, alcoholism appears to cost the individual about a decade in terms of level of cognitive ability."

That's a high price to pay for a problem many experts believe can never really be cured—only prevented.

ALZHEIMER'S DISEASE

A diagnosis of Alzheimer's disease is a grim one. Today, the cause and cure of this all-too-common disorder are unknown, but its outcome is certain. About 2.5 million Americans have this deadly degenerative brain disease; if you're over 80, there's a better than one-in-five chance of getting it. Alzheimer's is usually fatal within seven to ten years of onset, and it is now the fourth-ranking killer of adults in the country, exceeded only by heart disease, cancer, and stroke.

"Many years ago, when people lost their memory and became senile as they aged, it was thought that was a natural effect of getting older," says Mark Alberts, M.D., a neurologist at the Alzheimer's Disease Research Center at Duke University Hospital. "But we know now that senility is *not* a normal function of aging. It's not normal to get to be 70 or 80 and not be able to understand and remember things. That's clearly *abnormal*."

There are two types of Alzheimer's. Early-onset Alzheimer's strikes people in their forties or fifties, while the late-onset type targets people in their midsixties and older.

Autopsies of Alzheimer's victims reveal structural changes. "An Alzheimer's brain shows atrophy.

A DAUGHTER'S DEDICATION

Rita Hayworth's public persona in the 1970s had disintegrated: The former glamorous Hollywood love goddess was now intoxicated, agitated, and confused in public. The medical diagnosis was alcoholic dementia. It wasn't until 1980 that the correct diagnosis was found: Alzheimer's disease, which was almost unheard of at the time. "I later learned that drinking often accompanies the onset of Alzheimer's . . . out of sheer frustration," Hayworth's daughter, Princess Yasmin Aga Khan, told *People* magazine. The truth galvanized her to action. "I kept asking myself, 'Why can't I do more to relieve her anguish?' " The desire to help others with the disease led her to join the Alzheimer's Disease and Related Disorders Association and to serve as its vice president. A bedridden, insensate Rita Hayworth died in 1987, but her daughter Yasmin carries on in her memory.

It's much smaller than a normal brain should be." Millions of cells die in the cortex and the hippocampus—in other words, in the thinking, feeling, doing, remembering brain.

Generally, there's an early stage of three or four

years when memory, judgment, and intellectual abilities begin to fail and emotional imbalance appears. Later, the victim has trouble walking or talking. He may not recognize family members or even know himself when he looks in a mirror. Daily activities like eating, bathing, and grooming become difficult, and incontinence, insomnia, and behavior problems appear. The victim has become a shell of his former self.

In the final stages of Alzheimer's, the victim needs total care the entire time. Death usually comes from pneumonia, malnourishment, or other related effects.

Two to three times more women than men get the disease, but that's probably because men tend to die earlier from other causes before Alzheimer's can get to them, Dr. Alberts says. "Alzheimer's has probably always been around, but now more people are living long enough to express the gene."

"Express the gene" is a crucial phrase in Alzheimer's research, since genetics represents "the most exciting and promising lead," Dr. Alberts says. "In some families it's very clear Alzheimer's appears to be inherited." Scientists have traced the early-onset Alzheimer's gene to a site somewhere on chromosome 21. "It remains controversial," he says, "but I would say that at least 50 to 60 percent, perhaps as high as 80 to 90 percent, of Alzheimer's cases may have a genetic basis."

EPILEPSY

"An electrical storm in the brain" is an apt analogy for epilepsy, says neurology professor John Freeman, M.D., director of the Pediatric Epilepsy Center of Johns Hopkins Medical Institutions. "The brain works on electricity. That's how one brain cell talks to another. But for reasons we don't understand, sometimes the wires get crossed and static is the result. Then all the cells are talking at once."

A certain amount of this static is normal, but people with epilepsy either get more of it or are more sensitive to it. The associated seizures range from the simple to the generalized. The simple partial seizure strikes the parts of the brain that control sight, smell, hearing, memory, or motor controls, causing strange sensations or minor jerking or twitching while the person remains conscious.

If both hemispheres of the brain are involved, a generalized seizure can occur, causing alteration or loss of consciousness and painless convulsions (grand mal seizures) in some or just a trancelike (petit mal) state in others. Seizures usually last only a few minutes at most.

Causes of epilepsy are varied and age-related. Birth trauma ranks first as a cause in young children; brain injury is tops for 20-year-olds, tumors predominate in 30- to 40-year-old adults, and blood vessel disease is the most common culprit in older people.

Treatment of epilepsy depends on what kind of seizure you have, Dr. Freeman says. "We don't know what triggers a seizure or what ends a seizure," he says, "but 80 percent of people can have their seizures completely controlled by medication."

THE WORST DEMENTIA: BINSWANGER'S DISEASE

Up to 50 percent of people with Alzheimer's disease have a "Binswanger's-like" disease superimposed on the Alzheimer's, says Mark Alberts, M.D. The severely dementing Binswanger's disease is believed to be caused by a number of small strokes deep in the white matter of the brain. Binswanger's also hardens the arteries that supply the white matter, evidence of its close link with high blood pressure, which is a likely cause of stroke. "These strokes coalesce, and as they progress, the patients become demented," Dr. Alberts says. "It's not entirely clear what produces this pattern of strokes. It's one of the very interesting questions in stroke research."

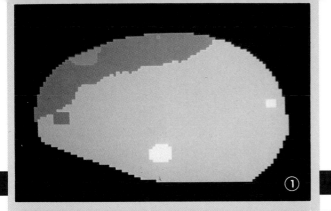

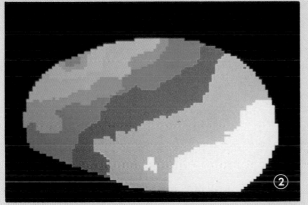

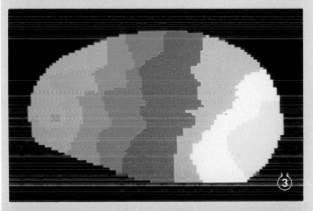

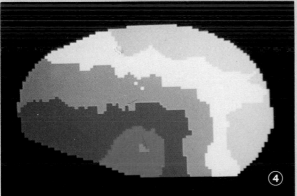

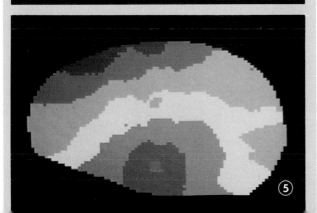

A SEIZURE'S SPECTRUM OF CHAOS

These images depict an epileptic seizure, showing abnormal electrical activity on the left side of the scalp (the front of the head is at the left). In these images, warm colors represent positive electric voltage; cool shades show negative voltage.

(1) The green spot shows the brain's electrical field moving toward a negative voltage. (2) Blue emerges in the same spot as the negative field nears its peak. (3) The less negative voltage sweeps backward across the scalp. (4) The field enters a positive voltage. (5) Red emerges as the field reaches peak positive voltage.

This cycle will repeat over and over until the seizure ends.

PARKINSON'S DISEASE

By the time the first symptoms of Parkinson's disease appear, the part of the brain it attacks is 80 percent destroyed. The symptoms are insidiously gradual and progressive: trembling, slowing of movement, stiffness, weakness, loss of balance. The facial muscles lose their ability to smile or frown; from the inside out the face crystallizes into an empty mask. The mind remains intact but imprisoned. Parkinson's affects 1 in every 100 Americans over age 60.

Doctors know what happens to the brain in Parkinson's, but they don't know why, and so they don't know how to stop it, says Juan Sanchez-Ramos, M.D., Ph.D., assistant professor of neurology at the University of Miami and a research associate for the National Parkinson's Foundation.

Parkinson's destroys a tiny but uniquely important area deep in the midbrain called the substantia nigra. Many of its neurons contain the neurotransmitter dopamine, a crucial link in a metabolic chain that enables us to move our bodies. Neurons need both dopamine and another neurotransmitter, acetylcholine, to communicate. Normally these two are in balance, but Parkinson's somehow kills the dopamine cells. Your muscles no longer can do what you tell them because they aren't getting the message.

Parkinson's fluctuates from day to day, even hour to hour, so sufferers are immobilized at some times and normal at other times. "That means the nervous system is intact, but the chemicals aren't," Dr. Sanchez-Ramos says.

Increasingly, evidence shows that still other chemicals may be the culprits. The street drug MPTP produces symptoms that "for all the world look like Parkinson's," Dr. Sanchez-Ramos says. "And there are at least 200 compounds in our environment that are structurally similar. So we're zooming in on environmental toxins that may cause the disease."

ADRENAL CELL IMPLANTS FOR PARKINSON'S?

The brain disease Parkinson's—and its symptoms of shaky limbs and slurred speech—is accompanied by the death of dopamine cells in the brain. Because similar cells are also found in the adrenal glands, surgeons have tried implanting bits of adrenal tissue in the brains of Parkinson's patients.

"At first it was very exciting to hear about adrenal cell implants for Parkinson's," says Juan Sanchez-Ramos, M.D., Ph.D. "But I'm afraid they jumped the gun. What very minimal improvement there is can't even be linked to the surgery. So there's a moratorium on further transplants in this country."

What's more, Dr. Sanchez-Ramos notes, if environmental toxins cause Parkinson's (a current theory), "the adrenal cells were probably exposed to the same thing."

Mild cases of Parkinson's can be treated with drugs—anticholinergics, certain antihistamines, and tricyclic antidepressants—that inhibit dopamine's opposite number, acetylcholine. When Parkinson's becomes more severe and disabling, the drug levodopa (L-dopa) is given so neurons can make their own dopamine.

SCHIZOPHRENIA

Schizophrenia is a beast of a brain disease. It terrifies its prey. It rips their thoughts into tattered shreds, snarls menace into their ears, carves florid frescoes of illusion before their eyes. It seizes them in their youthful prime and pounds them into fragments of what they might have been. And it grinds relentlessly at the lives of those who love them, chipping away at time, opportunity, resources, patience, and understanding. Schizophrenia strikes at the very heart of humanness, chews it up and spits it out.

No one knows what causes the abnormalities in brain chemicals that are associated with schizophrenia. Like most brain diseases, its origin is a mystery. Yet it's estimated that 1 in every 100 Americans will get schizophrenia.

Symptoms are usually divided into positive and negative: positive symptoms are distortions of normal functions like thought (delusions) or perception (hallucinations); negative symptoms are a loss of normal functions like emotional response (withdrawal) and drive (inactivity). A schizophrenic may have any or all of these symptoms dominating his confusing world.

SEARCHING FOR A CAUSE

What's behind these heartrending symptoms? "There is evidence of structural abnormalities" in schizophrenic brains, says Joel Kleinman, M.D., Ph.D., chief of neuropathology for the National Institute of Mental Health's Clinical Brain Disorders Branch. "But the cause of those abnormalities remains unknown." And whether the abnormalities are a cause or an

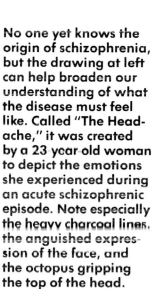

No one yet knows the origin of schizophrenia, but the drawing at left can help broaden our understanding of what the disease must feel like. Called "The Headache," it was created by a 23-year-old woman to depict the emotions she experienced during an acute schizophrenic episode. Note especially the heavy charcoal lines, the anguished expression of the face, and the octopus gripping the top of the head.

effect of schizophrenia is also unknown.

These abnormalities include enlarged ventricles, cavities in the brain that contain cerebrospinal fluid. One section of the cerebellum may be too small; it's theorized that this section may be involved in regulating the neurotransmitter dopamine. Cells in the basal ganglia (motor functions) and parts of the limbic system (some emotion and memory functions) become smaller, less numerous, and more disorganized. The differences between the left and right brains are greater than normal, which supports the theory that the schizophrenic's left brain is overactive.

Another hypothesis is that either too much dopamine is being produced or there are too many dopamine receptors, Dr. Kleinman says. Overactive dopamine-producing cells in the cortex and limbic regions (the emotional centers of the brain) have been linked to delusions, hallucinations, and disorganized thinking.

There's no cure for schizophrenia, but it can be controlled. Antipsychotic medications like chlorpromazine (Thorazine and others) are commonly used, although the side effects can be considerable for some, especially after years of treatment.

Earlier in this century psychoanalysis was tried, despite Sigmund Freud's opposition to the notion the disease could be traced to upbringing or traumatic emotional experiences. "It's difficult if not impossible to say psychology is effective," Dr. Kleinman says. "But a skilled therapist can use it to develop an alliance with the patient so he will take the medications." And it does seem to help some sufferers deal with the difficulty and pain of the disease.

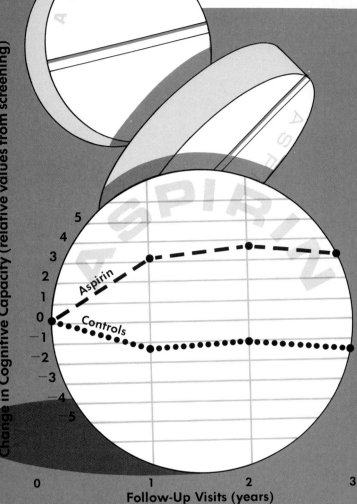

Change in Cognitive Capacity (relative values from screening)

Follow-Up Visits (years)

Aspirin

Controls

ASPIRIN REVERSES STROKE MIND DAMAGE

"Simplify, simplify," said Thoreau. Following his advice, scientists find the simplest solution is often the most elegant. So it is with multi-infarct dementia and aspirin. Caused by a series of ischemic strokes (which occur when blood clots block arteries that supply the brain), multi-infarct dementia is second only to Alzheimer's as a cause of mental deterioration. But unlike Alzheimer's, this dementia can be reversed, and very simply: with aspirin.

That landmark discovery was made by Baylor College of Medicine neurology professor John Meyer, M.D., director of the Cerebral Blood Flow Laboratory at the Veterans Administration Medical Center in Houston. He found one aspirin a day so effective in improving cognition in stroke patients that he ended his comparison study on ethical grounds and gave aspirin to the control (nonaspirin) group as well. "Many patients treated with aspirin improved to the point where families didn't have to supervise them anymore," Dr. Meyer says. Their cognitive test scores (a measure of thinking ability) jumped 17 percent the first year, 21 percent the second, and 20 percent the third.

STROKE

A stroke may seem like a bolt from the blue, but for most people it's actually a long time coming and highly preventable. Doctors know what causes more than half a million Americans each year to suffer a stroke. (More than 150,000 of these strokes are fatal.) Research suggests that by the age of 30, one-quarter of all Americans have had the kinds of changes in their brain arteries that set them up for a stroke at any time.

All this means that science has also learned how you can keep your arteries healthy and thus contribute to a continuing drop in the stroke death rate. And if you're one of the almost three million Americans living with the aftermath of stroke, modern rehabilitation methods may help you lead the most productive life possible.

What doctors call a cerebral vascular accident we call a stroke. "Stroke is a syndrome, not a disease,"

says neurologist John Marler, M.D., of the Division of Stroke and Trauma at the National Institutes of Health. "It's a set of symptoms and signs due to an injury to a part of the brain supplied by a blood vessel."

There are two major types of stroke—ischemic and hemorrhagic. Ischemic strokes account for 70 to 80 percent of all strokes. They're also the most preventable. In an ischemic stroke, a clot of blood sticks in an artery feeding your brain and starves your brain cells.

One type of hemorrhagic stroke, cerebral hemorrhage, occurs when a defective artery right in or on the brain bursts and blood spills into the tissue. Another type—the subarachnoid hemorrhage—is due to the rupture of a small blood vessel on the inner side of the lining of the brain. In either case, the accumulation of blood creates excess pressure on the brain.

Stroke deprives the affected brain cells of food

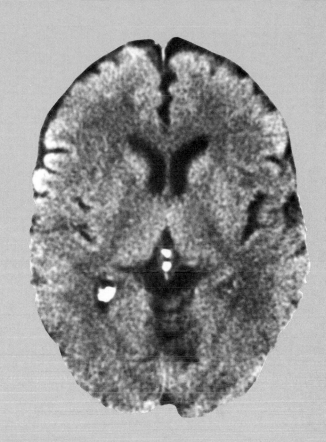

and oxygen, causing them to die. Forever. No healing here.

The results vary with the severity of the stroke and depend on which area of the brain is under siege. One of the most common effects is paralysis. If the stroke hits your right brain, your left arm and leg and left side of your face can become numb and weak, your face sags, your speech slurs as if you've gotten a huge dose of novocaine at the dentist. A stroke can also affect your memory, your emotions, and your ability to understand speech.

REDUCING THE RISK

Since stroke is a symptom of disease, treating a stroke is a bit like closing the barn door after the horse gets out. "Prevention is strongly advised," Dr. Marler says. "The risk factors to be concerned about are the same as those for heart attack.

"Ischemic strokes are associated with high blood pressure, heart disease, artery disease, and diabetes," Dr. Marler says. "These diseases cause perhaps 80 percent of ischemic strokes. And they are largely preventable." An ischemic stroke can occur when fat and cholesterol deposits in an artery stimulate blood to clot. In the case of hemorrhagic strokes, high blood pressure may push too strongly on an artery wall's weak spot and cause it to rupture or leak.

"Far and away the most important preventive thing you can do is to control your blood pressure," Dr. Marler says. Faulty diet, smoking, obesity, heredity, stress, and personality seem to play crucial roles in raising blood pressure to dangerous levels. High blood pressure, in turn, speeds up the development of atherosclerosis.

On the dietary front, America's love affair with high-fat foods has been linked to high blood pressure, although science hasn't pinned down the exact connection. It is known, however, that a high-fat diet also raises cholesterol levels in the blood, with atherosclerosis too often the next step. Smoking, too, is strongly implicated in atherosclerosis, while obesity makes you a plump morsel for heart disease and resultant stroke.

BETTER DIAGNOSIS, BETTER TREATMENT

A man who had left-side numbness and weakness also had a normal CAT (computerized axial tomography) scan (above). But an even "higher tech" MRI (magnetic resonance imaging) scan showed a small area of stroke deep in his brain (below, arrow). Surgery would be unnecessary in this case.

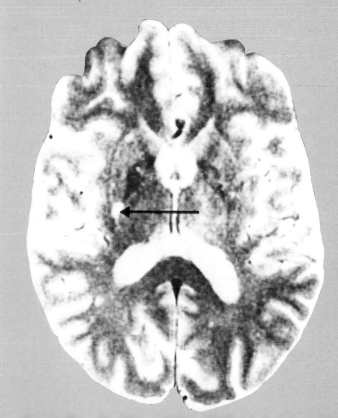

So if you could do just four things for yourself to reduce your blood pressure and prevent a stroke, experts suggest the following steps.

- Cut way down on fat in your diet.
- Lose excess weight.
- Stop smoking.
- Exercise.

Drugs are also very good at lowering blood pressure, Dr. Marler says, and at times they are critical. Treatment usually starts with a diuretic to get rid of excess fluid, a step that by itself can bring blood pressure down. An antihypertensive drug is often used in combination to further reduce pressure.

If a stroke does strike, experts say family support and involvement is the key to successful rehabilitation, and a team of rehab specialists probably is the best approach.

TRAUMA

By growing a hard, thick case of bone for your brain, the body does the best it can to protect its center of consciousness, its mainframe computer. But the protection is not evenly distributed. Your rear brain stays in one place during a blow or whiplash; your not-so-well-fixed forebrain bounces back and forth inside your skull. Nerve cells get pummeled, bruised, and squeezed, and nerve fibers stretch and

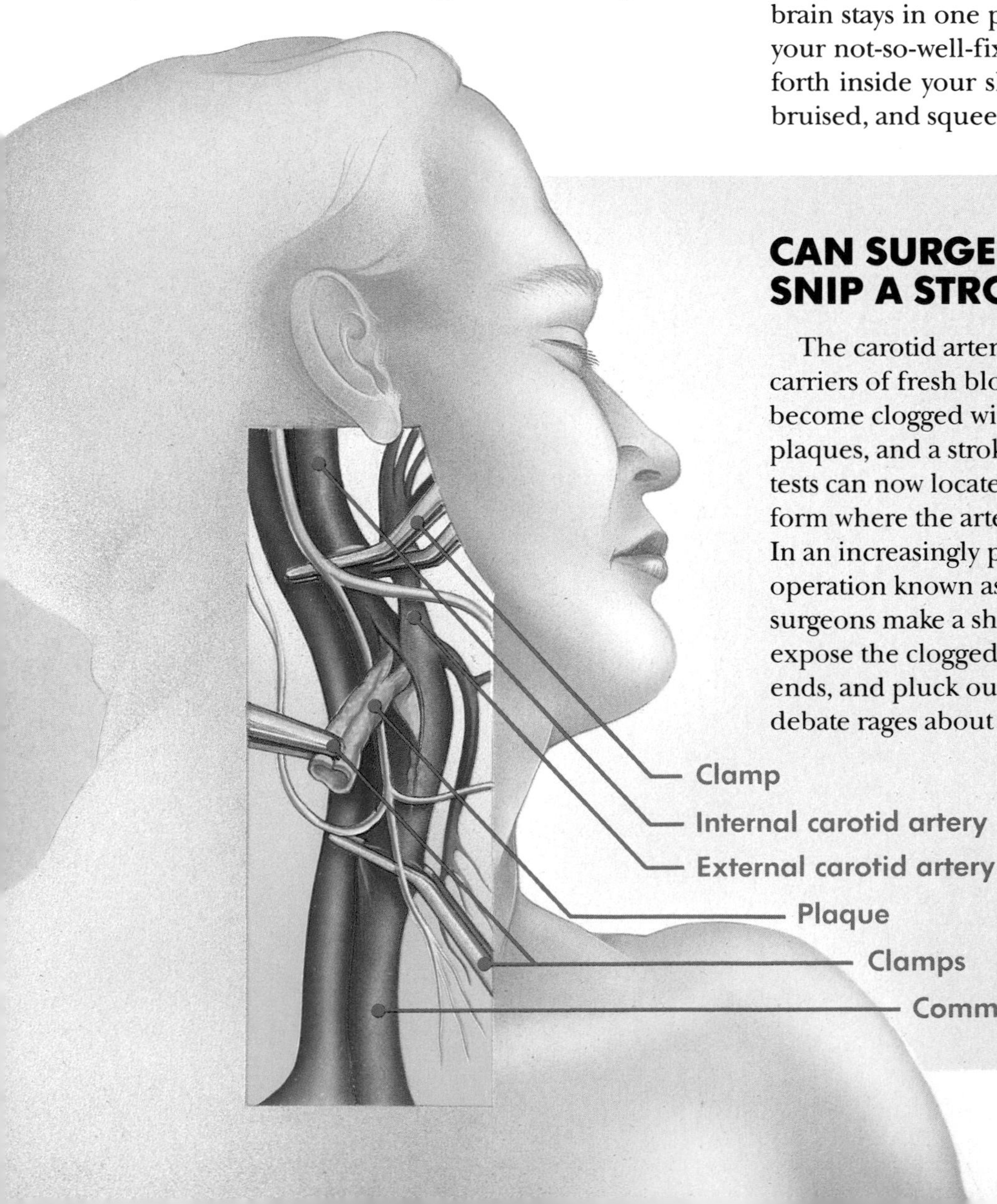

CAN SURGERY SNIP A STROKE?

The carotid arteries, which are the primary carriers of fresh blood to the brain, can become clogged with fatty deposits called plaques, and a stroke can result. Sophisticated tests can now locate the plaques, which usually form where the arteries narrow and branch off. In an increasingly popular but controversial operation known as a carotid endarterectomy, surgeons make a shallow incision in the neck to expose the clogged artery, clamp it off at both ends, and pluck out the plaque. A medical debate rages about the safety, necessity, and results of the surgery, which can itself cause a severe, even fatal stroke or other complications.

Clamp
Internal carotid artery
External carotid artery
Plaque
Clamps
Common carotid artery

snap. This front brain bounce is why most head trauma has long-term intellectual consequences. Memory and concentration difficulties, impaired judgment, emotional imbalances, and behavior problems all stem from injuries to the forebrain, the truly *human* brain.

There are two stages of brain damage, says neuropsychologist James Mikula, Ph.D., vice president of the Professional Council of the National Head Injury Foundation. Initially, the cells themselves are injured from a blow to the head, from fresh blood on the outer surface of the cells, and from pressure caused by fluid buildup. "When your body has any type of injury, it dumps water on it and it swells, as in a blister," Dr. Mikula says. "Your brain does the same thing. The only problem is that it's encased in a nice little shell and there's no place for it to swell." The resulting pressure squeezes some cells so much that their functioning declines or stops altogether. Once the cell bodies die, any remaining connections they have will also deteriorate and die.

If pressure continues long enough, the second stage of damage occurs. Blood flow in the brain is reduced. Surviving cells don't get enough oxygen, and their metabolic functions suffer. "In most cases, the loss of function tends to be permanent," Dr. Mikula says. "There may be major changes in overall metabolic rates as well. Some people may have a very high metabolic rate for months after their injury.

At least gladiators got it over quickly. But a boxer suffers a career of trauma: When gloved fist meets bare head, the forebrain is slammed against the skull. Nerve fibers tear, and swelling squeezes brain cells. This repeated pounding can produce a punch-drunk pugilist. And experts say even helmets don't offer adequate protection.

In others the rate is very suppressed."

Not all head injuries involve damage to the brain cell bodies themselves, however. Just as bad is injury to axons, the connectors that carry messages from one nerve cell to another. "In a whiplash injury, you've got a mass of cell bodies fixed in the rear of the brain, but when the rest of the brain starts to move, the axons or nerve fibers end up being torn and sheared," Dr. Mikula says. "A perfectly good cell body that doesn't have connections to any other cell is worthless."

Sometimes a damaged axon will reconnect itself. But other times it will degenerate right up to the cell body, which will then die.

Common sources of head trauma include automobile and bicycle accidents, boxing, and football. Sometimes small children are injured when parents shake them violently.

Each year more than 700,000 Americans are treated for head injuries; 100,000 die. Yet many injuries are totally preventable, often by as simple an act as buckling a seat belt.

ENDORPHINS

You may have heard a few things about them—intriguing things, exciting things. "The body's natural painkillers," some have called them. Others have linked them to "runner's high," the great feeling many get during exercise. They are the subject of a burgeoning field of research so young that new theories pop up every day and inconclusive results are the norm. But one thing is for sure: There's still lots to learn about these fascinating chemicals, and so far, the picture looks positively promising.

Endorphins were discovered by brain researchers in the late 1970s. The first evidence of their existence came with the discovery that certain brain

Getting needled by an acupuncturist may prompt production and release of endorphins that block pain and inflammation throughout the body, say researchers studying this ancient medical technique. Beta-endorphin levels of patients in one study showed marked increases during and shortly after acupuncture. Measurements of their tolerance for pain rose at the same time.

cells have opioid receptor molecules into which the opiate morphine seems to naturally fit itself, like a plug into a socket. Researchers immediately wondered why the brain would evolve such a mechanism for the extract of a poppy plant. Could it be, some surmised, that the human brain produces an opioid substance very similar to opium?

Yes, it could. Enkephalin (meaning "in the head") was the first such naturally produced opioid to be

discovered. Dozens more have been found since, not only in the brain but throughout the body. Now considered to be hormones, they are known to be produced in the pituitary gland in the brain, the adrenal glands near the kidneys, possibly in certain immune cells, and perhaps elsewhere as well. They appear to flow both down from and up into the brain. Present in the blood in infinitesimally small quantities, they nevertheless can be extremely powerful. One type called dynorphin, for instance, is more than 200 times more potent than morphine.

Beta-endorphin, produced in the pituitary, has been especially well researched. "Beta-endorphin slows the heart rate and respiration and lowers blood pressure," says Lee Berk, doctor of health science, assistant research professor of pathology and laboratory medicine at Loma Linda University, in California, who has been studying endorphins for a decade. "It is a euphoric substance, contributing to feelings of well-being."

NATURE'S ANSWER TO PAIN

Beta-endorphin, enkephalin, and others also seem to play an important part in relieving pain, possibly by blocking the transmission of a pain-carrying brain chemical called substance P. Studies have found that endorphin levels rise among pregnant women —nature's way, perhaps, of providing pain relief during delivery. On the flip side, people who suffer from chronic headaches and premenstrual syndrome may actually be suffering from low endorphin levels, some researchers theorize. Insufficient endorphins— which might result from a genetically weak endorphin system—might even cause psychological depression.

Overall, human beings need endorphins to lead an energetic, productive life, says Murray Allen, M.D., a researcher and consultant at the School of Kinesiology of Simon Fraser University in Canada.

"Endorphins help people thrive," he says. "Following physical activity, they have a major calming effect on the central nervous system, muscles, arteries, and a host of hormonal glands. They influence the body heat mechanisms so you can be active in a wide range of external temperatures. And they give you a sense of calm and fearlessness in the face of risks, enabling you to accomplish more, giving you a sense of achievement."

But all is not positive in the world of endorphins. Some types may impair learning or memory. Others may suppress the immune system: Studies show that one type, alpha-endorphin, along with some others, may reduce the effectiveness of the natural killer cells the body needs to fight infection.

RELIEF ON DEMAND

For the most part, though, it seems the goal is to have more endorphins working for you, not less. And researchers know that certain situations can prompt the body's production of these chemicals. Physical pain and stress top the list. One such stress is moderate exercise.

"Individuals who work out regularly, who are conditioned, release more endorphin as they exercise," says Dr. Berk, who has conducted extensive research in this area. "Exercise seems to somehow modify their pituitary, causing greater endorphin release." Endorphin release enables them to exercise longer and presumably with less pain, he says.

Acupuncture—the ancient oriental medical system in which needles are inserted at certain points of the body—can also stimulate endorphin production, some studies have shown. So can chiropractic adjustments. And although no one is necessarily advising it, binge eating or eating lots of sweets may boost endorphin levels, possibly to chemically counteract feelings of depression.

A good laugh seems to stimulate endorphins, too, says Dr. Berk, whose most recent research examines the hormones' links to humor. Blood samples taken from people chuckling through funny movies showed significant changes in the ratio of endorphins to other stress-related hormones, he says, although he adds, "I don't think anyone can say quite yet that endorphins increase with humor." But we certainly won't laugh if he discovers that they do.

Exercising more—or in some cases, less—may increase your chances of a "runner's high," says New York sports medicine specialist Lewis Maharam, M.D. Theorizing that each of us has a specific activity level that optimizes mood, he put runners on a treadmill, recorded their moods moment by moment, and came up with individualized "exercise prescriptions."

EXERCISE AND YOUR BRAIN

Your brain may be the seat of your intelligence, but to stimulate it you may have to get up off the seat of your pants. "If you want to stimulate your thinking process, it's probably not a good idea to be sedentary," says Bruce W. Tuckman, Ph.D., professor of educational research at Florida State University. "A sedentary body makes for a sedentary mind."

To prove his point, Dr. Tuckman got a group of more than 100 youngsters up and running. The fourth-, fifth-, sixth-, and eighth-grade students that he picked definitely had, as he says, "anti-aerobic attitudes." Translation: Running wasn't their favorite activity.

But after a 15-week program of jogging, Dr. Tuckman discovered that "the kids did substantially better on tests for creativity than kids who didn't exercise."

And on still another track, a Salt Lake City research psychologist at the Veterans Administration Medical Center has found that fast walking seems to help jog the memory of forgetful adults, and it does other good things as well. "Our fast-walking group significantly improved its mental ability," says Robert Dustman, Ph.D., who investigates the effect vigorous aerobic exercise—the kind that speeds heart rate and circulation—has on the brain.

In a four-month study, Dr. Dustman divided a group of 55- to 70-year-old people into three categories: aerobic exercisers, nonaerobic exercisers, who exercised less vigorously, and a control group of nonexercisers.

"The aerobic exercisers showed an improvement in short-term memory, had faster reaction times, and were more creative than nonaerobic exercisers," he says. And while the nonaerobic exercisers did show small improvement, "the nonexercisers showed absolutely no change in mental ability. We think this increase in mental performance relates to the fact that more oxygen gets to the brain during aerobic activity," says Dr. Dustman.

"Aerobic exercise will not only make a difference in how your heart, lungs, and muscles function," says Ted Bashore, Ph.D., associate professor of psychiatry at the Medical College of Pennsylvania. "It may also make a difference in how your brain processes information—how efficiently you can make split-second decisions, for example, like braking when a child darts in front of your car."

Keeping your *eye* on the ball can also keep your *brain* on the ball. "Ping-Pong and activities like it," says Miriam Ehrenberg, Ph.D., "are particularly good in helping develop coordination. And coordination develops neural connections in the brain."

In an ongoing study of the reaction times of more than 100 men of varied ages, Dr. Bashore says preliminary results indicate "that although older people have slower reaction times than younger people, older aerobic exercisers react faster than nonexercising older people. The older you are, the more important aerobic exercise is."

If you're looking to keep your brain lobes up to speed, try practicing your tennis lobs. Studies of sports like squash, tennis, and racquetball show that those participants have faster reaction times than runners or nonexercisers.

Another psychologist who has studied the benefits of aerobic exercise on brain power is Charles Emery, Ph.D., assistant professor of psychiatry at Duke University Medical Center. He agrees that older people could benefit the most from aerobic exercise. It's important, though, for anyone over 35 to check with a doctor before beginning to exercise.

After you get the okay, Dr. Emery recommends "low-impact aerobics like stationary bike riding, walking, or swimming. The improvements you'll see should last for as long as you keep exercising."

IDEAS AFOOT

Oh, to have been Einstein's shoemaker. Like many other creative thinkers, Einstein walked to help solve problems. And he walked a lot, sometimes becoming so involved in thought that he became lost.

Whether you're grappling with the theory of relativity or just trying to decide what to feed the relatives, walking might help. "There is a very dynamic action involving both sides of the brain when walking, and you tend to become more creative," says David Balboa, codirector of the Walking Center in New York City.

When you have a problem, "just get up and walk," he suggests.

GENDER AND YOUR BRAIN

You know what they say: Women and numbers don't add up; men and words are mutually incompatible. But recent findings are yielding a new and more complex picture of where our natural abilities lie—and what we can do to make the most of them.

"The role of sex hormones in prenatal brain development is quite dramatic and profound," says Doreen Kimura, Ph.D., professor of psychology at the University of Western Ontario. This role continues immediately after birth and perhaps even into adulthood. As a result, the verbal left hemisphere of the brain may develop faster in girls than in boys. Women tend to be "more verbally fluent," Dr. Kimura says. "In general, girls start talking sooner and articulate better than boys. They're better at fine motor-[movement] skills. Males tend to be better at certain kinds of spatial tasks [being able to picture how an object would look from different angles] and mathematical reasoning tasks."

Hormones aside, just two anatomical differences between human male and female brains have

BRAIN TRAITS: MEN AND WOMEN COMPARED

Here you see Joanne Average Female and Russell Average Male. Just as they differ below the neck, so they differ above. It's not likely that *you're* so average, though: Each of us is a unique, cornucopian blend of attributes and skills.

Men are better at spatial tasks, and they don't get lost as easily.

Men tend to rely more on a single hemisphere for certain abilities.

Women talk at an earlier age, articulate better, and are more fluent.

The connection between hemispheres is bigger in women.

The vast majority of mathematical geniuses are men.

Women are better at work requiring high levels of dexterity.

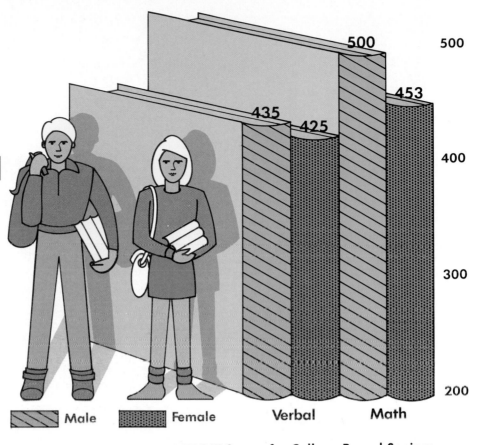

Does your sex make a difference in your aptitude for math and verbal skills? Yes and no, respectively, according to Scholastic Aptitude Test (SAT) results. Boys outreason their female classmates mathematically by an average of 50 points (especially among top scorers), but verbally there's little difference. In hot dispute is whether the SAT itself flunks, since girls consistently get higher math *grades*.

Sex Differences in 1987 SAT Scores for College-Bound Seniors

been proven. First, a typical male brain is bigger than a typical female brain, because the typical male is bigger than the typical female. Second, Roger Gorski, Ph.D., chairman of the Department of Anatomy and Cell Biology at UCLA, and others have shown that a portion of the corpus callosum, the connection between the two hemispheres of the brain, is larger in women than in men.

Research indicates males are more dependent on one hemisphere or area for a certain function, while women's functions are more scattered throughout the brain.

"So you could argue that the halves need to communicate with each other more in the female, and if there's more crosstalk, the connection would be larger," Dr. Gorski says. "But it's just inference. We don't really know what it means." And more recent studies show brain organization depends on what function you're talking about. For example, studies of brain-damaged people show that some of women's speaking abilities, for example, are *more* localized than men's.

YOUR SEX CAN'T STOP YOU

It's likely that environment has also played a role in this sexual differentiation of brains, Dr. Kimura says.

"The brain organization we enjoy today was probably present in its basic form as long ago as half a million years," she says. In other words, despite today's lessening of sex roles, men still have the spatial brain they needed to chuck spears and find their way home from the hunt, and women still have the motor and communication advantages they needed to watch passels of kids, prepare food, and make clothes, all close at hand and often all at once.

Your ability to do math, for instance, does not hinge solely on your sex, Dr. Gorski says. "There's no anatomical reason to tell a youngster, 'Since you're a girl, you can do well in language but not in math,' or to tell a boy, 'Stick with math, forget English.' Because the brain is such a marvelous organ, there's every reason to encourage people to do anything they want." Neuroanatomist Marian Diamond, Ph.D., of the University of California, Berkeley, says her research shows conclusively that while hormones have a role in "programming" the brain, "environment can go beyond that program." Here, environment means upbringing, education, encouragement, and challenge.

So, hormonal head starts and hindrances notwithstanding, the possibilities for all of us—regardless of gender—are virtually unlimited.

GENIUS

She had held human brain tissue before, many times. But this time was different. This time, there was genius lying in her palm. "It was the ultimate brain as far as our society is concerned," says neuroanatomist Marian Diamond, Ph.D., recalling that moment in the early 1980s.

In her hands, she cradled Albert Einstein's brain. Alone in her University of California, Berkeley, lab, Dr. Diamond carefully placed a section of it under her microscope. Holding her breath, she slowly turned a dial and suddenly one of the few geniuses of this century came into sharp focus. "I knew I was looking at something very precious," says Dr. Diamond. "Nobody had studied Aristotle's, Galileo's, or Newton's brain. But now I had the opportunity to examine the brain of a true genius."

She looked where even Einstein couldn't see. What she found confirmed what many others had thought all along. Einstein's brain was special. "Seventy-three percent more glial cells were found in a certain portion of his left hemisphere as compared to the same area of the brains of normal males."

Glia cells nourish and support neurons and are known to increase in number with learning, something Einstein obviously did a lot of.

Other researchers are finding, though, that the true nature of genius can't always be pinned down under a microscope's lens.

IQ ISN'T ENOUGH

Most people believe that to be a genius you must have a high IQ. But researchers who study geniuses say that if you want to be a genius, you have to be more than just smart. "We have to distinguish between a person who does well on conventional tests and someone who makes really unique contributions to knowledge," says Philip Powell, Ph.D., associate professor of educational psychology at the University of Texas at Austin.

The people who make the IQ tests characterize an IQ above 140 as genius, but those who've looked behind the numbers aren't so sure. "After 70 years of following a group of people with IQ's over 180, we found that none of them turned out to be geniuses in their lifetimes by anybody's definition," says David Feldman, Ph.D., professor of developmental psychology at Tufts University. "Genius is only very loosely related to IQ."

To find real genius, you have to look beyond the tests. "The operative word when describing genius is novelty," says Dr. Powell. "A genius is a person who comes up with unusual or unique ideas or products that end up transforming a generation. Buckminster Fuller was one. Shakespeare was one. Certainly da Vinci and Einstein were also geniuses."

Geniuses are like oysters. They can turn a tiny grain of sand into a sparkling pearl. Geniuses are driven. They get an idea, the grain of sand, and they continue to build on it, layer by layer. "Persistence pays off. They always keep their mind focused in on the problem," says Dr. Powell. "They can't stop thinking about it. They have an incredible need for completeness. They need to bring their ideas together to create a synthesis." The result could be anything from a symphony to a new scientific theory.

DO YOU HAVE IT?

So even if you didn't score 200 on that last IQ test, don't rule out your ability to reach "geniushood." "If you have a passion for some field or activity, that's a good sign," says Dr. Feldman, that there may be genius within.

Talent is another clue. "If you do something easily that's difficult for other people, that's also a really good sign."

You'll find that geniuses tend to do very well in many different areas "if you let them," says Dr. Powell. They also tend to do things on their own. "Many are self-educated, and that may actually help them. They are not caught up in accepting the usual viewpoints or approaches to problem-solving."

Don't underestimate the challenge facing you. But "if you have faith that you have potential to do something significant," says Dr. Feldman, "keep the faith and try to organize the resources to make it possible."

AUTISTIC SAVANT'S WORK DUPLICATES DA VINCI

At age 3½, Nadia could barely hold a crayon by herself, yet when this autistic child did manage to draw, her art works rivaled that of the genius Leonardo da Vinci.

Nadia drew the large image of the horse and rider above when she was 5½. (It is not known how old da Vinci was when he drew the image of the small horse in the upper right corner.)

Comparing the style of the master to the style of the child, you can't help but be struck by the similarity between the two.

Even for someone classified as an idiot savant (a severely retarded or autistic person who exhibits exceptional ability in one limited area), Nadia's talent was unique. "Nadia was in a class by herself," says Bernard Rimland, Ph.D., director of the Institute for Child Behavior Research in California. "She was extremely artistic."

Like a genius, a savant has a unique ability to focus on a problem. "It's a function of their disability," says Dr. Rimland. "They're compelled to stick to a very limited, almost tunnel-vision focus. It's as if they are walking around in a very dark room, but their flashlight is narrowly focused like a laser beam. Whatever they look at they see with great intensity."

THE HEALING BRAIN

She was recently married, with plans for a child. For Debby Franke Ogg, it should have been the best of times. Instead, it was the worst.

In September of 1984, she was diagnosed as having a nodular lymphoma, a cancer thought incurable. At age 42, she was told by her doctors (all three of them) that she had only a few years to live. "Every day when I went to sleep and every day when I woke up, I felt terror."

Today, the terror is a thing of the past. Debby Franke Ogg is alive and remarkably well. The tumor has shrunk almost to oblivion. She is now the mother of a little girl and an active member of her community in upstate New York.

Was it a medical miracle that saved her? A new serum or an advanced surgical procedure?

No, it wasn't any of the above. Nor was it a mistaken diagnosis. Nor, according to Ogg, was it luck. She will tell you without hesitation that she was healed by the thing that made her ill in the first place: her thoughts.

The notion that our thoughts can either make us ill or heal us did not originate with Ogg. It is a connection that has been recognized since the beginning of recorded history, says Jeanne Achterberg-Lawlis, Ph.D., author of *Imagery in Healing: Shamanism and Modern Medicine*.

Socrates said, "There is no illness of the body apart from the mind." But what may have been recognized by healers 2,400 years ago was generally *not* recognized by most healers of 10 or 20 years ago. For back around the turn of this century, allopathic medicine (based on vaccines and pills) came to so strongly dominate the scene in America that all oth-

The shaman, or traditional healer, conducts special ceremonies to mend his patients' spirits as well as their bodies. In the course of a single ritual, this masked medicine man may sing for several days and nights, to gather healing power. Centuries before we had cardiologists and dermatologists, most healers operated like the shaman.

er medical theories were summarily dismissed.

The allopathic approach emphasized that for every disease there was one germ and there was (or soon would be) one drug that could be administered to kill it. Legislation was enacted to outlaw many traditional healing practices, including those that suggested a patient's thinking might affect his health, says Dr. Achterberg-Lawlis.

Just *watching* others do good deeds may be healthy for you. So concluded David McClelland, Ph.D., a Harvard researcher who showed films of Mother Teresa in action to groups of students. He conducted postviewing tests of their saliva, which showed elevated levels of germ-fighting substances.

When she and her husband, G. Frank Lawlis, Ph.D., both at the University of Texas Health Science Center, conducted studies in the early 1980s showing that the life expectancies of terminal cancer patients could be accurately predicted by looking at each patient's attitude, "nobody wanted to hear about it," she says. "We found it very difficult to get published in medical journals."

But in the past several years those same journals have exploded with articles about the power of the mind to heal or to render sick.

PROFILE OF A WINNER

"I would rather know what sort of a person has a disease than what sort of disease a person has," said Hippocrates many centuries ago. What sort of a person is Debby Franke Ogg? What might she have had in her favor going into the steep uphill battle against an "incurable" cancer? In what ways might her mind have fortified her body—ways that no known medical treatment could?

First, it should be said that the connection between *bad* thoughts and *bad* health has been much more accepted by doctors than has the connection between *good* thoughts and *good* health. Few doctors would deny, for instance, that stress can undermine good health. Nevertheless, the latest research has looked at some mental profiles of the healthy. Here

are the factors that seem to make a difference.

Love and friendship. "I felt there were some things in my life that weren't right—and I set out to change them, with the help of my husband, who was just wonderful, and my very dear friends," says Ogg.

A large number of studies have shown that no man (or woman) should be an island. "We have clear, indisputable evidence that social relationships are a predictor of health and mortality," says James S. House, Ph.D., professor and chair of the sociology department and program director at the Survey Research Center of the Institute for Social Research at the University of Michigan.

Just how important is it to your health to have friends and loved ones in your life? Referring to dozens of studies which show that people with more social relationships live both longer and healthier lives, Dr. House says that social relationships are as important as "the health effects of smoking or not smoking."

Optimism. "I provided an environment where my mind, my body, and my spirit could thrive—and I knew they would," says Ogg.

If you tend to look at the world as a positive place, you'll not only be more fun to be around, you'll likely have better health for it. Such was the conclusion of a 35-year-long study that looked at 99 graduates of Harvard University's classes of 1942 through 1944.

As 25-year-olds, the graduates were asked a

series of questions to determine whether or not they looked at the world through rose-colored or mud-smeared glasses. When these same graduates were given physical exams 20 and 30 years later, the optimists were in much better shape than the pessimists (that is, the pessimists who were still alive).

The fighting spirit. "When my doctors were telling me when I'd be dead, well, we just didn't agree on that. I really didn't believe that I was going to die . . . There were days I felt nothing but rage," says Ogg.

Sure enough (although some physicians are undoubtedly loath to admit it), being a skeptical patient, not treating your doctor's prognosis as God's final word, refusing to accept anything as inevitable, and freely expressing anger about your condition seem to be critical personality traits among survivors of formidable diseases.

Looking forward to something. "I was diagnosed in September. By December, the nodes were starting to go down. By January, I was pregnant with Jenny. I had her on October 7, 1985—13 months after I was diagnosed with lymphoma," says Ogg.

Is it possible that looking forward to giving birth helped Ogg deal with her illness? It's more than possible, it's probable, according to studies that show major upcoming events in people's lives often foster a will to live that bolsters the body through rough times.

History gives us this striking example: Former presidents Thomas Jefferson and John Adams both passed away on July 4, 1826—seemingly postponing their deaths long enough to witness the 50th anniversary of the signing of the Declaration of Independence.

A study by researchers at the University of California, San Diego, has shown that the death rate among Jewish-American men is significantly lower just before Passover (the most frequently observed of all Jewish holidays) than immediately afterward.

Balance. "I believe that I carried around certain discomforts with me that depressed my immune system," says Ogg. "I believe that disease comes as a

THE MIND/BODY STRESS LINK

Traffic jams, tax forms, terrorism—the modern world is *full* of legitimate reasons to feel stressed. But what a toll stress can take on the body.

When the brain senses trouble, it sends a chemical message special express to practically all parts of the body. The message says "Hey, buddy, do something—run, fight, but *do something*." This fight-or-flight mechanism worked well for our ancestors in prehistoric times. A pumped-up system likely saved them from many a saber-toothed tiger.

But today, because the sources of stress are so varied and so omnipresent, the system can stay pumped up for too long—for some of us, almost permanently. And that can spell t-r-o-u-b-l-e. Doctors have linked a large number of modern maladies, such as stomach ulcers, migraine headaches, and coronary artery disease, to stress.

Let's call the man illustrated at right Joe Atlas. Joe has recently acquired a mortgage to buy a house, he's having marriage problems, his boss is an ogre, and his car is on the blink. Joe feels like he has the whole world on his shoulders, and someone has filled the oceans with lead.

Let's take a peek into Joe's body and see how it's reacting to all this stress.

The hypothalamus (1), a control center in Joe's brain, becomes aware of stress. It releases the chemical CRF, which acts as a messenger to tell the pituitary gland (2), located at the base of the brain, to get ready for action.

The pituitary gland then takes over as foreman, and like the hypothalamus, it shoots out hormones that give further instructions to other glands in the body, such as the adrenal glands (3), the thyroid (4), and the sex organs (5).

These glands work at pumping Joe up, readying him to fight or flee. What does getting "pumped up" involve? Well, if you've ever been on a roller coaster, been chased by a snarling dog, or had an angry truck driver drive within an inch of your rear bumper, you're familiar with the symptoms.

Joe's hair stands on end (6).

The pupils of his eyes dilate (7).

His mouth becomes dry, as saliva output drops (8).

Blood vessels supplying the skin contract, so that his skin becomes pale (9).

His chest expands as breathing gets faster to deliver more oxygen to his muscles (10).

His heartbeat is faster and harder (11).

His blood pressure soars (12).

Glucose is released from storage in the liver to feed his muscles (13).

His digestion is slowed as blood from the intestines is diverted elsewhere (14).

His muscles tense (15).

His body sweats (16).

Meanwhile, the thymus gland (17), the processing center for Joe's T-cells (key players in his immune system) slows down. And steroid hormones emanating from the adrenal glands also serve to depress T-cell activity. Joe's immune system is seriously compromised.

If Joe's stressed condition lasts long enough, it could land the poor guy in the hospital.

signal into your life. I had just married Oscar. I think there was something in me telling me that if I were happy then I would die."

John E. Upledger, D.O., D.Sc., head of the Upledger Institute in Palm Beach Gardens, Florida, and a frequent lecturer on the mind/body connection, is firmly convinced that "little voices of the inner self," deep in our psyches, are responsible for many illnesses.

He tells of a case in which a young man from New York City complained of terrible back pain for many years. Nothing showed up on any test. The man began to question his thoughts. He flashed to something that occurred when he was 6 years old. His older brother had just died of leukemia. At the funeral, his aunt turned to him, looked down, and said, "At least he's no longer in pain."

"This man grew up convinced that as long as he was in pain, he wouldn't die," says Dr. Upledger. Perhaps the single most important "pill" for good health, he says, is allowing our inner voices to speak their piece while we listen carefully. Without this outlet, an individual may alleviate the symptoms of one disease, but another illness is likely to pop up elsewhere soon, says Dr. Upledger.

Laughter. Are there any serious medical studies that show that laughter is good medicine? "I have a bibliography of thousands," says Patch Adams, M.D., director of the Gesundheit Institute in Arlington, Virginia. "But I laugh at all these studies on laughter—why do we need studies about something that is *so* obvious?"

Dr. Adams does not wear a white jacket as most of his fellow physicians do. He tends to his patients dressed as a gorilla, a Viking, a court jester, a Renaissance frog, a medieval knight, Louis the XIV, Santa Claus, or "something just as goofy," he says. Not only does he find such "goofiness" helpful to his patients, but "it's healthy for me, too," says the pony-tailed doctor through his handlebar moustache.

Norman Cousins, a writer and magazine editor stricken with the rare disease ankylosing spondylitis, was perhaps the first to bring the laughter connection to the public eye. He says that reruns of "Candid Camera" and old Marx Brothers films were instrumental in his recovering from an "unrecoverable" illness.

Today an adjunct professor at the University of California School of Medicine, Cousins says, "It is possible that laughter serves as a blocking agent. Like a bulletproof vest, it may help protect you against the ravages of negative emotion."

DON'T SUCCUMB TO SUGGESTION

You're lying flat on your back, unconscious, half-covered with a white sheet. A nurse has just handed a scalpel to the surgeon. "Doctor, there seems to be excessive bleeding coming from the patient's chest," you hear. Or your *unconscious* hears. It doesn't much matter. In either case, your *body* gets the message and can react in ways that may make matters worse.

To access that mind/body pathway for a more beneficial result, researchers in England gave a special tape to half of a group of 39 women scheduled for hysterectomies. During surgery, they "listened" through headphones to repeated positive and therapeutic suggestions: "You will not feel sick; you will not have any pain. The operation seems to be going very well and the patient is fine." The rest of the women got a blank tape.

Those patients who heard the soothing messages wound up spending significantly less time in the hospital, experiencing far less fever, and making—in the opinion of hospital nurses who didn't know which patients heard the positive tapes—extraordinary recoveries.

HOW THE MIND HEALS
What actually happens inside the body when laughter and other positive feelings are used as healing

NOT ALL HOSPITAL ROOMS ARE CREATED EQUAL

A Room with a View is more than a movie title. It's also an aid to recovering after surgery. So say researchers from the University of Delaware who looked at patients recovering from gallbladder operations. They found that those who were assigned to rooms with windows looking out on nature did considerably better than those who had to stare at nothing but a brick wall.

The patients with the pretty views had shorter hospital stays and fewer negative evaluations from nurses, they required fewer doses of painkillers, and they had slightly fewer postsurgical complications. One of the researchers speculates that a hospital window view could influence a patient's emotional state, and this might affect his recovery.

Although the patients in Delaware looked mainly at trees, it's suspected that any kind of natural vegetation will do—and a water view might be even better.

tools? According to Alison Crane, executive director of the American Association for Therapeutic Humor, researchers have found that a good chuckle stimulates the heart and respiratory system, decreases muscular tension, and tends to lower blood pressure.

But the most potent connection between the body and the mind, at least in Ogg's case, would seem to be the effect of thoughts on the immune system. In the past few years, scientists looking into this connection have acquired a name for themselves: psychoneuroimmunologists.

These doctors have measured levels of germ-fighting agents in human blood and saliva and found that they fluctuate in tune with the individual's level of stress and other emotional factors. Widows and widowers in their grief, for instance, are known to have fewer active lymphocytes (white blood cells that lead the attack on foreign invaders in the body). In another study, researchers at the State University of New York at Stony Brook found a definite correla-

tion between good moods and high amounts of immunoglobulin A in the saliva. Conversely, people who reported feeling down on the day of the test showed lower than normal amounts of this antibody.

Researchers at the Ohio State University College of Medicine who took blood samples from 38 married and 38 separated or divorced women came up with similar conclusions. Married women with marriage problems were generally depressed in both spirit and immune function. Women suffering through the first year of separation from their husbands had "significantly poorer" immune defenses.

The mind/body connection is more, however, than just a series of measurable physical effects, says Larry Dossey, M.D., author of *Beyond Illness* and former chief of staff at Medical City Dallas Hospital. There's a vaster dimension involved. "Almost everyone who wants to talk about the mind is actually talking about the brain—the physiology, the neurotransmitters, the endorphins—but there's a huge dif-

63

ference between the brain and the mind," he says.

The latter is much more difficult to pin down, though its influence should never be ignored. "There is no such thing as a strictly *physical* examination, and the error of the patient who thinks he is getting one is exceeded, perhaps, only by that of the physician who believes he is performing one," says Dr. Dossey. As proof of the nonphysical dimension of the mind, Dr. Dossey cites a study done by California cardiologist Randy Byrd, M.D. Dr. Byrd separated nearly 400 coronary patients at San Francisco General Hospital into two groups. The members of one group unknowingly had their names given to five to seven people elsewhere in the country who prayed for them every day over a ten-month period. The members of the other group did not have their names given out.

The result? Members of the "prayed-for" group had far fewer complications. What does it mean? That "the mind is nonlocal," says Dr. Dossey. "It is an entity outside of the body as well as within." It is this understanding, he says, that makes for healers and healing.

"I've even begun doing healing rituals in my office," says Dr. Dossey. "I meditate, holding visions of the patient in my mind. I burn incense and shake the rattle [a Navajo medicine-man rattle]." Crazy? Dr. Dossey maintains that it is well known within medical circles that some physicians seem to always have patients in the hospital, while others almost never do. The difference, he maintains, hinges on the willingness of the healer to connect minds with the patient.

Does your spouse show his or her love? Demonstrations of affection might help protect your heart. One Israeli study found that men suffering from angina pectoris (chest pain associated with coronary blockage) were more likely to report that their wives didn't express their love.

Playing boccie ball—or doing just about *anything* with close friends on a regular basis—is good medicine. Studies show that people with strong social ties tend to live longer and healthier lives.

THINKING OF HEALTH

You can exercise for hours every day, eat only raw vegetables and whole wheat toast, drink only pure spring water, and *still* be unhealthy. Studies suggest, for instance, that the so-called Type-A behavior found in individuals who are always racing the clock is just as likely to lead to coronary artery disease as is high blood pressure, a cholesterol-packed diet, or heavy smoking.

So stress is a good place to start this discussion of what you can do to turn all your thoughts into healthy ones.

Destress your life. There's little disagreement among doctors that stress, whether it's physical or the more subtle psychological varieties such as anger, anxiety, fear, and frustration, is responsible for, or contributes greatly to, many modern maladies.

What can be done about stress? Well, you could quit your job, sell your house, and move to the mountains of Nepal to tend goats. Or you could find a patch of deserted beach somewhere in the South Pacific and live on coconuts.

Or you can take the advice of experts who say you can beat stress right on its own turf. One researcher studied corporate executives, high-powered lawyers, and others who face more than their share of stress every day. He's found that it's not the *amount* of stress in our lives that matters, but rather how we choose to deal with it.

How well we deal with stress depends on our hardiness, or more specifically, "three sets of beliefs about ourselves and the world," says Salvatore Maddi, Ph.D., professor of psychology with the social ecology program at the University of California, Irvine, and president of the Hardiness Institute. He calls these sets the three C's—commitment, control, and challenge. If you've got the three C's, chances are you are going to be a lot healthier than someone who doesn't, he says—regardless of whether you work on Wall Street or Sesame Street.

Commitment, according to Dr. Maddi, refers to the ability to find something to provoke your interest and curiosity in whatever you're doing. People with commitment are good at getting involved, and

Why did the Laugh Mobile cross the road? To bring funny tapes, cartoon books, and toys to patients at the Shady Grove Adventist Hospital in Rockville, Maryland. The van belongs to Carolina Ha Ha— short for Carolina Health and Humor Association —a group that believes in the old saying, "Laughter is the best medicine."

they find their activities interesting. People who lack commitment are alienated and bored. They hang back and say, "I don't want to get involved."

Control, says Dr. Maddi, is a gut feeling that your life's course is determined by you—not by your boss, your spouse, or anyone else. People who lack this sense of control often feel like victims of circumstance.

Challenge rests on the belief that human life is all about growth through learning. If events are painful, a challenge-oriented person will see them as opportunities to grow despite the pain. People who shun challenge see the world as a threatening place. They say, "Comfort and security is what it's all about."

Practice your new skills daily. Those in the fast lane need to remind themselves to take it slow on a regular basis, according to Meyer Friedman, M.D., a San Francisco cardiologist and an expert on Type-A personalities. He recommends the following "drills" to be done as often as possible.

● Announce to your spouse and friends that you intend to turn over a new leaf and whip your Type-A behavior patterns.

● Start smiling at other people and laughing at yourself.

● Play to lose, at least some of the time.

● When something angers you, immediately make a note of it. Review the list at the end of each week and decide objectively which items truly merited your level of anger.

● Listen, really listen, to the conversations of others.

Tend to friends and family. There's no question about it: Plentiful, strong social ties are good for our health. All the same, when presented with the evidence, people often say, "Well, that's good—but there's nothing I can do about it," notes Dr. House. "But that's not true," he asserts. "We have direction over our relationships just like we do over whether we smoke or exercise."

Dr. House maintains that we certainly don't need people around us all the time to be healthy, but we should make sure that we have a healthy amount of contact with other folks. These contacts, says Dr. House, generally come from three sources.

● Family relationships: parents, siblings, spouse, and children.

● Informal relationships: friends, neighbors, and distant relatives.

● Work relationships: colleagues.

A number of well-publicized studies have linked marriage to good health and longevity. But Dr. House says that if you're single, you shouldn't fret—it's not the marriage certificate that makes for a healthy bond. "There are many other possibilities for building healthy relationships," he says.

Laugh it up. "I act silly every minute I can," says Dr. Patch Adams. He quotes Mary Poppins: "In every job that must be done/There is an element of fun/ And every job you undertake/Becomes a piece of cake." Dr. Adams suggests that if your life is not filled with wonder, curiosity, and *fun,* you should make it so.

Find inner peace. Chronic worry can lead to chronic physical problems. "Recognize that your mind can create disease, and it can create health," says Dr. Upledger. "The mind and the body are not separate entities—they are one."

If you have an occasional cold, that's one thing. If you are chronically sick, that's another. If your health is constantly a problem, Dr. Upledger suggests you "explore the possibility" that your mind is somehow contributing to your condition. Don't feel guilty about it, he says. Just try to get to the bottom of it.

Dr. Upledger suggests you find a good therapist to help you through the discovery process that leads toward better health.

Go dig a hole. Sun Bear is medicine chief of the Bear Tribe Medicine Society, a frequent lecturer on traditional North American Indian healing, and the author of several books, including *Sun Bear: The*

Whether you're a fan of Beethoven or the Beatles, the *Genesis* biofeedback system plays your favorite music while numerous sensors measure your body's degree of tension or relaxation with each variation in sound. Then the computerized device responds by amplifying those tonalities that best reduce stress.

Path of Power. When people ask him how to heal the spirit, he often suggests digging a hole.

"Go out into the land and dig a hole in the ground. Speak into the hole, say everything you feel badly about in life . . . all the things your ex-husband, or boyfriend, or father and mother did to you . . . everything. Then fill the hole with dirt and say good-bye to those things forever. Before you do, however, throw in a pine cone or an acorn, so that some good grows out of it. Your bad feelings will serve as fertilizer, compost for the Earth Mother."

Imagine yourself healthy. By visualizing yourself as a healthy person, you may contribute to your healthiness.

Debby Franke Ogg used several specific imaging techniques to overcome her lymphoma. (See "Visualizations That Heal" on page 68.) She believes the power of the imagination to create a new reality goes even beyond creating personal health. She believes the healing power of the mind is virtually limitless: "If people would visualize world peace, I know we could create it—I know it would happen."

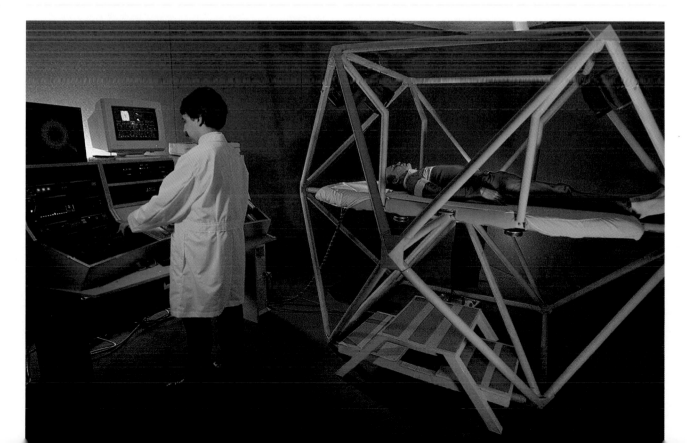

VISUALIZATIONS THAT HEAL

"I saw my lymphoma as gray puddles, and the sun would come up and dry up the puddles. Or, as I became more enraged with it all, I would see myself with an axe, chopping the lymphoma to bits and pieces," says Debby Franke Ogg, who believes that such visualizations helped her fight off cancer.

The projector in her head has been running for several years, changing films at times during the course of her disease. "Now I imagine my thymus as enormous, easily the size of my chest and shaped like a sun, with radiating spikes. Millions of T-cells and B-cells [the immune system's attack forces] fill up the points of the sun and shoot out into the parts of my body that need them."

Is this an exercise that merely helps pass the time, or can such use of the imagination create health miracles? According to a growing number of doctors working with imagery as a tool to fight everything from headaches to cancer, the theater of the mind can indeed be a real savior of the body—in certain instances.

One such doctor is Errol R. Korn, M.D., a San Diego County, California, practitioner who counsels many of his patients in imagery techniques. "I think imagery is the most important thing for determining health," he says. "If you know what a person's images are, you know whether a person is healthy."

Dr. Korn explains that imagery is visualization (seeing something in your mind's eye), but it also may, and in fact *should,* involve feeling, tasting, hearing, and smelling—using all the senses of imagination.

Imagery, say some doctors, can work wonders in both relaxing us and giving us the positive attitudes necessary for good health. But, says Dr. Korn, "the time to learn imagery techniques is not once you're sick or dying—the time is now."

EXERTING CONTROL

Achieving relaxation or altering your attitudes might not seem enough to ensure good health. But imagery has also been shown to change body chemistry and control bodily functions that we normally think of as being beyond our control.

Certain yogis, for instance, are known for their ability to slow their heartbeat and breathing down to fractions of normal rates for hours on end—simply by using their thoughts.

But yogis aren't the only people who can control their body chemistry with their thoughts. You can, too. Just try the following "lemon trick."

Imagine picking up a big, fresh lemon. Imagine slicing it in half and squeezing the juice into a glass. Visualize a few bits of pulp falling into the yellowish juice. Imagine the smell of the juice as you raise the glass to your lips. Now take a mouthful and let it swish around in your mouth.

Are you salivating?

Studies have shown that imagery can affect more than your salivary glands. At Michigan State University, for example, students used imagery to induce changes in neutrophil activity in their blood.

More recent studies by Jeanne Achterberg-Lawlis, Ph.D., have used imagery to similarly alter the activity of T-cells, another component of the immune system.

Another study involved two groups of gall-bladder patients in three Louisiana hospitals. Before and after their surgery, some of the patients listened to tapes inviting them to take a mental journey through their bodies to the healing area and to picture in their minds the phases of successful wound healing. The results? Those who listened to the tapes healed better.

Such healing visualizations seem suited to a wide variety of conditions. "There are...certain symptoms and illnesses that seem to be more readily responsive to imagery than others," Martin L. Rossman, M.D., author of *Healing Yourself*, says. "These include headaches, neck pain, back pain, 'nervous stomach,' spastic colon, allergies, palpitations, dizziness, fatigue, and anxiety."

Other, generally more serious health problems such as cancer, heart disease, arthritis, and neurological illness "are often complicated by or themselves cause stress, anxiety, and depression. The emotional aspects of any illness can often be helped through imagery, and relieving the emotional distress may in turn encourage physical healing," says Dr. Rossman. He emphasizes, however, that good medical care for serious health problems is essential and "perfectly compatible with imagery."

PICTURES OF HEALTH

Patrick Fanning, author of *Visualization for Change*, suggests you begin to practice imagery by lying down, closing your eyes, and relaxing. The next steps call for using all your senses to see what you want to see. (If you want to see an apple, you should also imagine its feel, its taste, and the sound it makes as you bite into it.)

Gaining the ability to make images appear real will take time and patience, says Fanning. But with practice, you can perfect it to an art form. In his book, he gives many examples of the kinds of imagery that might prove helpful for various conditions.

If you have heartburn, caused by acid reflux, imagine a strong, industrial-strength valve at the top of your stomach. Imagine yourself shutting off the valve firmly to keep the burning juices down where they belong. Visualize other little valves that dispense acid into your stomach. Close them all off tightly.

If you suffer from hemorrhoids, visualize the blue, bulging veins shrinking back to normal size. See the blood flowing smoothly and evenly.

If you have a skin condition, like dermatitis, eczema, or acne, picture sores drying up like mud puddles. Watch your skin change from red to a healthy, normal color.

Books and tapes on imagery can be useful in developing a visualization program. But Dr. Korn stresses that personal, one-on-one instruction by an expert is most likely to produce the exact healing image that's right for you.

IMAGERY IN ACTION: TWO CASE HISTORIES

These two cases of successful healing through imagery are described by Gerald Epstein, M.D., assistant clinical professor of psychiatry at Mount Sinai Medical Center in New York City and author of *Waking Dream Therapy*. Dr. Epstein originally wrote about the first case in the medical journal *Advances*.

"A young man came to see me with chronic eczema, which appeared on his face and other parts of his body. He had tried all forms of conventional medical treatment without lasting success and was currently using cortisone cream and gaining some relief. He understood that we would be working with imagery, and he agreed to cooperate with the treatment mode, which excluded the use of all medication.

"I directed the man to imagine the following: *'See your fingers becoming palm leaves. Put the leaves on your face. Feel the flow of water and milk becoming a river of honey that heals the area. Leave a drop of oil on the healed area after finishing, seeing your face becoming all clear.'*

"I instructed him to do this exercise with his eyes closed three times a day for 21 days, at roughly the same times each day. Before beginning each session, which could last up to 3 minutes, he was to tell himself he was doing it with the intention of healing the eczema.

"He phoned me a week later to let me know that his face had improved considerably but that he was experiencing difficulty with eczema on his body. I instructed him to imagine encasing his body with ten palm leaves using all ten fingers so as to swaddle himself in them, and see his body becoming clear.

A GOLDEN BRUSH

"Again the patient contacted me a week later to let me know that his body had cleared up but that he was now experiencing itching. I gave him an exercise in which he was to take off his skin on the banks of a stream, turn it inside out, and wash it in the stream, then to cleanse it thoroughly, scrubbing the reversed skin with a fine golden brush. He was then to turn the skin right side out and put it back on, knowing that the itching would be gone. He contacted me one week later to tell me that the itching had stopped.

"After four weeks, his skin was free of itching. He was actively making changes to improve his life."

BARBOUR

In the second case, Dr. Epstein tells of Mary, a 50-year-old woman, who summoned him to the hospital. She had just been admitted suffering from severe cardiac arrhythmia, an irregularity in her heartbeat.

"Her husband had died suddenly some months before. She was deeply in love with this man and I felt that her heart was responding to the shock of this loss.

"When I came to see her, I found her hooked up to a cardiac monitor that was being monitored in the nurses' station at some distance from her room. I closed the door to ensure privacy after telling the nurses that we did not want to be interrupted for the next 30 minutes.

"I then instructed her in the 'musical triangle' exercise: *'Close your eyes. Breathe out three times and see a musical triangle that you place in the center of your heart. With a soft golden mallet, play each of the three sides, hearing a harmonious sound, knowing that as you play, the heart is quieting down. When the sound is completely harmonious, the heart will be in tempo. Then, open your eyes.'*

"It took Mary about 30 seconds or so to get the hang of the exercise and to get the sounds of the triangle in harmony.

"IS SOMETHING WRONG?"

"A few minutes later, the nurse on duty came bursting through the door, charging into the room, shouting to see if Mary was all right. We were both stunned at first, and when Mary pulled herself together she demanded to know what the nurse was doing there.

"The nurse said she was watching the cardiac monitor screen in the nurses' station and she saw the electrocardiogram signal become normal. She thought that something must be wrong with Mary because of the sudden change in the cardiogram, and so she rushed to the room to check.

"I told the nurse that we were doing mental imagery, but she didn't seem to understand.

"Mary was released from the hospital shortly afterward. Over the next three weeks, I had her do the musical triangle exercise at least three times a day, for 1 to 2 minutes each time. In addition, if she felt the onset of any symptoms associated with arrhythmia, such as dizziness, faintness, or blacking out, she was to immediately sit down and do the exercise.

"Within three weeks, she returned to her cardiologist (who had never asked her about her husband dying or about any other emotional disturbances in her life). He checked her heartbeat and told her her arrhythmia was gone.

HOW YOUR
BRAIN WORKS

If the human brain were simple enough to understand, the saying goes, humans would be too simple to understand it.

Indeed, such paradoxes are the norm when researching the workings of the brain. After all, when a scientist studies this wrinkled mass of neurons and nerve fibers, he uses the workings of his own brain to study the workings of *the* brain, leaving us to wonder whose brain is being studied after all. Can we understand what we are when it's what we are that controls our understanding?

Welcome to the brain.

Composed of somewhere between 50 billion and 100 billion neurons (science isn't sure) and countless nerve fibers, the brain demands one-fifth of the body's blood and oxygen supply, though its energy output barely equals that of a 25-watt light bulb.

What does the brain do with all the energy it consumes? For one thing, it allows you to look at these dark squiggles of pigment printed on a former pine tree and hear the voice of another human being inside your head. That's no small feat in itself, but the brain also permits you to analyze, synthesize, compare, and recollect the ideas conveyed by that voice. And then, quite remarkably, the human brain lets you write down and store those ideas outside your body, leaving room for more ideas inside.

Reading, analyzing, creating, contemplating. Such are the lofty functions of this soft, mushroom-shaped organ, but the brain has to take care of many other tasks before abstract thinking takes place. How it controls so much so well testifies to the beauty of its engineering—a fully integrated brain system capable of governing the beating of your heart, the awareness of your senses, the state of your moods, and the knowledge of your very being—all without a bit of conscious effort on your part.

How can one organ control so many things at once? Well, it can't, really. Truth is, the brain that allows you to ask such a question sits atop other brains, much more ancient than the one you know, and much more primitive and ugly at times. But survival is rarely a pretty business, and the lower brains are survival brains. By taking care of the basics—increasing your blood pressure when you start to run and decreasing it when you walk, for example, or increasing gastric juice secretion when you're eating, then decreasing it when you sleep—they leave the higher brain free from such mundane concerns.

The lower brains, in essence, have liberated the conscious brain, leaving it free to ask questions, consider alternatives, apply reason, make changes. Such deep, profound thinking by the conscious brain is our most distinguishing characteristic as a species, and it's proved to be our best survival tool as well. "The upper and lower brains all need to work together and are integrated into a whole," says Peter Fox, Ph.D., assistant professor of neurology and radiology at Washington University School of Medicine in St. Louis.

THE BRAIN STEM—BASIC BRAIN

Our brain evolved from the inside out. Peel away the layers and you move back in time. Scrape away the topmost layer and watch science and the arts disappear, replaced by moods, emotions, and instinct. Scrape more and aggression, territoriality, and ritual behavior surface. Dig deeper still, to the point just above where the spinal cord enters the skull, and you find the brain stem—the heartbeat-and-breathing center of life.

In evolutionary terms, the brain stem developed quite early; worms and insects have a brain stem very similar to our own. But that's where "thinking" ends for them. For us, the brain stem is only the beginning, though no less vital for it. The brain stem links the newer parts of the brain, which create your intellect and will, to the hypothalamus and limbic system, which govern your moods and appetites. It also houses the centers that control heart rate, respiration, blood pressure, pupil dilation, swallowing, wakefulness, and numerous other functions without which life would end. Though less than 3 inches long, the brain stem is, in essence, the key to life itself.

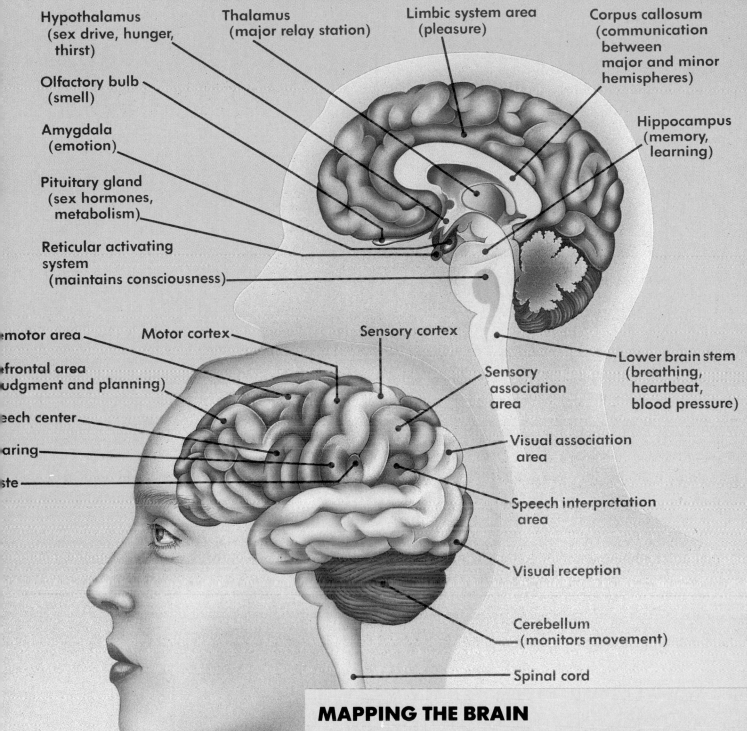

Hypothalamus
(sex drive, hunger, thirst)

Olfactory bulb
(smell)

Amygdala
(emotion)

Pituitary gland
(sex hormones, metabolism)

Reticular activating system
(maintains consciousness)

Thalamus
(major relay station)

Limbic system area
(pleasure)

Corpus callosum
(communication between major and minor hemispheres)

Hippocampus
(memory, learning)

motor area

frontal area
(judgment and planning)

eech center

aring

ste

Motor cortex

Sensory cortex

Sensory association area

Visual association area

Speech interpretation area

Visual reception

Cerebellum
(monitors movement)

Spinal cord

Lower brain stem
(breathing, heartbeat, blood pressure)

MAPPING THE BRAIN

Like explorers recording landmarks in a strange new frontier, scientists have mapped each valley, hill, and lobe of the brain. On its surface *(bottom)* lie the areas responsible for our senses, as well as the areas used in movement and higher thinking. The prefrontal area of the brain, where abstract thoughts occur, is large in comparison to that of other mammals. Such differences become less noticeable deep inside *(top)*. This cross-sectional view of the interior shows the life-maintaining brain stem and surrounding limbic system components responsible for our emotions.

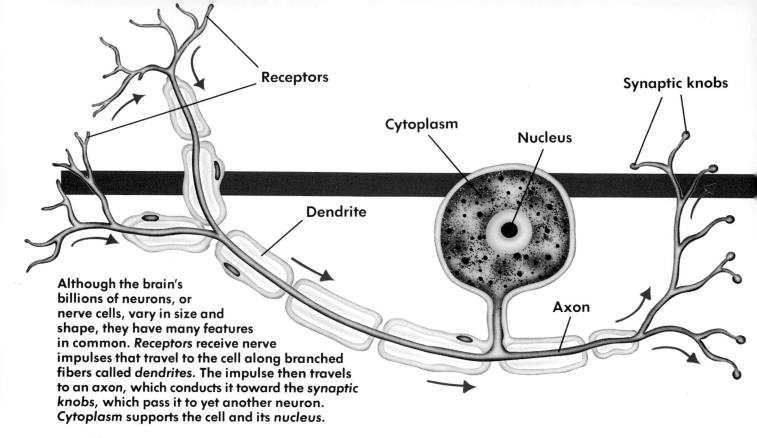

Receptors

Synaptic knobs

Cytoplasm

Nucleus

Dendrite

Axon

Although the brain's billions of neurons, or nerve cells, vary in size and shape, they have many features in common. *Receptors* receive nerve impulses that travel to the cell along branched fibers called *dendrites*. The impulse then travels to an *axon*, which conducts it toward the *synaptic knobs*, which pass it to yet another neuron. *Cytoplasm* supports the cell and its *nucleus*.

The brain stem is located in what might be described as the basement of the brain. Its top begins just beneath the cerebrum, or conscious brain, while its bottom ends at the base of the skull. Along its length are four sections—the diencephalon, the midbrain, the pons, and the medulla oblongata. Each is unique in design and purpose, and very much a specialist in the maintenance of life.

Diencephalon. The topmost section, the diencephalon (considered separate from the brain stem by some researchers, though not by others), contains two dense areas of gray matter called the thalamus and the hypothalamus. Though only an inch in length, the importance of the thalamus cannot be overstated. "It serves as the central relay station for all the sensory information you receive," says David Friedman, Ph.D., a neuroscientist and director of preclinical research at the National Institute on Drug Abuse. "From here, taste, sight, hearing, and touch are directed to the appropriate spot in the conscious brain for interpretation."

Below the thalamus is the hypothalamus, a group of specialized nerve cells that is no larger than a sugar cube but is responsible for controlling numerous body functions and emotional responses. "The hypothalamus controls many of your basic drives," says Dr. Friedman. "Hunger, thirst, sex, all the glands, stress responses, water content of the body—all the things we don't think about but that keep us going every day." The hypothalamus is what lets you know

when you've had enough water to drink or when you need more. An area inside the hypothalamus produces the signs of hunger. When artificially stimulated in laboratory animals, it causes them to eat and drink until they become obese.

Other structures in the general region of the diencephalon play important roles in controlling emotional responses. Parts of the cortex—the thinking and reasoning part of your conscious brain—are interconnected with the hypothalamus, thalamus, and other nearby regions, forming a complex called the limbic system (more on that later).

Midbrain. Below the diencephalon and its encircling limbic system components lies the midbrain, a short section of the brain stem that helps control pupil size and the coordinated movement of the eyes. If you look at something to your left, for instance, then turn your head to view it straight on, it's the midbrain and the pons that keep your eyes locked on the object while your head swivels. It also contains the auditory reflex centers that tell you when to move your head in order to hear something more distinctly. Interestingly, the midbrain possesses a sound-activated center, much like that in a dog, that's designed to prick up the ears for better hearing. In people, though, it no longer functions.

Pons. The pons appears on the underside of the brain stem and separates the midbrain from the medulla oblongata, a final section of brain located just above the spinal cord at the very bottom of the

Electrical activity in the cortex creates patterns called brain waves. The four waves typically produced are (top to bottom): alpha, found when you're awake and resting; beta, the waves of high mental activity; theta, produced during stress; and delta, the waves of peaceful sleep.

skull. Several parts of the inch-long pons relay sensory impulses from peripheral nerves to higher brain centers. Nerve centers that help control chewing, taste, salivation, and facial expression are found in the pons, as are those of balance and equilibrium. Still others help control the rate and depth of breathing.

Medulla oblongata. The medulla oblongata is an inch-long group of nerve cells and fibers located at the very base of the skull. Anatomically, the medulla oblongata looks like nothing more than an enlarged continuation of the spinal cord, and it serves as the primary thoroughfare for almost all nerve traffic flowing from the brain to other parts of the body. While that function sounds fairly simple and basic, the medulla oblongata manages to throw in a twist, literally. For reasons quite beyond our understanding, most of the nerve fibers traveling from the left side of your brain cross over to the right side of your spine when they reach the medulla oblongata, while most of the fibers traveling from the right side of your brain cross over to the left.

As a result, the movement impulses that originate on the left side of your brain only control muscles on the right side of your body, and vice versa. Coming back the other way, nearly all the sensations you feel on one side of the body are perceived on the opposite side of your brain. The value of this strange phenomenon, if any, is still unknown.

More important, the medulla oblongata also contains a number of vital areas that function as control centers for other organs, including the heart, blood vessels, and lungs. The cardiac center, for instance, can cause the heart to speed up or slow down, while the vasomotor center causes constriction in the walls of small arteries, forcing blood pressure to rise. This center can also lower blood pressure by dilating the arteries, while the respiratory center, which works with a similar system in the pons, helps regulate the rate and depth of breathing.

Scattered throughout the medulla oblongata, pons, and midbrain is a complex network of nerve fibers called the reticular activating system, which connects many centers in each of those sections. Most important, perhaps, the reticular activating system is what alerts your brain to pertinent information in a world filled with many more sights, sounds, and sensations than the human brain can process at once. The auditory nerve running from your ear to your brain, for instance, is stimulated by thousands of sound waves every moment. If your brain were forced to give its undivided attention to each and every sound you hear, you'd probably go mad by the end of the day.

Fortunately, the reticular activating system automatically filters out background noises for you, but it instantly alerts your conscious mind the moment an important sound is heard (the doorbell ringing, someone calling your name).

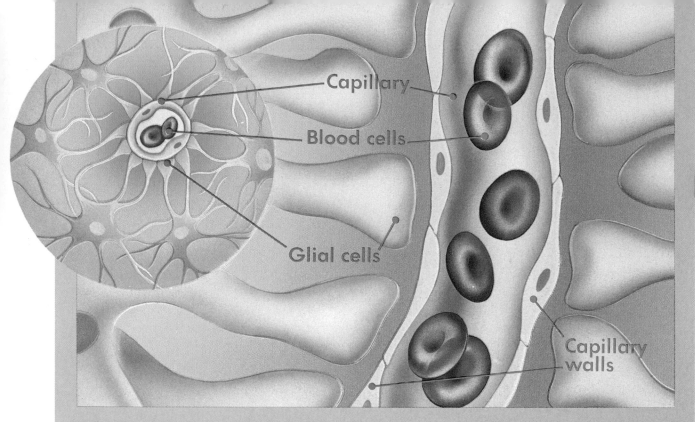

Capillary

Blood cells

Glial cells

Capillary walls

HOW THE BRAIN BARS ITS DOOR

The brain is isolated from the rest of the body by a protective mechanism called the blood/brain barrier. No other organ in your body is so uniquely encapsulated, but no other organ needs to maintain such a constant chemical environment to survive.

In the brain, the walls of each small capillary, like the one shown above (and in cross section at left) are tightly fused and surrounded by large numbers of support neurons known as glial cells. As a result, blood-borne substances that readily leave the capillaries and enter other tissues in the body have a hard time reaching this organ. Entry to and exit from the brain is limited to a select group of specific molecules.

The blood/brain barrier usually works in our favor. While substances such as glucose (the brain's main energy source) and the essential amino acids can cross it, toxins and infectious viral and bacterial organisms have a much tougher time getting in. On the down side, however, if an infection does reach the brain, many drugs that would normally help (like penicillin) cannot penetrate the blood/brain barrier in sufficient concentrations to treat the disease.

THE ANIMAL INSIDE

Ever wonder why an animal, or human, for that matter, suddenly attacks its neighbors when frightened or frustrated? What's going on in the brain? That type of behavior is largely controlled by the limbic system, a kind of lower brain that involves the hippocampus, amygdala, parts of the thalamus, hypothalamus, and parts of the cortex. If you think of your conscious brain as president of a major information-processing corporation, then think of the limbic system as the vice president in charge of emotion.

The limbic system produces feelings of pleasure as well as fear and anger, and it seems able to recognize upsets in a person's physical or psycholog-

ical state that might threaten survival. By causing us either pleasant or unpleasant feelings about our experiences, the limbic system helps guide us into behavior that can increase our chances of survival.

"The limbic system is a very old part of the brain," Dr. Friedman notes. "It receives information from all the senses and integrates it with emotion. Without a limbic system, you don't have emotions." Normally, the more rational upper brain is able to inhibit or control activity in the limbic system beneath it, keeping emotions like fear, frustration, anger, and rage in check. But what if the mature "president" decides to go out for a few drinks and gulps down more than he intended? As his conscious control begins to wane, the ever-alert "vice president" is ready, and quite willing, to assert his power. What was formerly a rational, sober human being slowly becomes an intoxicated, emotional wreck—crying in his beer or ready to fight the whole bar.

The limbic system also plays a role in letting us store memories, says Dr. Friedman. "Memories are stored in the conscious brain, but it's the limbic system that tells you to either store the information or forget it."

THE CEREBELLUM— MOTION CONTROLLER

Though some people believe the brain functions like a computer, it is in fact far more complex than any machine, and nothing created by the brain of man functions quite as well or in quite the same way as the original.

There is, however, one part of the brain that does its job by processing information in a very logical, straight-line fashion that would make even the most talented computer programmer green with envy. It's called the cerebellum, which is Latin for "little brain." Though relatively small—it makes up only 10 percent of the brain's total volume by weight —the cerebellum contains fully half of all the nerve cells found in the entire brain, making it a powerful little package. It needs to be, for nearly every movement you make today will be modified and fine-tuned by the cerebellum, including the movement of your eyes across this page right now.

Located low in the back of your skull, where it has ready access to both the conscious brain and the brain stem, the cerebellum's precise positioning and massive capacity allow it to monitor your every need for motion—from the moment such thoughts arise in your brain until they end with the response of a muscle.

That's a process quite profound but one we largely take for granted. The reason for this easy flow of thoughts and action is found in the cerebellum's organization. Unlike the relatively haphazard array of nerve cells found in the conscious brain (where neurons chatter back and forth while considering options and weighing the consequences of your decisions), those in the cerebellum are laid out in precise, parallel rows. While research has shown that these rows may play a role in the timing of motions, they also seem to cut down on chatter between nerve cells, which lets the cerebellum speed its directions from the conscious brain to the muscles in short order.

That well-ordered structure allows the cerebellum to repeat the same movement instructions over and over again along the same exact nerve cell pathways until the mind's desire to move and the

Much like the hatchlings pictured here, the brain is constantly hungry. Though it accounts for only 2 percent of adult body weight, it receives one-fifth of the body's total supply of blood and burns up 20 to 30 percent of the body's total available energy. Why this high metabolism? The brain's constant electrical activity eats up plenty of energy and may account for its massive appetite. The brain also has no way to store energy, and thus demands a constant supply of fresh nutrients.

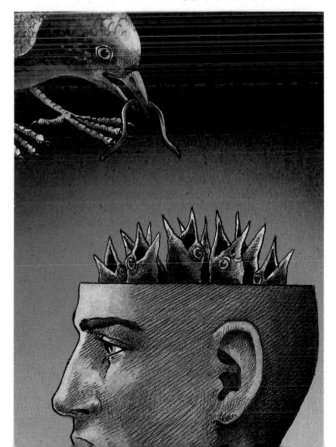

body's ability to move correctly happen as a single "thought-free" act. But it's important to understand that the cerebellum is involved only in the *control of movement*. It does not produce the desire to move or initiate the act of moving. Those functions are located in a special part of the conscious brain called the motor cortex. This section of the brain is where you find both the will to move and the nerve impulses that start the body moving in the right general direction.

THE SPORTING BRAIN

"The motor cortex sets up the 'motion program' that tells the muscles what to do," says Dr. Friedman, "but it's the cerebellum that takes over after that." He uses a well-known sports figure to explain: "When Dr. J [basketball star Julius Erving] jumps up and lets the ball roll off his fingers into the basket, several things take place. First, he has to jump up in the air and maintain his balance, then look at the basket and dodge around other players in midair. Then, at the top of this incredibly powerful movement, he delicately lets the ball roll off his fingertips and into the basket. The cerebellum controlled all of that except the decision of when to jump. The motor cortex took care of that."

Though few people develop the skill of a Dr. J, given a bit of time and many repetitions of the same or similar movement, the cerebellum will develop and store away massive blueprints of how each motion should be made.

Chris Evert, for example, can bring a racket into nearly perfect contact with a moving tennis ball almost every time she swings—her brain instantly computing the angles and timing required for a winning shot. And Jack Nicklaus can bring a club into perfect contact with a tiny golf ball almost every time he swings. Yet the new golfer misses or swats the ground with every other stroke, while the novice tennis player hits more net balls than not. Why? Because Nicklaus and Evert, through constant repetition (and perhaps some better-than-average wiring), have embedded the correct nerve responses for swing-

ing golf clubs and tennis rackets into the pathways inside their cerebellums.

THE CEREBRAL CORTEX— THE THINKING BRAIN

The brain that allows you to read these words has evolved over millions of years, starting out as genetic codes, then slowly developing into the ancient brain stem. From there it evolved into the limbic system, or old mammalian brain, eventually becoming the cerebrum and its crowning glory, the cerebral cortex— the magnificent thinking machine you're putting to use right now. It is with this highest part of the brain, the cerebral cortex, that we read and write and contemplate our existence. It's this part of the brain that sets us apart from the other animals sharing this planet with us. This is the part of the brain that tells us we are different, that tells us who we are. It is the essence of our being, the home of humanity.

The cerebral cortex that makes you human is a thin, wrinkled layer of about eight thousand million specialized nerve cells covering the outside of your brain. No thicker than the sole of your shoe, this thin layer of neurons is responsible for your ability to initiate movement, to sense, to remember, to reason, to laugh, and to be. Just how this layer of cells stores or produces thought remains a mystery, however, for there's nothing to suggest that there is anything responsible for thought—for our knowledge that we exist— other than the electrical connections nerve cells make with one another.

But is there nothing more to human thought than electrical connections? It seems there must be more. A neurologist wouldn't think of probing inside your spinal cord in search of language ability or memories, yet the cells located there make electrical connections that are identical to those in the brain. But the neurologist could stimulate a group of neurons in just the right part of your cortex and make you perceive sounds, colors, emotions, and memories. And while he might know where these are located, none can say why or how they exist.

"It's a very interesting problem," Dr. Friedman

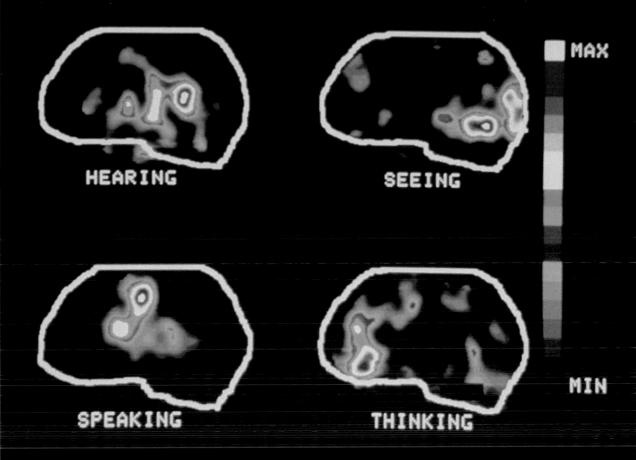

HEARING

SEEING

MAX

SPEAKING

THINKING

MIN

SEEING WHAT SEEING IS ALL ABOUT

Study of the living brain has been revolutionized in recent years by the development of such imaging techniques as PET (positron emission tomography) scanning. Researchers can now study the workings of the brain while people are actually thinking, seeing, and initiating voluntary movements. In hospitals, physicians can locate brain tumors and other lesions without risky exploratory surgery.

The scans shown here were taken from the left side of the head and depict, clockwise from right, activity centered in the occipital lobe when viewing a scene, in the frontal lobe during abstract thinking, in Broca's speech center as words are spoken, and in the temporal lobe upon hearing words.

Such scans can be remarkably sensitive. In one study, researchers asked a subject to memorize parts of a Sherlock Holmes story, then watched as neurons in the hippocampus "lit up" while the memory was being stored!

concedes. "And entirely unresolved." Perhaps it will always be. All we have for now is a map of the brain to guide us, and the human need to understand residing in our heads.

THE PINNACLE OF OUR POWERS

The cerebrum that underlies and supports the cerebral cortex is the largest part of the brain, responsible for two-thirds of its total mass. It sits atop the older, smaller brain stem and cerebellum like a giant mushroom on a stick. Most of the cerebrum is made up of white matter, insulated nerve fibers that connect the cerebrum and cortex to the older brains beneath, and from them to the spinal cord.

The cerebrum is divided in half by a deep valley running from front to back. The two large halves created by this valley are called the major and minor hemispheres, each of which is responsible for its own type of thinking. The minor hemisphere (on the right for right-handers) gives us intuition, sensitivity, and spatial reasoning, while the major hemisphere gives us rational, analytical and critical thinking, and language. Strange as it may seem, you would actually have two separate brains—and essentially two separate people inside your skull—if not for a wide bridge of nerve fibers called the corpus callosum, which connects the brain of imagination to the brain of reality. Joined together, these hemispheres let us generate ideas and test them, too.

In addition to the deep valley separating the hemispheres, the surface of the cerebral cortex is marked by many mounds and grooves—an ancient evolutionary device that greatly increases the amount of surface area available to the cortex for information processing and storage. A shallow groove in the cortex is called a sulcus, while a deep one is called a fissure. Certain prominent fissures divide the brain into roughly four lobes, and these are named after the skull bones that cover them—the frontal, parietal, temporal, and occipital.

Research has shown that each of these lobes has a rather specialized function. The frontal lobe is the newest and largest of the four, and probably the most complex. Parts of it have conscious control over all voluntary movement (the motor cortex that works with the cerebellum), while other frontal lobe areas let you participate in some very abstract ways of thinking, such as weighing the consequences of future action and making plans accordingly.

"The frontal lobe appears to be involved in long-term planning, in setting goals and in integrating information from other parts of the brain," Dr. Fox says, noting that people with damage to the frontal lobe sometimes lose these abilities and are unable to plan out anything that doesn't involve their immediate circumstances or environment. "The ability to apply learning or previous experience is also lost," he says. In addition to voluntary movement and long-term planning, the frontal lobe contains the center that allows us to translate our thoughts into speech. It's also believed to play a role in our personalities and overall intelligence.

Just behind the frontal lobe and high up on each side of the brain are the parietal lobes. These contain the areas responsible for your sense of touch, as well as the neurons responsible for taste. The sense of touch is wired to the parietal lobes in a very specific way that does an amazing job of keeping you out of harm. Each individual receptor cell in your skin is hooked directly to its own specific nerve region there. This direct line from skin to brain lets

you know instantly, for example, that someone has tapped you on the left shoulder—you never have to wonder about where a sensation is coming from. And, because the parietal lobe is located right next to the motor cortex of the frontal lobe, your body responds instantly to this sensation.

Located just beneath the parietals and running laterally along both sides of each hemisphere are the temporal lobes. Their nearness to the ears makes them an ideal location for the sense of hearing, which is one of their major functions. But the temporal lobes are deeply involved in other forms of communication as well. They contain a center that's important for understanding language when you hear it. This language interpretation center works hand-in-glove with the speech center of the frontal lobe, giving you the ability to both receive and respond to spoken messages.

The temporal lobes may also be home for your long-term memories—that is, the information stored in your permanent memory banks. "The inside areas of the temporal lobes are involved in letting you acquire a memory," says Dr. Fox. "If those are damaged, you have great difficulty doing that." In patients who've had both temporal lobes removed for the treatment of epilepsy, the ability to form long-term memories has been profoundly impaired. The manner or form that memories take, however, remains unknown. "They could be something stored in various places and pulled together to form a specific memory," Dr. Fox notes, "or they could be something tucked away in specific cells, though that theory's no longer popular. It doesn't explain forgetting."

At the very back of the cortex and just above the cerebellum is the occipital lobe. All sensations received by the eyes are sent to the occipital lobe to produce sight. Though the occipital is the smallest of all four lobes, psychologists estimate that two-thirds of our knowledge about the world is gained through sight. Vision may also be the most complicated of the senses: The auditory nerve that controls hearing contains perhaps 30,000 fibers, while the optic nerve that controls vision contains one million.

THE TEAMWORK IT TAKES TO WIN

As the gymnast descends toward the balance beam, her eyes work in conjunction with her motor cortex to prepare for a landing. To perform a graceful, skilled movement such as this, her motor cortex must rely on a storehouse of skilled movements established in the cerebellum through practice. Messages sent to the cerebellum tell it what the cortex *intends* to do to prepare for the landing, while messages returning from her body tell the cerebellum what is *actually* being done. After comparing the intended motion with the actual motion taking place, her cerebellum works to bring intention and execution in line. This coordinating information originates in the brain, then travels down the brain stem and spinal column to the muscles, resulting in a perfect landing and, we're told, a solid 9.7 from the judges.

PUTTING IT TOGETHER

Included in the four lobes just described, several *association areas* in the cortex help the brain integrate and understand the massive amount of information it receives from the senses. The association area concerned with such things as planning, problem-solving, and judging the consequences of behavior is located in the frontal lobe. The area located in the parietal lobes aids us in understanding speech and choosing the words we need to express ourselves. The association area of the temporal lobes help us understand the meaning of written words, memorize visual scenes, music, and other complex sensory patterns, while association areas near the occipital lobe help us make sense of what we see.

"If you look out your window," Dr. Friedman explains, "you'll see a complex picture, but the information that reaches your brain through your eyes is broken down into a very simple code. The brain has to reconstruct the code so you have a representation of what the outside world is really like. The association areas put the simple code back together."

The brain also puts that information together with "inside information" about your body and state of mind, thus giving you a complete picture of the world around you and your place in it.

In this and countless other ways, our senses, muscles, and emotions work together through the brain to make us the individuals we are. But we may, in fact, never realize just how much the brain does, or just how individual we are. "Most people equate thought with what they can form into words and say," explains Dr. Fox. "But there are many other high-level thoughts produced by your brain that never have access to the speech center in the cortex. If we can't verbalize our thoughts, we may never know the extent of our thinking." Nor, perhaps, all that we are or could be, inside this human brain.

THE MANY FACES OF EMOTION

The cerebrum sits astride it "like a rider on a horse without reins," wrote one early researcher. His subject was the brain's limbic system, home of our emotions—the place where happiness, as well as anger and grief, reside in tenuous balance side by side.

Working with the cerebrum and the senses, the limbic system provides us with an entire menu of emotions to choose from. These we communicate to others with our words and body language, but many are communicated most profoundly with the muscles of the face.

Joy, love, laughter, and contentment are registered on the face, as are fear, grief, hate, disgust, and surprise. (Interestingly, the emotion of shame, which some researchers have termed "the master emotion," apparently has no facial representation.)

Why we use our faces to communicate as frequently and fluently as we do is largely unknown. But we do, and our facial muscles are so finely tuned and our ability to read meaning into them so finely honed that a single glance can tell as much as a thousand words.

NO TRANSLATION NEEDED

It's a remarkable talent for giving and receiving messages, but one that leaves science with many questions yet unanswered. Why, for example, do people blind from birth use facial expressions the same way sighted people do, though they've never seen another person smile or frown?

And why do facial expressions, unlike bodily gestures, remain constant from culture to culture and across time? Unlike the handshake or the curtsy, a smile means the same thing in Tokyo that it does in Toledo, and it always has. Is there a biological reason why we as a species wear our emotions so readily and universally on our faces? Is there, perhaps, a direct link between the facial muscles that express emotion and the limbic system that produces them?

"Yes, there probably is," says Carrol E. Izard, Ph.D., a psychologist at the University of Delaware. "Although," he adds, "there still isn't that much known about the neural control of facial expressions—believe it or not."

It's not hard to believe, for the mysteries of facial expression run deep. In one landmark study, for example, actors told to mimic the facial expressions of sadness, anger, and fear, reported experiencing those emotions as they moved their facial muscles into the appropriate pattern for each feeling.

Moreover, physiological changes associated with those emotions took place inside the actors' bodies, meaning that emotions and facial expressions may be joined in a strange, two-way loop.

That loop fits into a theory of expression known as facial feedback, which maintains that sensory information from face muscles actually help the brain understand what emotion it's feeling.

WARM SMILE, WARM BRAIN

Other theories abound. One, developed by French physician Israel Waynbaum in 1906, maintains that the facial muscles themselves help create our emotions by controlling the brain's blood flow and temperature. The muscles used for smiling tend to hold blood in the brain and warm it, says this theory, producing feelings of happiness. The facial muscles used to express grief let blood rush out of the brain and cool, producing feelings of sadness. This theory has undergone some revision in modern times and now has a number of supporters.

Studies have also demonstrated that two independent pathways work through the brain to produce facial expressions. Victims of stroke, for example, often cannot pose a smile if asked to, but are able to smile automatically upon hearing a funny joke. "They

can smile spontaneously, but not deliberately," says John Cacioppo, Ph.D, at the Ohio State University.

Conversely, patients with Parkinson's disease can pose a smile when asked, but show no emotion upon hearing a funny joke. "They'll tell you they thought it was funny," says Dr. Cacioppo, "but they can't express it spontaneously."

Findings like these have led researchers to investigate the minute differences between true and false smiles. Forced smiles actually produce a different muscle pattern than those that express real delight, and the trained eye can spot the difference.

Proper training in the science of expression could help physicians and psychiatrists tell when someone is trying to hide physical or emotional pain behind the mask of a smile. Such knowledge could sure come in handy at a poker game, too.

83

HYPNOSIS

Slowly now: TEN—your eyelids are growing heavy. NINE—your eyes are closing. EIGHT—your breathing is slow and deep. SEVEN—your heartbeat is calm and regular. SIX—imagine a bundle of warm, relaxing energy slowly pouring through your head, your arms, your chest. FIVE—feel the energy pour through your stomach and legs and feet. FOUR—see yourself standing at the top of a long staircase. THREE—you are now descending the staircase, step by step. TWO—you are aproaching the bottom of the staircase, feeling more and more relaxed. And . . . ONE—you step off the staircase and come to a comfortable place, a special place, the most peaceful place in the world.

You have just entered . . . The Hypnotic Zone, a mysterious world where strange and wonderful things can happen—if you let them. Under hypnosis, you may be able to visit your dentist and, without a drop of novocaine, feel not the slightest twinge of discomfort while he drills away. If you suffer from allergies, hypnosis might help you relieve them. The same goes for migraines, high blood pressure, ulcers, and the myriad symptoms of stress. You might even be able to give your immune system a boost in fighting off infections like colds and the flu. Under hypnosis, you might finally be able to rise above your fear of heights, quit smoking, lose 10 pounds or 100. Or perhaps you'd like delving into your psyche, reliving childhood experiences in vivid detail, or gleaning lessons from your dreams. You might even use it to improve your self-esteem and motivation, learn new things more effectively and cultivate your creativity.

What you *won't* be asked to do under hypnosis is bark like a dog or croon out a tune à la Frank Sinatra in front of a cackling audience of strangers. Unlike the old-time stage hypnotists, modern-day practitioners prefer to use hypnosis for more legitimate ends. In fact, they're quick to point out that the practice originated as a *medical* technique.

Developed by 18th-century Viennese physician Friedrich Mesmer to treat a variety of his patients' ailments, hypnosis (then called mesmerism) was at first believed to work by balancing "magnetic body

CHILDBIRTH WITHOUT PAIN

"You feel no discomfort. You are in control, breathing, pushing, relaxing. One part of your mind is engaged in the birth process, while another part—the part that registers pain—is far away, sitting on a blanket in the sunlit forest where you once spent a wonderful vacation."

Suggestions like these can often short-circuit the pain and trauma that accompany giving birth, say those who use hypnosis medically. It can make anesthetic unnecessary by reducing or eliminating pain, enabling the woman to take a more active part in the birth process. Hypnosis can also shorten labor, foster positive feelings, and promote a speedy recovery.

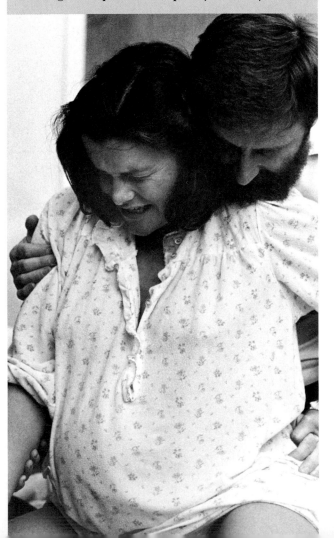

fluids" that caused disease. In 1784, a commission headed by Benjamin Franklin determined that health improvements did indeed occur but were actually produced by the patient's imagination rather than by magnetic fluids. Fifty years later, an English surgeon renamed the technique hypnosis after *Hypnos,* the Greek god of sleep, and regularly used the technique to perform pain-free surgery.

But hypnosis isn't really sleep. "The hypnotic state is a natural state of mind that we enter and exit a hundred times a day," says California hypnotherapist Josie Hadley, coauthor of the book *Hypnosis for Change.* "You enter a light trance state, for example, every time you drive down a highway. Your mind wanders. The part of your mind doing the driving is your subconscious rather than your conscious mind."

SHORTCUT TO THE SUBCONSCIOUS

Your subconscious mind is home to your habits and patterns, freeing you from having to constantly think about everything you do, Hadley explains. This subconscious state also happens to be extremely responsive to suggestions for change. Hypnosis, then, takes a shortcut to your subconscious and opens the door to healthier ways of being.

Most people experience hypnosis as a kind of intense attention, says psychologist Julie Linden, Ph.D., president of the Greater Philadelphia Society of Clinical Hypnosis. You can direct this attention toward specific goals, she says—for example, away from your dentist's drill and onto "a very pleasant visual scene in which you're out on a boat in the middle of a lake, enjoying your surroundings and feeling very relaxed."

You can also choose at any point to follow or ignore suggestions, a factor that makes two things clear: You're ultimately in charge, and hypnosis is no magical solution to all your problems.

Everyone responds to hypnosis differently, says Josie Hadley, and it doesn't work for everyone. The effects grow on you and are most dramatic after three to six hour-long sessions, she says. If you feel no different after your first couple of sessions, "then

hypnosis is not for you." You may also find that the techniques are great for, say, improving your efficiency on your job but useless when it comes to losing weight—or vice-versa. This type of variation is perfectly normal, Hadley says.

HYPNOTIZING YOURSELF

Hypnosis is a skill that just about anyone can learn, says Dr. Linden. Start with a relaxation exercise much like the one at the beginning of this chapter, stated in a soothing voice. (You might want to consider recording your own personal tape.) Then add "suggestions" designed to guide your imagination to make the changes you desire. Suggestions should be concise, positive, and believable, says Hadley. Repeat them for maximum effectiveness.

One suggestion for weight loss, for example, might be: "You are enjoying a healthy meal of fresh, delicious vegetables and fruits. You eat modest portions and then stop, and feel fine. You are totally satisfied, totally satisfied."

A suggestion to help improve your self-esteem could state: "Imagine yourself talking to your co-workers. See yourself as confident, capable, and talented. You are kind to yourself, and you no longer have time for negative thoughts or feelings. You fill your mind with positive ideas and productive goals. You look at life as an adventure."

Conclude your session by slowly counting from one to ten while interjecting that when you awaken, you will feel as if you have had a long rest. At "ten," open your eyes. You should feel relaxed and refreshed—and on the way to changing your life.

IMAGINATION

The white-coated scientist peers at the cells under his microscope, wrinkles his forehead, then sits back and gazes at the white-tiled wall in front of him.

Down the hall another scientist, sitting in front of a computer terminal with his shirt sleeves rolled up and his tie loosened, leans back, props the keyboard across his knees, and stares at the blank screen.

Who are these people? They're dreamers. They're people who use their imaginations to develop solutions to complex cellular puzzles that may one day rid the world of a major disease.

A hundred times a day they stare into space and wonder, "What if we . . . ?" They're not so different from the rest of us except, perhaps, in one important way: They allow themselves to use their imaginations to the fullest. They don't dismiss a new thought with, "Ah, that'll never work."

Think about the person who invented yellow sticky notepads, for example. Nine-tenths of the people in his company were trying to figure out how to make a stronger glue. He thought about the glues already available—Super Glue, KRAZY Glue, Elephant Glue, whatever—then turned the problem around and asked, "What happens if we make a *weaker* glue?"

Today most of us have his answer fluttering around the edges of our lives—on the refrigerator, the dashboard, the bathroom mirror, everywhere. "Post-it" note pads—those little yellow stickers that allow us to attach our comments and reminders to almost anything—have taken over the world. How did we ever do without them?

YELLOW STICKY ANSWERS

How can you dream up yellow sticky answers to the problems of everyday life?

Jeffrey Goelitz, teacher and author of *The Ultimate Kid,* suggests that reading mythological stories such as Homer's *Iliad* and *Odyssey,* the *Epic of Gilgamesh,* or *Norse Myths* will fire your imagination by drawing attention away from the mundane thinking of television plots that dominates our culture and refocus-

DAYDREAMING: IT'S NOT FOR THE LAZY

What do people daydream about? Their problems, says Eric Klinger, Ph.D. Daydreams are an inherently spontaneous burst of imagination in which you work out problems, dream up solutions, and plan for the future.

"Daydreaming seems to be a natural way to use brainpower efficiently," explains Dr. Klinger.

You might replay an argument you had with a friend, then visualize how the two of you will go to lunch and work it out. Or, if you're planning a dinner, you might recall the foods your guests like to eat, take a mental inventory of what's in your pantry, and then plan what you'll need to pick up at the market.

What we daydream about, although it's usually related to figuring out a problem, is largely determined by social differences, says Dr. Klinger.

A businessperson is far more likely to think about a new product line, for example, while a day care worker is more likely to daydream about conflict resolution on the playground.

"But daydreamed thoughts are not random," Dr. Klinger points out. They only occur when you run into emotionally arousing cues that trigger a new thought related to an ongoing problem.

The smell of diesel oil might make you think about how your car stalls at stop signs, when you can take the car to a service station, and whether the amount of money in your checking account will cover any necessary repairs.

In such instances, think of daydreaming as personal brainstorming, says Dr. Klinger. Then use what it reveals.

THINK YOURSELF RICH

In the early 1930s, Andrew Carnegie—pictured here in front of New York's Carnegie Hall—commissioned writer Napoleon Hill to ask 504 of the world's richest men how they accumulated their wealth.

Their answers, which Hill subsequently published, boiled down to a single magic "secret": That ideas, which are born and developed in our imagination, are the "beginning points of all fortunes."

How can you stimulate your imagination to produce "rich" ideas? Hill himself had a group of nine imaginary advisors—Lincoln, Ford, Edison, Carnegie, Darwin, and the like—that he consulted every night before bed.

"The procedure was this," wrote Hill. "Just before going to sleep at night, I would shut my eyes and see, in my imagination, this group of men seated with me around my council table."

At first he used his imagination to learn how these men had thought—how they had approached problems and solved them. Then once he felt that he knew them intimately enough to have absorbed their intellectual and emotional characteristics, he began to consult them as equals regarding any problem that came up.

Did such an imaginary board of directors help stimulate "rich" ideas? Well, Hill subsequently wrote the book *Think and Grow Rich,* which his publisher claims has reached seven million readers. At $7 a book, Hill certainly didn't think and grow poor.

ing it on the realm of the infinite. In a world where horses can grow wings, goddesses can become stags, and gods can turn into half man, half beast, clearly nothing will limit your imagination.

Goelitz also suggests that listening to classical music—Wagner's *Ride of the Valkyries,* for example—then drawing a detailed picture of what you "saw" as you listened will also stimulate your imagination.

You can also ignite your imagination when you run into a particular problem, adds Eric Klinger, Ph.D., a psychologist at the University of Minnesota at Morris, by learning as much as possible about as many different facets of the problem as you can. Then just sit back and allow yourself to "hear the solution."

It *will* come, promises Dr. Klinger.

INTELLIGENCE

Take an informal poll. Go out and ask the next 477,218,588 people you meet what their IQ's are. What you'll find is that, among all those people, *1*—just 1—will have an IQ of 194. So what do you think your odds are of finding that person by, say, next Tuesday?

Well, we can make your search a little easier. Romero Anton XIV Montalban-Anderssen is your one-in-four-hundred-and-seventy-seven-million man.

Anton Anderssen, as he sometimes calls himself, knew at a very early age that something was up when it came to his IQ. "I've been tested many times and in many ways, beginning when I was in kindergarten," he says. The tests Anton took showed he had an IQ of 194. (To put that in perspective, consider that those who score over 132 are classified by some as "gifted," while scores of 140 or more denote "genius.")

Sometime after high school, Anton took a test measuring right-brain intelligence and achieved a perfect score. Then in college, from his freshman year until receiving his doctorate, he earned straight A's in every class.

While Anton speaks 27 languages, he prefers to describe in plain English what his high IQ means to him: "It's a passport to growing. It's been a motivation for me to not put limits on myself as far as what I could learn and what I felt I could accomplish."

What about your own IQ? Before you can tell how you stack up against Anton, or anyone else, you'll have to take an IQ test.

"Standard IQ tests focus on basic levels of thinking, like retention of information," says Robert Swartz, Ph.D., founder of the Critical and Creative Thinking Program at the University of Massachusetts-Boston

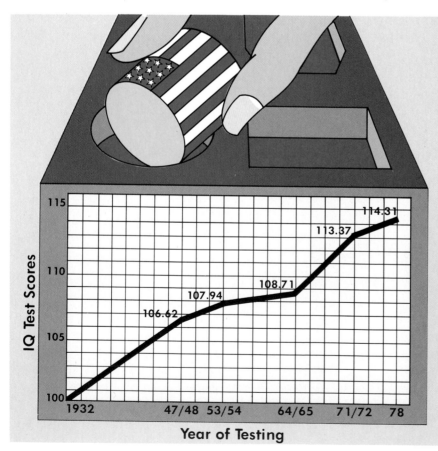

IQ IS INFLATING

In just one generation, penny candy now costs a dime, and a ten-cent phone call takes a quarter to make. It seems that everything is going up, including America's IQ scores. "Americans gain about $3/10$ of an IQ point a year," says James Flynn, Ph.D., a researcher at the University of Otago in New Zealand, who conducted a study of IQ levels in 14 countries. "From 1932 to 1978, the American IQ rose 15 points."

While Dr. Flynn still can't draw any firm conclusions based on the data from 1978 on, he says, "The assumption is the gains have kept going. Test performance in the United States still seems to be improving."

RAISING A SUPERKID

Jimmy's not quite out of diapers yet, but he's already reading *Hamlet*. Three-year-old Debbie is dwarfed by her violin, but she plays like a virtuoso all the same. And then there's 1-year-old math whiz, Mark, who prefers square roots to building blocks.

These advanced toddlers have been dubbed "Superkids," but the person most responsible for their development says that any child could join their club. "Every child born has at the instant of birth the potential to be a genius," says Glenn Doman, founder of the Philadelphia-based Institutes for the Achievement of Human Potential.

During a week-long intensive course, Doman shows mothers special techniques for teaching their babies subjects like reading, math, foreign languages, music, and gymnastics. Much of the action centers on learning drills using 11-inch-square poster boards as giant flash cards.

"All kids are capable of all things," says Doman. You can teach a tiny child anything."

and an expert on IQ. "By and large the tests measure what we know in terms of facts and routine thinking abilities."

HOW SMART ARE YOU?

Okay, you've taken a test, and you have the magic number, so what does it mean? "IQ stands for intelligence quotient," says Jonathon Baron, Ph.D., professor of psychology at the University of Pennsylvania. "It's your mental age divided by your chronological [actual] age and then multiplied by 100."

Unlike your Social Security number, your IQ number doesn't have to be cast in stone. There are ways to *increase* your intelligence.

You might think that the only way you could increase your IQ score is to have Anton use *your* name on his next IQ test. But there are other, more creative ways to boost your intelligence.

"You have to think creatively. Everybody has the capacity to do that, but often we allow lots of things to get in the way of creative thinking," says Dr. Swartz.

"Don't be afraid to take risks. Don't be afraid of what people will think about you. When you overcome those attitudes, you will be available to use the information you have more effectively and in a sense become more intelligent."

You also need to have a mind that is open to the intelligence locked within. "Most people don't think enough about things that are important," says Dr. Baron, "and when they do they tend to favor things they already believe. "But to be truly intelligent, you need to look for reasons why you might be wrong. Always consider the other point of view."

For another point of view, you might want to listen to Anton explain why, with an IQ of 194, he still seeks to expand his intelligence.

"The universe is constantly expanding," he says, "so it seems to me that we should constantly expand *our* horizons, whether that means spiritually or intellectually."

When asked how he does that, Anton replies modestly, "I read a lot."

"Poetry is a way of taking life by the throat," said Robert Frost, speaking of the linguistic intelligence that brought him fame.

Dancer Fred Astaire embodied the bodily/kinesthetic type of intelligence that turns motion into magic. Who can forget his sense of effortless but total body control?

THE MANY FLAVORS OF INTELLIGENCE

Pretend for a moment that your mind is a Baskin-Robbins ice cream parlor. When you peer through the frosted glass case, you don't see just one round cardboard tub of ice cream, you see many colors and many flavors.

Well, what if that ice cream were really intelligence—would you still see an assortment of flavors? You would if psychologist Howard Gardner, Ph.D., professor of education at Harvard Graduate School of Education, was dipping into your mind. So far in his studies he's managed to come up with at least seven different flavors.

"The seven intelligences are a set of categories that might help you to better understand why *your* mind isn't like everyone else's," says Dr. Gardner.

"The more that all of us are aware of our plurality of capacities, the less likely we are to become pigeonholed into one way of thinking for life."

VANILLA AND SIX MORE

Let's start with the plain vanilla and chocolate types.

Logical/mathematical intelligence. This is the old standby that most IQ tests measure. It's the type of reasoning intelligence found most often in scientists, and it's the intelligence most valued in Western society.

Linguistic intelligence. Another category most often measured on tests, this type of intelligence is used mostly by writers and public speakers.

According to Dr. Gardner, these first two are the flavors of choice. "Most psychologists, when they speak about intelligence, are talking about a certain combination of language and logic which is important in school but doesn't have as much meaning once you get outside of school."

Now for the butter brickle and tutti-frutti flavors.

Musical intelligence. This type often appears by age 2 or 3. Naturally it's the type of intelligence found in composers and performers.

Spatial intelligence. This type gives you the ability to envision how objects appear in space. It enables you, for example, to flip a cube around in your mind and see it from all sides. Architects

Hers was more than a gift for carrying a tune. Musically intelligent people like Billie Holiday are, as anthropologist Claude Lévi-Strauss says, those "whose minds secrete music."

Frank Lloyd Wright designed buildings half a century ago that are still ahead of their time today. His spatial intelligence allowed him to turn concrete and glass into works of art.

and engineers have this intelligence down pat.

Bodily/kinesthetic intelligence. Your ability to control your physical motion and your skill in handling objects both depend on this intelligence. If you have two left feet, you may have been left out in this area, whereas dancers, athletes, mechanics, and surgeons have more than enough.

Interpersonal intelligence. This category comes into play in your successful interaction with other people. It's found most often in salespeople and politicians.

Intrapersonal intelligence. To "know thyself" is to have this intelligence. It helps you access your own feelings and moods.

WHAT'S YOUR FLAVOR?

The scoop here is that "every normal person has all seven intelligences to some extent," says Dr. Gardner. But if you look carefully across a wide range of abilities you'll find that most people do have areas of strengths that they can build upon."

While there aren't yet any tests available that would determine which intelligence you may lean toward, "most normal adults who are relatively reflective have an intuitive sense of how good they are in these different areas," Dr. Gardner says.

If you have a feeling about which area you may be strongest in, "just knowing that will help you increase your competence in that specific intelligence," he adds. "It will also help you in the other areas because now you will be aware of them, and you can work on increasing those kinds of intelligence."

But what if you could choose only one flavor? Which one would it be? The man who brought you all these intelligences knows which one he would pick. "I think intrapersonal is of extreme importance, but it tends to be ignored," Dr. Gardner says. "To have a good sense of yourself, your strengths and weaknesses, your own intelligences and how to build on them, gives you a real leg up on others. I wouldn't say any intelligence is intrinsically more important than another, but I'd give special billing to intrapersonal . . . at least this week."

THREE WAYS TO BE SMART

While Dr. Gardner looks into the ice cream store of your mind and sees many different kinds of intelligence, psychologist Robert Sternberg, Ph.D., looks into the same store and sees only *one* kind. But it has three different parts—sort of like a gallon of chocolate with marshmallows and M&M's.

"The triarchic theory says there are three *aspects* to intelligence," explains Dr. Sternberg, who is a professor of psychology and education at Yale University. "A person can have all three, although not many people do." And if you have one aspect more than the others, it's possible that "you can improve each aspect that needs improving."

The best way to do this, Dr. Sternberg says "is to buy and read my book, *The Triarchic Mind*," which goes to show that he's at least improved the aspect of his own intelligence that guides what he calls street-smarts. (More on that later.)

KNOWING WHAT YOU'RE GOOD AT

"Intelligence boils down to your ability to know your strengths and weaknesses and to capitalize on the strengths while compensating for the weaknesses. In other words, you need to make the most of what you have," says Dr. Sternberg.

And what you have is one intelligence that comes in three parts.

The *componential* aspect is the brainy you who keeps scoring well on IQ tests. It's your ability to break things down into their component parts and analyze them. "It's what gets you good grades, gets you into college, and keeps you there," says Dr. Sternberg. "If you're an accountant, for example, this is the type of intelligence that is important."

The *experiential* aspect refers to the artist inside you—the part of you that has the ability to take various experiences and combine them in insightful new ways. "It's your creative or intuitive abilities. These come into play once you get beyond the school business (taking tests), and they're really important."

Those of you who don't get high test scores but who come up with creative ideas nonetheless fit well here—as do writers and scientists.

The third or *contextual* aspect is the street-smart veteran in you. It's part of you that learns from experience and adapts to the environment. "H. Ross Perot [the billionaire businessman] probably didn't score 1600 on the SATs," says Dr. Sternberg. "But so what? He's done remarkably well. There are plenty of very successful managers and entrepreneurs who don't do well on standard intelligence tests."

These include people like Dr. Sternberg himself, who admits, "I did terrible on IQ tests when I was young." That got him thinking not about himself but about the tests.

"IQ, SAT, and similar tests are very narrow in their scope. As a result, a lot of people go through their lives thinking that they aren't smart, or that their kids aren't smart.

"What I'm saying is that there is more to intelligence than a test score, and if you don't do that well on tests, there are other areas where you may do very well."

MAKING SENSE OF LIFE

"Intelligence is what happens when all three of these aspects come together," says Dr. Sternberg. "Intelligence is really mental self-management—how we order and make sense of the events that happen around and inside us."

One way we do that is through what Dr. Sternberg calls practical intelligence. (See the box "Can You Spot the Strangers?") "It's how our intelligence operates in the real world. Some people are very good at reading nonverbal cues, for instance, and that's an important skill. Under-

standing nonverbal cues is just as important as understanding verbal cues. In relationships, when things start to go wrong, the initial communication is always nonverbal."

Bottom line time. "Intelligence is not something you have, it's more like something you use," Dr. Sternberg says. "The real test is not how *much* intelligence you have in your brain but how you go about using the intelligence you have to make this a better world for yourself, and other people."

CAN YOU SPOT THE STRANGERS?

If you're good at reading nonverbal signs, then you shouldn't have any problem picking out which of the four couples pictured here are romantically involved and which ones just met.

In this exercise designed to test what Robert Sternberg, Ph.D., calls practical intelligence, see if you can spot the two pairs who are involved, and the two pairs who saw each other for the first time right before the photos were taken.

Having trouble? Here are some clues.

To sharpen your practical intelligence, look for nonverbal signs like the angle formed by the two bodies. Genuine couples tend to lean toward each other. Also, they tend to touch each other more and to stand closer together.

Other things to watch for: Real couples tend to position their arms and legs more naturally, instead of just posing. "Fake" couples have more tenseness in their hands, faces, and bodies, while real couples seem more relaxed.

Finally, real couples tend to resemble each other in style of dress, age, and socioeconomic class.

The answer is on page 170.

INTUITION

How many times have you really had *all* the information you needed to make a decision? Once? Twice? Never?

When you stop and think about it, you realize that each day we all must make many decisions—some important and many minor—with only partial information. Sometimes, in fact, we make decisions with very few hard facts to go on.

But that doesn't mean our decisions are reduced to chance. You couldn't possibly have known everything about your doctor, or the house you live in, or the car you drive before you selected them. But you didn't choose them by the flip of a coin or a roll of the dice, either. You chose them using a combination of rational thinking and what you would probably describe as instinct, a hunch, or a gut feeling.

Whether you knew it then or not, you used intuition. You sensed something or felt something guiding you one way or another, and, quite likely your decision was influenced by that "feeling of knowing." You may have even said, "I just feel comfortable with this doctor," or "Buying this house feels so right to me; I know I should do it."

Locating the source of that feeling isn't easy. "Intuition is when you know something, but, like, where does it come from?" says a 15-year-old girl quoted in Philip Goldberg's book, *The Intuitive Edge*.

Science can't answer that question yet. "It will be a while before we know what goes on [in the brain] when we do something as routine as recall a telephone number, and longer still before we sort out the neurophysiology of intuition," Goldberg says.

But that doesn't mean intuition is a complete mystery. "It is not magic," he explains. Rather, it is a mental faculty that leaps across chasms of missing information, makes sideways detours, and brings together unusual, even illogical combinations."

TWO WAYS OF KNOWING

Although rational thought and intuition often work together as allies, it is important to distinguish between the two.

"Rational thought is drawn out over time," according to Goldberg. "It takes place in a definable sequence of steps with a beginning, middle, and end."

But intuition is a "single event. A snapshot as opposed to a motion picture. And it just seems to happen, often when least expected, without the application of specific rules."

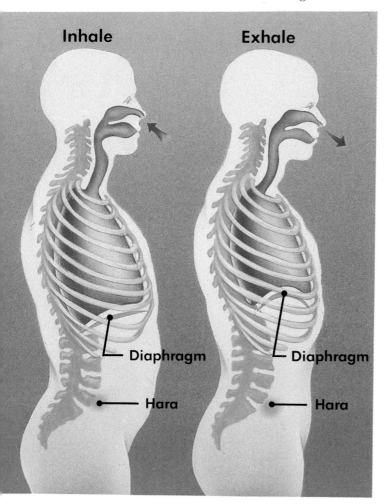

Inhale   Exhale

Diaphragm   Diaphragm

Hara   Hara

Want to get more in touch with your gut feelings? Then try stimulating your gut—or more specifically a point three finger-widths below the navel. According to oriental tradition, breathing deeply into the lower abdomen, extending your stomach as you inhale and drawing it in as you exhale, energizes the "hara" and awakens intuition.

"Intuition is direct knowing independent of the senses, rationality, and memory," says William Kautz, director of the Center for Applied Intuition in San Francisco. "By every indication, intuitive powers come with being human. But they are blocked by emotional problems or early conditioning."

If people are born equally intuitive, that equality "disappears pretty fast," says Malcolm Westcott, Ph.D., professor of psychology at York University in Ontario. Dr. Westcott found different levels of intuitive powers in children as young as 3 years old. His research also showed girls to be more intuitive than boys.

Society has preserved the notion of "women's intuition," and there appears to be some evidence that women are more intuitive about people than men are, says James Greeno, Ph.D., professor of education at Stanford University. But Dr. Greeno suggests this could be merely a matter of women paying more attention to other people's behavior; it's not necessarily an indication that they are born with more intuitive ability.

Regardless, Goldberg is sure of two things: successful people tend to be intuitive people, and *all* of us can improve our intuitive powers.

Every now and then a serious bettor gets that special feeling. Call it intuition. Ron, a frequent bettor at Philadelphia Park, had it when he picked a long shot named "Woodshole." He felt calm—"no butterflies in the stomach," he says. The horse came in and paid $162 (on a $2 bet). "The trick is knowing when you're 'on,' " says Ron, "and being able to act on it."

AN INGREDIENT IN SUCCESS

Winners in business realize intuition is important and work to develop it, says John Harricharan, a consultant to Fortune 500 companies. "They are listening to themselves instead of just to lawyers, accountants, and comptrollers," he says.

Take the now-legendary Ray Kroc story, which Goldberg mentions in *The Intuitive Edge*. Kroc's consultants advised him not to buy the McDonald's hamburger chain. But Kroc, after some closed-door ranting and raving, defied his advisors. "I felt in my funny bone it was a sure thing," he said. The rest, of course, is McHistory.

Of course, learning to recognize your own intuition won't come automatically, especially if you treat it as something alien that you don't quite trust. "It is possible to believe in something intellectually

HOW INTUITIVE ARE YOU?

Some people, if given the chance, would let a computer plan their lives for them. Just plug in the data and wait for modern technology to produce a life script. Other people, though, like to follow their own inner voice. They'll write their own script, thank you—and produce and direct on the spot. How about you? Take the following quiz and decide.

1. When I don't have a ready answer, I tend to be
    (a) patient.
    (b) uneasy.
2. When faced with uncertainty, I usually
    (a) become disoriented.
    (b) remain comfortable.
3. In challenging situations, I am highly motivated and deeply committed
    (a) most of the time.
    (b) infrequently.
4. When my intuition differs from the facts, I usually
    (a) trust my feelings.
    (b) follow the logical course.
5. When working on a difficult problem, I tend to
    (a) concentrate on finding the solution.
    (b) play around with possibilities.
6. When I disagree with others, I tend to
    (a) let them know about it.
    (b) keep the disagreement to myself.
7. Generally speaking, I
    (a) prefer the safe way.
    (b) enjoy taking risks.
8. When working on a problem, I change strategies
    (a) seldom.
    (b) often.
9. I prefer to be told
    (a) exactly how to do things.
    (b) only what needs to be done.
10. When things get very complicated, I become
    (a) exhilarated.
    (b) insecure.
11. When faced with a problem, I usually
    (a) create a plan or outline before getting started.
    (b) plunge right in.
12. In most cases,
    (a) change makes me nervous.
    (b) I welcome unexpected changes.
13. My reading consists of
    (a) a variety of subjects, including fiction.
    (b) factual material mainly related to my work.
14. When my opinion differs from the experts, I usually
    (a) stick to my beliefs.
    (b) defer to authority.
15. When faced with a number of tasks, I
    (a) tackle them simultaneously.
    (b) finish one before going on to another.
16. When learning something new, I
    (a) master the rules and procedures first.
    (b) get started and learn the rules as I go along.
17. At work I prefer to
    (a) follow a prearranged schedule.

and yet harbor mistrust on an emotional level," Goldberg notes. "And the impact of the emotions will be stronger." Try to banish any negative attitudes or skepticism about intuition beforehand.

In addition, Goldberg advises not taking your problems or yourself too seriously—that works against intuition as well. And intuition works better when allowed time and space, he suggests, adding, "A desire to shift gears may be a message from the intuitive mind telling you to withdraw; it needs a little solitude. Knowing the difference between that need and laziness or escapism is a key factor in developing one's intuition."

Just giving your intuitive mind quiet time every day is a "good first step," Kautz says. But if you are serious about improving your intuition, you will want to do more.

Meditation, when practiced regularly (twice a

(b) make my own schedule.
18. At school I was (am) better at
    (a) essay questions.
    (b) short-answer questions.
19. Basically, I am
    (a) an idealist.
    (b) a realist.
20. When I make a mistake, I tend to
    (a) second-guess myself.
    (b) forget it and go on.
21. The following statement best applies to me:
    (a) I can usually explain exactly why I know something.
    (b) Often I can't describe why I know something.
22. When offering a description or explanation, I am more likely to rely on
    (a) analogy and anecdote.
    (b) facts and figures.
23. I can usually be convinced by an appeal to
    (a) reason.
    (b) my emotions.
24. When I am wrong, I
    (a) readily admit it.
    (b) defend myself.
25. I would rather be called
    (a) imaginative.
    (b) practical.
26. When faced with a difficult problem, I am likely to
    (a) ask for advice.
    (b) tackle it myself.
27. Unpredictable people are
    (a) annoying.
    (b) interesting.
28. When setting an appointment for the following week, I am likely to say
    (a) "Let's set an exact time now."
    (b) "Call me the day before."
29. When something spoils my plans, I
    (a) get upset.
    (b) calmly make a new plan.
30. When I have a hunch, I usually react with
    (a) enthusiasm.
    (b) mistrust.
31. Most of my friends and colleagues
    (a) believe in the value of intuition.
    (b) are skeptical about intuition.
32. I am best known as
    (a) an idea person.
    (b) a detail person.

SCORING

Before you start adding up the numbers, remember that this test does not make you intuitive, nor does it prohibit you from becoming more intuitive if you scored low. Intuition is far from an exact science, and you are likely to feel more comfortable following your intuition in some situations than others.

That understood, give yourself 1 point if you answered (a) on questions 1, 3, 4, 6, 10, 13, 14, 15, 18, 19, 22, 24, 25, 30, 31, and 32.

Give yourself 1 point if you answered (b) on questions 2, 5, 7, 8, 9, 11, 12, 16, 17, 20, 21, 23, 26, 27, 28, and 29.

If you scored 24 or above, you lean strongly toward an intuitive approach to decisions and problems. More than likely you trust your intuition.

If you scored between 16 and 23, you tend to vary in style but are more intuitive than analytic or systematic.

If you scored 8 or below, you lean heavily toward a systematic, rational approach to problems and decisions. Chances are you do not trust your intuition very much.

day for 20 minutes), is probably the most effective route to expanding consciousness, says Goldberg. And "it is *after* meditation, when the mind is quiet and clear, that intuition is likely to be at its best."

Other suggestions from Goldberg for improving intuition include:
• Make quick decisions on minor matters, such as ordering from a menu or choosing a movie.
• Practice making predictions—who is calling when the phone rings, which line will get to the bank teller's window first, what will be in the morning mail.
• Cover the caption on newspaper cartoons and try inventing your own.

Finally, Goldberg offers this: "A feeling of wholeness or completion is a good guide to whether intuition has run its course. With experience, you will know when it is futile to wait for more."

LEARNING

You never stop learning. Every time you flip on the TV, pick up a newspaper, or watch people line up at a restaurant, you're learning. You're learning about people, about yourself, about the world. You're noting facts, taking them in, turning them over, and figuring out how you can use them in the future.

Learning is an ongoing process, experts say. It's what your mind does naturally, effortlessly, without pause or complication. It's only when you sit down, open a book, pull out a notebook, and announce sternly to yourself, "Now I'm going to learn!" that things start to mess up. All of a sudden you remember that little kid wedged between desk and chair who couldn't spell "geography." Or divide 5,382 into 1,283. Or recite Lincoln's Gettysburg Address—backward.

Learning as an adult is different from learning as a kid. For one thing, you've matured—you're not going to put up with being asked to memorize any-

SEE TOM LEARN TO READ

Who wants to read "Tom's nag is fat; his dog is not fat. Nat is on Tom's nag. Nat's dog, Rab, can not catch the rat," when Nat and Tom, if they had any sense, could simply have jumped on the nag, whistled for Rab, and taken off?

Fortunately, teachers began to realize that if they wanted kids to read for any reason other than the threat of a hickory stick, the basic reader, such as *McGuffey's Eclectic Primer (bottom right),* was going to have to change.

And change it did. Although Tom and Nat are still alive and well in supplementary phonics workbooks, basic readers today *(left)* are far more sophisticated—and interesting—than they were in the McGuffey era. Today dazzling graphics team up with well-chosen words to involve youngsters in the real-world action.

You can find animals here, too.

What animals can you see here?

36   ECLECTIC SERIES.

LESSON XXX.—REVIEW.

There is ice on the pond, and the mill wheel can not go round.

The boys are all out on the ice with their skates.

I will let you and Tom try to skate; but do not fall, for you will be hurt.

Look! here come the cars. John and Nat try to skate as fast as the cars go, but they can not. John has had a fall.

The girls are not on the pond; but some of them have skates which roll on the floor.

McGUFFEY'S PRIMER.

LESSON XXXI.

wŏrk   ăx   pile   Nĕd   thĭn

woŏd   sąw

härd   cŭt

ō   th   n

Ned and John are hard at work. John has a saw, and Ned h

thing backward. And for another, you've gotten smarter. Probably without your even realizing it, the things you've done and the experiences you've had since you left school have actually *increased* the part of your thinking abilities that scientists call crystallized intelligence—literally the ability to perceive relationships among facts and make rational deductions about how they can work together.

Moreover, unlike children who are frequently working to "get good grades" or "make Mom and Dad happy," adults generally have very specific—and powerful—motivations for setting out to learn something new.

HER STUDY PAID OFF

One woman, for example, who was newly widowed, was tired of having her eyes glaze over every time she tried to do her income tax. She'd open the IRS instruction book, look at the forms, try to figure out whether or not she was a "head of household," and become so confused that at one point she figured that even if *she* was widowed, her money must still be married.

Fortunately, she finally figured out that the problem was not her inability to learn who was and who was not an IRS-approved head of household. Learning is a two-way street, she realized, and the IRS's convoluted language had broken down at the curb. So she bought herself one of those do-your-taxes-in-less-than-a-day drugstore paperbacks and learned that not only was she a head of household, she was also a head of household who had been paying the United States government far more in taxes than it deserved, claimed, or wanted. She filed her return, reclaimed her nearly purloined dollars, and used them to finance a new paint job on her house.

Learning may indeed be its own reward. But it's nice when you can actually see the results in living color—in this case, nut brown with Chinese red trim.

The average adult is motivated to launch at least one learning project a year, either "formally" as 1 of the 23 million adults enrolled in an accredited

THE PERFECT PLACE FOR LEARNING

What kind of environment is the best in which to learn? Not the one pictured above, at least not unless you're planning to learn demolition housekeeping. If you're trying to grapple with almost anything else, however, try another room.

The best learning environment, experts say, is one with an operable window through which you can see vegetation or water and can breathe fresh air. The best lighting is a combination of both natural and artificial, with a desktop lamp beside or behind you as you study.

Make sure those noisy radios and TV's are turned off, a pad is under your typewriter, and all unauthorized pets and people are banned from the vicinity. If there's noise coming from outside your room, either use earplugs, tune out with a softly playing personal radio with headphones, or forgo the fresh air and think about replacing your window with the kind of thick glass used in store windows. If you do shut up the room, however, you might want to buy a small air cleaner with a negative-ion generator to keep your air—and your thinking—fresh.

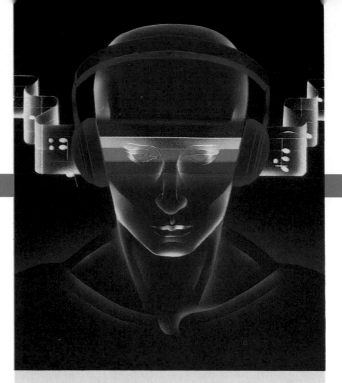

course of study at various schools, colleges, or universities; "nonformally" as a member of a local workshop, Sunday school class, or Y; or "informally" as someone who has simply set out to know as much as there is to know about investing in stock, raising blue-ribbon sheep, or starting a business.

A SUCCESSFUL ADVENTURE

Yet whether your goal is a college degree, a workshop certificate, or simply a new body of information, there are ways to prepare yourself for the experience that will make the learning process a successful adventure guaranteed to enrich your life.

Plan. First decide exactly what it is you want to learn, suggests Jerold W. Apps, Ed.D., a professor of adult education at the University of Wisconsin-Madison. Pick a topic, then sit down with a tablet and write pages and pages of questions. Then plan how you're going to answer them. Pull down a book from the library shelf, sit in on a class, doodle around with pencil and paper at home. Which way feels right to you?

We all have our own learning style that's based on our world views and the kind of assumptions that guide us, explains Dr. Apps. You may be the kind of learner, for example, who prefers to start with little pieces of information and go to the big picture. Or you may prefer to start with the big picture and add the pieces that make it work.

You also need to consider how you like your information delivered. Do you prefer to listen, read, or take something apart with your own hands? Do you like face-to-face lectures or is TV okay? Do you like being part of a group, or do you prefer to be off on your own?

What feels right to you? Figure it out and then commit yourself to learning what it is you need to learn.

Open your mind. "Get past the barrier that everything that's to be learned has to be taught by someone," says Dr. Apps. "You must already have learned thousands and thousands of things on your own just to survive in this society."

HOW SUPER IS SUPERLEARNING?

How would you like to increase your learning ability several times over? Well, according to three education theorists who've looked into the Eastern European learning system called Suggestology, you can. The trio wrote a book called *Superlearning,* in which they claim, basically, that if you learn to relax and use your whole brain, you can learn more than if you stay uptight and half-brained.

"Superlearning is an easy, relaxed way to learn that speeds up learning 2, 5, 10, or more times," write the authors. "This Westernized, modernized way of accelerated learning taps the reserves of the mind to release better mental abilities, supermemory, and other powers."

Sounds good. But does it work?

Unfortunately, the evidence is slim. Accelerated learning techniques frequently combine physical relaxation, mental concentration, guided imagery, and suggestions about the benefits of learning to the accompaniment of background music, reports the National Research Council's Committee on Techniques for the Enhancement of Human Performance. And although there is evidence supporting individual elements of the program—relaxation does reduce stress, for instance, and that can affect learning—there is none that supports bringing all these elements together as a whole.

You also need to leap over the idea that the adult mind's capacity to learn is somehow limited. It's not.

Sharpen your skills. Read everything you can get your hands on—fiction, poetry, plays, nonfiction, everything. Take notes. Reread important paragraphs. Question the author's statements. What's he trying to say? How does it relate to your own experiences? Does what he has to say make sense?

Relax. Relaxation exercises reduce the anxiety that can cause you to forget every word on this page 30 seconds after you finish reading it. And they improve your concentration.

Before his students even begin to tackle the day's learning in a writing class he teaches, Dr. Apps asks them to close their eyes and think about the space within the big toe on one of their feet. Left or right, it doesn't matter. Then he draws their attention upward to the spaces within the ankle, the knee, the shoulder, and finally the head.

"Focus on the space within your head," Dr. Apps encourages his students. "This is your personal space within all the universe." Then he asks them to open their eyes and write anything that comes to mind. It's amazing what his students learn—and teach themselves—in the following 45 minutes.

ARE YOU PLUGGED INTO THE M-FIELD?

Is windsurfing easier to learn than horseback riding? If biologist Rupert Sheldrake is to be believed, the answer is no. But it's not necessarily because of any sport-related problems like choppy water. No, in Sheldrake's view, learning how to ride a horse should be easier than learning how to windsurf simply because people have been doing it for centuries. And windsurfing, historically speaking, is a new guy on the block.

The idea, writes Sheldrake in the journal *Psychological Perspectives,* is that how easily any particular individual learns any particular task is based upon how many times someone—anyone —has done it before.

And why not? "If we tune into our own memories, then why can't we tune into other people's as well?" Sheldrake asks. "I think we do, and the whole basis of the approach I am suggesting is that there is a collective memory to which we are all tuned." He hypothesizes the existence of *morphic fields*—M-fields—around every person, tree, rock, and grain of sand on the planet.

The M-field sets up a soundless resonance that—along with genetics—influences and shapes every fiber of every being. This is only a theory, of course, but if it's true, the lack of guiding resonance in the M-field of our muscles could explain why those windsurfing lessons so often end with a splash.

LEFT BRAIN, RIGHT BRAIN

Y ou can't buy shoes one at a time. Pants need two legs or else they'd be skirts. Try rolling up just one sleeve and see the looks you get. Mittens may do away with our fingers, but they still come in pairs.

And why? Because we humans love the concept of two. We have a couple of this, a couple of that, two feet even if they are both left, two legs, two arms, two eyes, two ears, and now it seems, we even have two brains. The right brain and the left brain.

Examine a typical human brain and the split brain concept all but screams out at you. There it is, a gelatinous mass of tissue that looks like nothing so much as a gigantic pink and gray walnut. Just check out that cleavage and you know what started the whole right brain/left brain controversy.

Scientists looked. They questioned. They conducted endless experiments. And they *did* find differences in the two sides of the human brain. But while researchers are still sifting through their data trying to understand what those differences mean, clever entrepreneurs are already offering workshops on how to harmonize the two halves of the brain.

Popcorn psychology aside, what exactly *do* medical researchers know about the two halves?

THE LEFT (VERBAL) BRAIN

"Can we talk?"

When comedienne Joan Rivers shrieks out her trademark question, she's using her left brain. (It seems we all use our left brains for both shrieking and everyday speech.) If the flashy Miss Rivers knew as much about the left brain as Johnny Carson apparently does, perhaps show business history might have taken a different turn.

More than 150 years ago, an observant physician first noticed that the left side of the brain seemed to be more involved in speech.

"In 1836, a country doctor in France named Marc Dax reported at a small medical society meeting that after examining more than 40 people with language impairments due to brain injuries, he found that all of the injuries were to the left hemisphere of the brain," says Sally Springer, Ph.D., a psychologist

affiliated with the program in human development at the University of California, Davis, and coauthor of the book *Left Brain, Right Brain.* "Unfortunately for him, nobody paid much attention to what he said."

That Dr. Dax's fortuitous discovery fell on deaf ears does not detract from his accomplishment. Most physicians at the time did not believe that particular functions like language were localized in specific parts of the brain. When they took the time to think about the brain, they assumed that all parts of the brain were equally involved in all the different processes of thought.

A few years after Dr. Dax read his paper to deaf ears, his countryman Dr. Paul Broca made a discovery that caused the medical world to sit up and take notice. "Dr. Broca had convincing evidence that the left hemisphere appeared to control speech and language," says Dr. Springer.

In honor of his discovery, a small part of the brain (toward the front of the left cerebral hemisphere) is now called Broca's area. "It's the area where control of expressive language [talking] appears to take place," says Dr. Springer. "Many times when a person has an injury to Broca's area, he can understand what you say, but he has difficulty saying anything back to you."

As Dr. Broca and others discovered, the left side of the brain—in addition to controlling all the functions for the opposite side of the body—is very involved in the production of language, including "the grammar component of written or spoken language," says Joseph Hellige, Ph.D., a cognitive neuropsychologist at the University of Southern California. "The left side is also better able to recognize numbers and symbols."

And the left brain may also be better able to interact wittily with talk show guests. "Johnny Carson always looks to his right to his guests," points out Roger Drake, Ph.D., a cognitive neuroscientist in the Department of Neuroscience, Johns Hopkins University School of Medicine. "This activates the processes of his left hemisphere. In experimental studies, it's been found that when people look to the right, they're more optimistic, they have a more positive view, they're happier, and they have a faster reaction time for verbal questions and problems."

So the next time you're center stage and have to come up with quick, sharp answers, Dr. Drake suggests "you arrange yourself so that you are looking toward the right. That way your left hemisphere, the verbal one, the one that deals with the more positive emotions, has the most blood flow and is primed and ready to go."

Makes you wonder if all those failed talk shows had the guests sitting on the left side.

THE RIGHT (SPATIAL) BRAIN

Moving across the corpus callosum (the band of fibers that connects the two hemispheres), we find ourselves not only in the right brain but also in the middle of a controversy. First the noncontroversial aspect: The right side of the brain controls all the functions on the left side of the body, and "it's superior for processing spatial relationships," says Dr. Hellige. "That is, it's very good at figuring out how one thing in space stands in relation to another thing. It's also very good at making music. We know that many aspects of musical ability reside in this side."

Now the controversy: In recent years some peo-

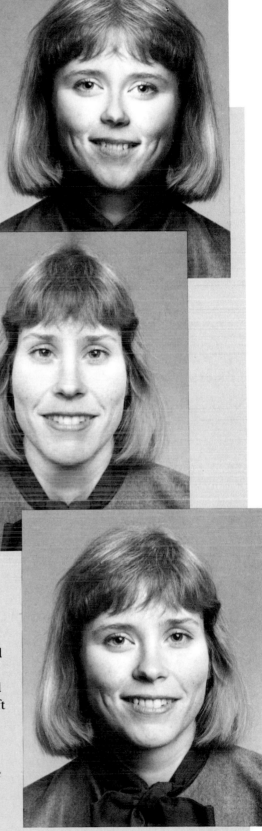

THE TWO FACES OF YOU

Face it, your mug isn't perfect. Go look in a mirror, closely. You'll see that your face is not symmetrical. Scientists believe this may reflect the fact that each side of your face is controlled by the opposite side of the brain.

At right, we've taken a normal photo of a woman *(bottom)* and then made composite pictures of her by combining her two left sides *(middle)* and her two right sides *(top)*.

Researchers found that when people were shown composite left/left and right/right photos like these, they consistently "reported that the left side of the face is much more expressive than the right," says Martin Skinner, Ph.D., a psychologist at the University of Warwick, in Coventry, England, who has conducted many studies of this phenomenon.

BALANCE YOUR BRAIN WITH BREATH

Can't find the words to write that letter to a friend? Maybe you have writer's block because your nose is blocked.

"When airflow is more free in one nostril, the opposite brain hemisphere is currently more dominant," claims researcher David Shannahoff-Khalsa of the Khalsa Foundation for Medical Science in Del Mar, California. Breathing through the congested nostril should stimulate the less-dominant hemisphere.

"It's a noninvasive mechanism for self-regulation," Shannahoff-Khalsa says. Supposedly you'll do better writing that letter or balancing your checkbook when you're breathing through your right nostril (left brain), while music may have more appeal when you breathe through your left nostril (right brain).

You can tell which hemisphere is dominant at the moment by pressing one nostril closed. Inhale and exhale through the other side a couple of times, then reverse it and see which side has the least resistance.

If, for instance, your right nostril is more congested and you want to open up the left side

of your brain, take your index finger and press the left nostril closed, exhaling slowly through the right side. Continue for a maximum of 11 minutes. The deeper the breath, the more powerful the effect, say practitioners.

ple have been singing the right brain's praises for being the seat for lots of other things like artistic ability, insight, imagination, and emotion.

But the scientists who look deep within the recesses of the brain believe that "something as complex as creativity or emotion is going to involve collaboration between both halves of the brain," says Dr. Hellige, "rather than being simply a product of one side or another."

"Cortical blood flow measurements allow us to measure the cerebral blood flow very precisely," says Georg Deutsch, Ph.D., associate professor of neurology at the University of Alabama in Birmingham. "Since blood flow is very much regulated by the amount of activity in a particular region of the brain, we can track the flow to see which areas are recruited for the performance of specific tasks."

In experiments, scientists can watch how much blood flows to each hemisphere as a person tackles a particular job. When someone is asked to do a language task involving analogies, for example, blood flow increases to *both* sides of the brain. However, it

increases slightly more on the left.

So what does it all mean? According to Dr. Deutsch, "There is no question that there are hemispheric differences, but they are very subtle ones. Almost any task involves teamwork between both sides of the brain."

WHICH SIDE ARE YOU?

While there's no hard scientific data to show there's a direct link between a person's abilities and the hemisphere they favor, it is tempting to say that most people intuitively know or can easily determine which side of the brain they favor.

Scientific research suggests that there may be differences in people who favor their right brain or their left brain. And a number of popularizers of the left brain/right brain theory believe that we can learn a lot about ourselves by using it as a tool for self-evaluation.

If you have a lot of trouble reading maps, for instance, you probably favor the left, or verbal side. If, on the other hand, you can follow a map but not the fine print of a new car lease, you probably favor the right, or spatial side. (Now you know why you may feel spaced out in the car dealer's "closing" office.)

Another way to tell which way you lean is to read the following sentence and count the number of f's in it: FINISHED FILES ARE THE RESULT OF YEARS OF SCIENTIFIC STUDY COMBINED WITH THE EXPERIENCE OF MANY YEARS.

Be honest now, did you come up with six? If not, you're not alone. Only 15 percent of those who take this test get the correct answer. Why? If you counted less than six, you probably didn't count the f in each "of." Of is pronounced ov, so your verbal left hemisphere took the verbal clue and overrode the right, "seeing" hemisphere—which some people claim left you with a wrong answer.

Want another clue as to which side you favor? The eyes have it. "Some people claim that when a person looks to the right or the left after being asked a question, that gives you insight into which hemisphere is dominant," says Dr. Springer. But it's not always as simple as that. "Investigators are finding that what *kind* of question you're asked may influence which way you look. There tends to be movement to the right if you're asked a question involving verbal stimulation, and movement to the left if you're asked a question dealing with spatial relationships." In any event, the eyes are definitely worth watching.

Even though people are never exclusively right- or left-brained, researchers believe that it's valuable just to know that there are differences in emphasis. "To know that different people have different styles of interacting with each other, and the world, is very important," says Dr. Hellige. "It's also important to know something about your own style of interaction, because that will help you broaden your capabilities."

In other words, try to strengthen and balance *both* sides of your brain.

You, at least, have that option. For a few very unique patients, working with both sides of their brain takes on a whole new meaning. These people are split-brain patients. They have undergone a form of brain surgery that was deemed necessary for them to lead normal lives. And from their operations, medical science has learned even more about the mysterious duality of the human brain. James is one such patient.

LIVING WITH A SPLIT BRAIN

To be an epileptic is to live your life as if your finger were stuck in a wall socket. Suddenly, without warning, James's brain would short-circuit and he would experience a seizure. Then he would wake up, only to dread the next electrical storm in his mind.

Some epileptics can control or at least reduce the intensity and frequency of their seizures with medicine, but most cannot. James was one of those unfortunate ones. So at 36 years of age, this Canadian turned to a surgeon for relief.

Cutting through the skull at the hairline, James's surgeon performed the operation of last resort for severe epileptics—a commissurotomy, or split brain surgery. James's corpus callosum was partially severed in the hope that this would localize his seizures to just one area of his brain.

No longer would electrical outbursts cross from his left brain to his right. But what about his thoughts, ideas, and feelings? Was James condemned to be a man with two separate brains, the right not knowing what the left was thinking—and doing?

"If you see him across the table from you, there is no way you could pick him out as a 'split-brain person,' " says Justine Sergent, Ph.D., a cognitive neuroscientist at the Montreal Neurological Institute who studies split-brain patients before and after their surgery.

"We all hear of one or two cases where a patient reports not knowing what his right or left hand is doing," she says. "But for the most part such people function as you or I do. You can only detect a difference in laboratory situations where you present information to only one hemisphere at a time."

In the real world that's a near impossibility: both hemispheres get their information almost simultaneously. When asked how he now gets along with almost two separate brains, speaking in a heavy French accent, James replies, "I feel perfect now. I can do anything anybody else can do. Sometimes I have a poor memory. I don't remember what I'm talking about, but eventually I get it out . . . it may be just a bit slower. Last Friday I went to work for the first time ever."

Even with two brains operating independently of one another, the only difference in James is that now he doesn't have seizures. "He's still very loving and caring. He still has emotions and feelings," says his mother. "My son who went in for the operation is the same son who came out."

"From knowing these split-brain patients, I believe that both hemispheres can do just about any sort of task, with the possible exception of speech," says Dr. Sergent. "Each half of the brain is doing all sorts of things, not to the same extent, but in different proportions.

"It's a puzzle. Is the brain like a computer made up of independent components, each one doing a specific function? Or is the brain made of interactive components in such a way that a function is distributed throughout? Both of these views are probably true to some extent. There is cerebral localization of function, but it is not rigid."

Even if functions are spread throughout the brain, it's still fun trying to determine which side you may lean toward. And if analyzing two sides doesn't provide you with enough challenge, maybe you should meet Ned Herrmann.

BECOMING WHOLE-BRAINED

Ned Herrmann describes himself as a physicist, musician, author, entrepreneur, and brain researcher. As a result of his research, he has divided the brain into what he calls "four different but equal quadrants. The upper left is the logical, rational, analytic, quantitative quadrant. The lower left is the planning, organizing, sequencing, implementating quadrant. The lower right is the feeling, emotional, interpersonal, spiritual, value-oriented quadrant. And finally, the upper right quadrant is the synthesizing, holistic, risk-taking, artistic part of the brain."

The name of one of Herrmann's companies, the Whole Brain Corporation, gives you a pretty good idea of what he does. Working with large multinational corporations such as IBM, GE, Shell, Goodyear, and General Foods, Herrmann's goal is to get employees to make optimal use of all four quadrants of their brain.

If you're looking to become more whole-brained yourself, Herrmann has some tips. "If you're a dominant left-mode person, you're a logical, rational engineer type. So I recommend that you learn how to draw as a routine kind of thing. Once you've accessed the part of your mental process that permits you to see clearly enough to draw, you will be using a part of your brain that you don't normally use.

"When that happens, then you will have learned a transferable skill. The fact that you can now draw gives you the permission to do other things like being more creative, more innovative, more playful, and more free and open. You don't have to give up the valuable characteristics of the left mode, but you've added to and enhanced that part of you by bringing the right mode into play as well."

But what about you artistic types who can balance a mobile, but not a checkbook? "It's much harder for the artist, because moving from the right mode to the left is basically like going back to school," says Herrmann. "It requires a value shift, a change from not giving a damn about the checkbook to wanting to work with numbers as easily as you work with paint. If you say you can't do it, that becomes a self-fulfilling prophecy. But once you see the value in learning to work with numbers, it will be easier for you to do so."

Knowing there is a bookkeeper in every artist and an artist in every bookkeeper is the key to becoming a more whole-brained person. "It's important to understand the nature of right mode/left mode differences, first with other people and then within yourself, and to know how to access them. Tapping into those differences will open up a whole cluster of possibilities," says Herrmann.

DRAWING ON THE RIGHT SIDE OF YOUR BRAIN

If there were an art category known as "stick figures," you would be the da Vinci of the genre. After painstakingly drawing a portrait of your spouse, you hear the compliment, "That's a nice picture of a tree, dear." Oh, to be able to draw! But *you* must not have what it takes, right? Wrong.

"If your handwriting is readable, or if you can print legibly, you have ample dexterity to draw well," says Betty Edwards, Ed.D., author of the best-selling book *Drawing on the Right Side of the Brain* and professor of art at California State University, Long Beach.

So how do you draw out the artist within? Dr. Edwards, who has had dramatic success in teaching people how to draw, says the first step is to learn how you see. "People process information in two different modes. The L-mode is the language mode. It's the sequential, verbal, analytic mode thought to be in the brain's left hemisphere. The R-mode is the visual, spatial way of thinking that is often associated with the right hemisphere."

One of the secrets of learning to draw involves shutting off the L-mode. "Drawing upside down is one technique designed to trick the verbal brain to stay out of the task," she says. "The L-mode has difficulty naming things that are upside down."

Seeing things in new ways, in this case upside down, is the key. "If you want to learn how to draw," Dr. Edwards says, "find someone who will teach you how to see, not someone who will sit you in front of a still life and say, 'Draw this.' Remember, you draw with your eyes, not your hands."

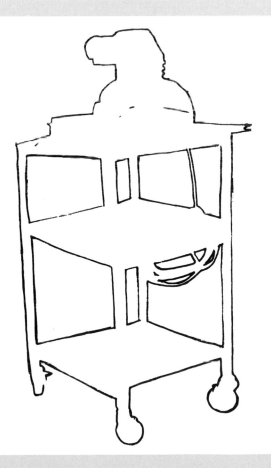

These drawings of a slide projector on a cart demonstrate the dramatic improvement that can occur when we draw on the right side of the brain. At the top, a student tried drawing exactly what he saw by using his L-mode, but the better bottom drawing (by the same student) shows what happened when he switched to his R-mode through a technique called drawing negative space. "It works the same way that upside-down drawing does," says Dr. Betty Edwards, "By concentrating on the empty space around objects rather than the objects themselves, we can cause the L-mode to bow out. Then the spatially oriented R-mode takes over."

MACHINES THAT MASSAGE THE MIND

It's like being on the inside of a pinball machine and looking out. Directly in front of your eyes, brightly colored lights are flashing on and off. Various tones assault your ears, and a tingling sensation cascades over your body.

Your eyes begin to close as your mind starts to open. Time is no longer meaningful. Parking hassles, demanding bosses, hungry kids, sloppy spouses, all the everyday tension in your life starts to disappear. You seem to drift back into your body. The inner reaches of your brain beckon. You feel like you're floating. You hear a voice, a soft, gentle voice, calling to you. Straining to listen, you hear. . . .

"Time's up!"

And suddenly, it's over. The lights stop flashing, the headphones are removed, and you're yanked back to reality.

What you've supposedly been doing for the past 30 or so minutes is exercising your brain. Electronically. It's a pastime that's catching on with more and more Americans. The idea is that every couple of weeks you plug into a device that serves as a kind of mental massage parlor for your brain.

SYNCHRONIZING RIGHT AND LEFT

In this case, the machine is called the Synchro-Energizer, and it's designed to help bring your right and left hemispheres into synchrony, or balance. The machine, according to its inventor, Denis Gorges, M.D., Ph.D., seems to "have a powerful effect in learning and psychotherapy. It appears to help reduce stress and anxiety, relieve phobias, and control substance abuse. It seems to have the same effect as hypnosis or meditation does."

Many other machines are on the market. All stimulate neural activity to some degree, either with electricity, motion, light, or sound. Some people claim the devices can boost your IQ, soothe pain, or even increase your creativity. The Graham Potentializer, for example, is designed to re-create the mental effects of the rolling, tumbling, swinging games you played as a child. To use it, you lie down on a bed that rotates around in a magnetic field while you listen to relaxation tapes.

The Mind Mirror is another brain machine that is gaining in popularity. It is an EEG-type device used for biofeedback.

If you're looking to one of these machines for pain relief, Dr. Gorges says, "the only devices that have been shown to relieve pain are the TENS (transcutaneous electrical nerve stimulation) devices, like the Alpha-Stim or the Relaxpak. They block the pain to the brain, but they don't stop the pain. They simply hinder the brain's ability to perceive it."

All the machines can be used at home. But since they are often very expensive—up to $70,000 in some cases—they are most often found in walk-in centers like Altered States in Los Angeles, MindWorld in Miami, Less Stress in San Francisco, and Synchro Energize in New York City.

People who plug into the devices seem to become very attached. "The Synchro-Energizer helped me achieve a very deeply relaxed state after using it for just 30 minutes," says David Harris, an industrial sales representative in Los Angeles who continues to use the device about once a month. "The effects from the machine stay with me for two or three days, even with all the stress and hassles here in L.A."

USING YOUR HEAD FIRST

If you want to try any of the numerous brain machines, Dr. Gorges recommends, "First ask how much research has been done on the machine and for how long. Then ask if hospitals or clinics use it. Has a federal agency approved it? [All machines that put electrical stimulation into the brain must have been reviewed and/or approved by the Food and Drug Administration.] If you get a no answer to any of these questions, using the machine could be risky."

"You also have to distinguish between brain toys and brain tools," adds Dr. Gorges. "If something is too cheap, under a couple of hundred of dollars, it's probably a toy. The more expensive and complex it is, the more research that backs it up, then the more likely it is to be a serious tool. The more sophisticated the hardware and software built into the device, the more likely it will be an effective piece of equipment."

But some neurologists wonder if the devices are effective at all, and they worry about other problems that the machines may cause. In some cases, for instance, flashing lights may trigger epileptic seizures in susceptible people.

"The idea that you can sit and listen to tones or see lights flash, and that will somehow balance your brain or increase your intelligence, has no basis in scientific fact," says Stephen Peroutka, M.D., an assistant professor of neurology at Stanford University Medical Center.

While most of these machines might indeed help you relax, Dr. Peroutka says, "listening to Mozart on a stereo Walkman will give you the same result for a lot less money."

MEDICATIONS AND YOUR BRAIN

You may think the only drugs that could affect your brain are ones you've heard about on the news—drugs like cocaine and LSD. Think again. Chances are that your medicine cabinet is *full* of mind-altering drugs—the kind that you pick up not from the street-corner pusher, but from the corner pharmacy.

Time to "just say no" to these drugs, too?

That question is not so easy to answer. True, many medications, both prescription and over-the-counter, can play with your mind. They can make you drowsy, confused, nervous, or depressed. In some cases, they can cause paranoid thinking, irrational behavior, even hallucinations. The flip side, of course, is that these same medications also relieve your sniffles, muffle that cough, or numb that throbbing in your head.

Many medications warrant consideration of a "benefit-risk ratio," says Roger Maickel, Ph.D., pro-fessor of pharmacology and toxicology at Purdue University's School of Pharmacy and Pharmacal Sciences. The *benefit* of taking an allergy tablet, for example, is that you'll feel more comfortable not having to constantly wipe your runny nose. The *risk* is that your alertness may conk out, because antihistamines can make you drowsy.

BIZARRE BEHAVIOR

Consider the case of a 49-year-old Canadian man, a mathematical scientist, who was taking the drug digoxin following a coronary bypass operation. As he reports in a letter to the medical journal *Lancet* he found himself unable to work out even the simplest algebraic expressions. The drug had seriously dulled his mental capacities, although he didn't initially realize it was the drug. Fortunately, he was able to discontinue the medication before he would have had to apply for long-term disability.

Or consider the case of three neuroscientists who thought they could beat jet lag if each belted down a couple of drinks with a sleeping pill (Halcion) during a flight. As reported in the *Journal of the American Medical Association*, they awoke several hours later in a hotel room in a foreign country—with no idea whatsoever how they got there. They couldn't remember landing, clearing customs, exchanging money, or checking into the hotel.

In another case, a man in his early fifties had serious trouble with his job at the phone company. Working with color-coded wires, he found himself continually fouling up his connections. The problem, however, was not carelessness. According to Dr. Maickel, it was the cardiac glycoside tablets the man was taking for his heart condition. They made everything he saw have a yellow tinge, so that white wires looked yellow, red wires looked orange, and blue wires seemed green.

WHY DRUGS DO FUNNY THINGS

You may be wondering why, if medications sometimes have these strange effects on the brain, the manufacturers don't just fix them. Well, they would

MEDICATION MAD

You've undoubtedly suffered dry mouth, fatigue, or perhaps a queasy stomach after taking a certain drug. But have you ever heard voices ordering you to jump out of a fourth-floor window?

A doctor in England reports in the *British Medical Journal* the case of a 50-year-old man who not only heard just that, he *obeyed*. He was given a single tablet of the painkiller buprenorphine following an operation to remove hemorrhoids. That was all it took.

The man, with no history whatsoever of mental illness, began to hear voices instructing him to perform various chores on the ward. A hospital official asked him into her office to discuss his bizarre behavior. That's when he jumped—four floors to the ground.

Although seriously injured as a result of the fall, the man lived to tell the tale.

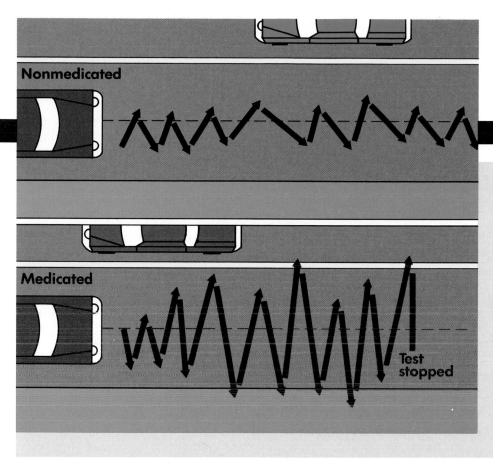

Nonmedicated

Medicated

Test stopped

if they could. But there are a few complications involved. Foremost, "there is no one drug that has only one action," says Dr. Maickel.

Take aspirin. It will help relieve a headache. It can lower your temperature if you have a fever. It relieves arthritis pain. It can also keep the blood from clotting. But let's say you want the aspirin today only for the headache. Does that mean it will no longer have any of these other effects? Of course not.

Another problem with drugs is that individuals react to them differently. No two people (except perhaps identical twins), weigh the same, have the same metabolic rate, and produce the same amounts of hormones, says Angele C. D'Angelo, a registered pharmacist who is assistant dean and associate professor at St. John's University College of Pharmacy and Allied Health Professions, Jamaica, New York.

What can you do to make certain the drugs you're taking do what they're supposed to—and no more? How do you make rational decisions about what drugs to take? Here's some advice from the experts.

Take only your own medicine. "*Don't* take some pill because Aunt Elvira once had the same problem that you do now, and it worked for her. You should *never* take anyone else's prescription," says Arthur H. Kibbe, Ph.D., director of scientific affairs at the American Pharmaceutical Association.

Be careful about mixing medications. Combining certain drugs can augment the effects of one or both drugs, negate their effectiveness, or create entirely new problems. If you're taking any kind of medicine whatsoever, let both your physician and pharmacist know before taking another, says Dr. Kibbe.

Beware of what you wash your pills down with. Not all drugs are in medications. The caffeine in coffee and the alcohol in beer are drugs, and they can mix with certain prescription or over-the-counter medications to make for big problems.

Follow instructions religiously. If your doctor's prescription or the instructions on the box say "three times a day," that *doesn't* mean one pill at noon, and the other two at dinnertime, says Dr. Maickel. It means one roughly every 8 hours.

Be quick to react. You should know as much about a medication as you can, including its possible side effects (which you can read about on the box or in the little insert that comes inside). If *anything* unusual occurs after taking a drug, get in touch with your physician or pharmacist as quickly as possible.

DRUGS THAT TAMPER WITH YOUR MIND

Don't expect that if you take any of the drugs below you will necessarily experience altered behavior or start swinging from chandeliers. Just be aware that unexpected side effects—including abnormal thinking patterns—are possible in some instances. These responses are fairly infrequent, but they can be quite alarming and potentially dangerous to you or others, says James W. Long, M.D., author of *The Essential Guide to Prescription Drugs* (where this information originally appeared).

DRUGS REPORTED TO IMPAIR CONCENTRATION AND/OR MEMORY

Antihistamines
Antiparkinsonism drugs
Barbiturates
Benzodiazepines

Isoniazid
Monoamine oxidase (MAO) inhibitor
    drugs
Phenytoin

Primidone
Scopolamine

DRUGS REPORTED TO CAUSE CONFUSION, DELIRIUM, OR DISORIENTATION

Acetazolamide
Aminophylline
Antidepressants
Antihistamines
Atropinelike drugs
Barbiturates
Benzodiazepines
Bromides
Carbamazepine
Chloroquine
Cimetidine

Cortisonelike drugs
Cycloserine
Digitalis
Digitoxin
Digoxin
Disulfiram
Ethchlorvynol
Ethinamate
Fenfluramine
Glutethimide
Isoniazid

Levodopa
Meprobamate
Para-aminosalicylic acid
Phenelzine
Phenothiazines
Phenytoin
Piperazine
Primidone
Propranolol
Reserpine
Scopolamine

DRUGS REPORTED TO CAUSE PARANOID THINKING

Bromides
Cortisonelike drugs

Diphenhydramine
Disulfiram

Isoniazid
Levodopa

DRUGS REPORTED TO CAUSE SCHIZOPHRENICLIKE BEHAVIOR

Amphetamines
Ephedrine

Fenfluramine
Phenmetrazine

Phenylpropanolamine

DRUGS REPORTED TO CAUSE MANICLIKE BEHAVIOR

Antidepressants
Cortisonelike drugs

Levodopa
Monoamine oxidase (MAO) inhibitor drugs

Listed next are some mood-altering side effects of drugs that have been observed often enough to establish recognizable patterns. These effects, of course, are quite unpredictable and will vary enormously from person to person.

DRUGS REPORTED TO CAUSE NERVOUSNESS (ANXIETY AND IRRITABILITY)

Amantadine
Amphetaminelike drugs (appetite suppressants)
Antihistamines
Caffeine
Chlorphenesin
Cortisonelike drugs
Ephedrine
Epinephrine
Isoproterenol
Levodopa
Liothyronine (in excessive dosage)
Methylphenidate
Methysergide
Monoamine oxidase (MAO) inhibitor drugs
Nylidrin
Oral contraceptives
Theophylline
Thyroid (in excessive dosage)
Thyroxine (in excessive dosage)

DRUGS REPORTED TO CAUSE EMOTIONAL DEPRESSION

Amantadine
Amphetamine (on withdrawal)
Benzodiazepines
Carbamazepine
Chloramphenicol
Cortisonelike drugs
Cycloserine
Digitalis
Digitoxin
Digoxin
Diphenoxylate
Estrogens
Ethionamide
Fenfluramine (on withdrawal)
Fluphenazine
Guanethidine
Haloperidol
Indomethacin
Isoniazid
Levodopa
Methsuximide
Methyldopa
Methysergide
Metoprolol
Oral contraceptives
Phenylbutazone
Procainamide
Progesterones
Propranolol
Reserpine
Sulfonamides
Vitamin D (in excessive dosage)

DRUGS REPORTED TO CAUSE EUPHORIA

Amantadine
Aminophylline
Amphetamines
Antihistamines (some)
Antispasmodics, synthetic
Aspirin
Barbiturates
Benzphetamine
Chloral hydrate
Clorazepate
Codeine
Cortisonelike drugs
Diethylpropion
Diphenoxylate
Ethosuximide
Flurazepam
Haloperidol
Levodopa
Meprobamate
Methysergide
Monoamine oxidase (MAO) inhibitor drugs
Morphine
Pargyline
Pentazocine
Phenmetrazine
Propoxyphene
Scopalamine
Tybamate

DRUGS REPORTED TO CAUSE EXCITEMENT

Acetazolamide
Amantadine
Amphetaminelike drugs
Antidepressants
Antihistamines
Atropinelike drugs
Barbiturates (paradoxical response)
Benzodiazepines (paradoxical response)
Cortisonelike drugs
Cycloserine
Diethylpropion
Digitalis
Ephedrine
Epinephrine
Ethinamate (paradoxical response)
Ethionamide
Glutethimide (paradoxical response)
Isoniazid
Isoproterenol
Levodopa
Meperidine and monoamine oxidase (MAO) inhibitor drugs
Methyldopa and monoamine oxidase (MAO) inhibitor drugs
Methyprylon (paradoxical response)
Nalidixic acid
Orphenadrine
Quinine
Scopalamine

MEDITATION

"Are you going to be awake for your life or not?" demands Jon Kabat-Zinn, Ph.D., director of the University of Massachusetts stress reduction and relaxation program in Worcester.

That's the choice you make when you decide whether or not to meditate, he adds. Because most of us—most of the time—are on automatic pilot. And it takes meditation to wake us up.

How? "Meditation is basically awareness or attentional training," explains Mark Epstein, M.D., a clinical instructor in psychiatry at New York Hospital-Cornell University Medical College. Most people think of it in terms of creating a relaxed state, says Dr. Epstein, but relaxation is really only a by-product of meditation. Its real use—and value—is teaching you to concentrate. It can interrupt the chatter of thoughts and create a stillness within the modern swirl of human activity that will permit you to pay attention to your life one moment at a time.

Meditation takes your mind off "automatic" and tunes you in to the present on a moment-by-moment basis, adds Dr. Kabat-Zinn. It teaches you to pay attention. And its benefits carry over into the rest of your life, even when you're not meditating.

Think how much more effective that can make you in almost any area. If your husband is rattling along about his day, for example, and you're just muttering, "Uh-huh . . . Uh-huh . . . Oh really?" every few minutes, how will the interaction change if you turn off that automatic pilot and turn on some concentrated brainpower?

What would be the different quality of your response if your mind was totally concentrated on your husband? asks Dr. Kabat-Zinn. Would it make you a different kind of spouse? Would it make your husband a different kind of person?

Quite probably, says Dr. Epstein. Because anchoring yourself in the present and focusing the entire

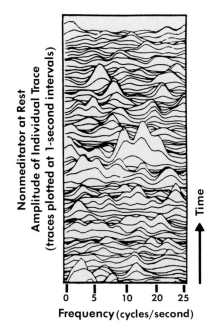

Nonmeditator at Rest
Amplitude of Individual Trace (traces plotted at 1-second intervals)

Time

Frequency (cycles/second)

0 5 10 20 25

Here's a topographical map of your brain waves when you're at rest. A mess, aren't you? The electrical impulses generated by your brain say you're a random, inconsistent, mixed-up burst of electrical energy.

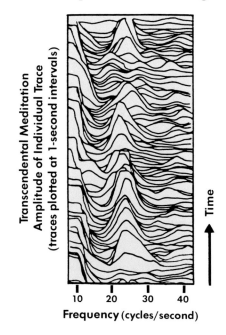

Transcendental Meditation
Amplitude of Individual Trace (traces plotted at 1-second intervals)

Time

Frequency (cycles/second)

10 20 30 40

Here's a map of your brain waves when you're meditating. They're organized, coherent waves of a constant, fast frequency. The electrical energy is focused and so are you.

power of your mind on a single instant allows you to see and judge what's going on in that instant more clearly than you normally would.

LEARN HOW TO SEE

Ready to give it a try? The best way to begin is to sit down in a comfortable spot, says Dr. Epstein, then close your eyes and concentrate on the physical sensation of your breathing.

Listen to the sound of air as it almost imperceptibly enters your body and gently swells your lungs.

Some people also like to focus on the word "stillness" as they breathe—quietly hearing "still-" as they inhale, and "-ness" as they exhale.

"The important thing is not how long you can keep your mind on your breath—that's difficult—but how willing you are to bring your mind back to your breath when it wanders," says Dr. Epstein. "When you can bring your mind back easily, begin to expand your awareness so that any feelings, thoughts, or sensations can become the object of your awareness."

Then, "Concentrate on the object with a calm acceptance, an inner stillness that allows you to see a thought coming, blossoming, and leaving," suggests Dr. Kabat-Zinn. "You will begin to see things that you haven't seen before. And you will see them in a

So you think you're hot stuff? These gentlemen, Tibetan monks by trade, are participating in a secret Buddhist ritual at a monastery tucked away in northern India. The temperature is 40°F. The sheets have just been dipped in ice-cold buckets of water. And—as filmed here by Herbert Benson, M.D., a Harvard University researcher—the sheets are steaming because while meditating, the monks can voluntarily raise their body temperatures high enough to vaporize water. The sheets were completely dry in 40 minutes, reported Dr. Benson.

360-degree way. You'll be self-accepting. Nonjudgmental. Uncritical.

"I don't think we need magic solutions to the problems we face as individuals or as a society," adds Dr. Kabat-Zinn. "The magic's inside ourselves,"—if we can learn to see it.

How often should we take a look? "Try meditation once a day for 20 minutes and find a way of integrating it into your life," advises Dr. Epstein. "Then give yourself a period of time to practice.

"People usually see benefits immediately," he adds. "They feel it's right. They see the wisdom. They see how cluttered their minds have been."

And how clear they can really be.

MEMORY

Imagine life without your memory.

You wake up in the morning, look around at the flowered wallpaper, the photographs that line the dresser top, and the crumpled bedclothes and think, "Where am I?"

You sit up, legs dangling from the edge of the bed. Your toes touch a pair of well-worn slippers. "Whose are these?" you ask yourself. Your feet slide into them. Surprise! They fit perfectly.

"Are you up? Breakfast is ready," a voice calls from the hallway. A face peeks around the edge of the bedroom door. "You *are* up. Good morning!"

"Who is this person?" you wonder.

Tough way to start a day, huh? Well, thank your memory that every day doesn't start out with questions instead of answers. Because memory is many things: A diary of the past. A guide to the present. A calendar for the future.

Memory can help by recording information just long enough for you to look up a phone number, dial, and say hello before the number fizzles. Or memory can span decades, registering the bouquet of an evergreen that you enjoyed as a child so that you carry the piny scent in your head and heart for a lifetime.

But memory isn't just what we think of as remembering. It's also a tool for the simplest tasks: turning on a light, understanding dialogue, or walking around the block. If you had no memory, you couldn't read this page. You wouldn't know how to turn the pages of this book.

"Memory is the heart of our knowledge," says memory investigator H. B. Eichenbaum, Ph.D., associate professor of biology at Wellesley College in Massachusetts. "It is our conception of the world. It is the closest thing to consciousness."

FINDING THE DEPOT

There's no particular spot in the brain that serves as a giant warehouse for memories. Scientists speculate that memory is stored in various places as a combination of chemicals and nerve networks, says Neal Cohen, Ph.D., assistant professor of psychology and neurology at Johns Hopkins University and Johns Hopkins Hospital.

"Memories are often associated with the region doing the processing," Dr. Cohen says. "If you are riding a bicycle, for instance, the brain areas that control your leg movements and your eye/hand coordination may also store the memory of the skills needed to perform the feat.

Researchers have pinpointed some parts of the brain that are especially important to memory by studying amnesia victims, says Dr. Eichenbaum. Damage to the hippocampus, the amygdala, the thalamus, or the hypothalamus, areas located near the lower central part of the brain, "causes an inability to remember new things, to add new information to long-term memory."

TEST YOUR SPATIAL MEMORY

Are you one of those people who can work a puzzle or a maze with little effort? If so, you probably have a good spatial memory. You can look at a map once or twice, then find your way without getting lost. You remember colors well. You recognize music and voices with little prompting. You are usually good at learning new faces.

Here's a tough test to challenge your spatial memory. Look at the eight shapes pictured above for a minute and try to add them to your memory. Then, turn to the larger display on page 127 to see how many you can correctly recall.

Long-term storage, he says, is throughout the cerebral cortex, the gray matter of the brain.

Exactly how the brain controls memory is still mostly unknown. Scientists continue to probe, hoping new discoveries will lead to a cure for, or prevention of, memory disorders.

What experts do agree on is this: For most people, memory is a tool with a lifetime guarantee. Less than 20 percent of people over 60 experience memory loss due to disease or disorder. Memory does slow a little with age, but it carries most of us faithfully from cradle to grave.

PRECOCIOUS MEMORIES

Picture this: darkness all around. You are curled in a tight place, squeezed by the walls surrounding you. There is a continuous pulsating sound. Sometimes you hear music; sometimes a soft, low voice. Then suddenly it is light. You shiver. Your warm, dark world is gone.

For some people, this is their first and oldest memory. It is a memory of birth.

"Although the idea of babies remembering birth seems a recent one," reports psychologist David Chamberlain, Ph.D., "birth memories have shown up periodically for the last hundred years . . . as recurring dreams, thoughts, habits, fears, or other phenomena."

In his book *Babies Remember Birth*, Dr. Chamberlain reports babies develop memories in the womb, as early as five months after conception.

He tells of a Canadian symphony conductor who knew the cello line of some scores before seeing them. His mother, a professional cellist, had practiced those pieces over and over during her pregnancy.

In another study, pregnant women repeated the words "beguile" and "tinder" ten times each six times a day for two weeks before giving birth. After birth, their babies turned their eyes, raised their eyebrows, and moved their heads more often in response to those odd words than they did in response to their own names.

Does memory begin in the womb? In a study at the University of North Carolina, 12 pregnant women read *The Cat in the Hat* to their unborn babies. A few days after birth, the newborns were presented with two special nipples— sucking on one activated a tape of *The Cat in the Hat*, while sucking on the other activated another Dr. Seuss story. Ten of the 12 newborns repeatedly picked "The Cat."

Amazing? Yet, in spite of a growing number of studies documenting infant memories, many adults say they can't remember much about their childhood.

So what gives some people good memories and some people poor ones? Scientists charting the process called memory have some theories. But first you must know how memory works.

A FINELY TUNED FILING SYSTEM

Using memory is like sitting at a desk in an office.

Short-term memory, often called a working memory, is like a desktop scattered with papers you are using at the moment. This is the memory that keeps track of conversation, notes where you set your pen and paper, or registers what you have read so you don't have to keep rereading to follow the story.

Potential memories land on the desktop through one of the five senses: seeing (visual), hearing (verbal), touching, smelling, or tasting (physical or kinesthetic). But short-term memory is just that, short. It lasts 10 to 15 seconds. Then the papers disappear—you for-

get the information—or they zip to the long-term memory cabinet. Long-term memory is what most people think of when they think of memory. It contains data decades old as well as information stored a few minutes ago.

Long-term memory is broken down further into two categories. The first type is declarative memory. It contains your autobiography: your name and address as well as images we might call a mental photo album of the events in your life.

The other category involves procedural memories, or skills. These might include a great tennis swing, the knowledge of how to tie your shoe, or the ability to read, says Dr. Eichenbaum.

To get to long-term storage, your memories must pass a short-term gateway. To send data to the permanent collection—to memorize—you must practice the information or link it with a memory already in storage. To recall information, a link or cue travels to the storage file, where it acts like a magnet, pulling out related information to remind you of something tucked away.

You are at a custom car show, for example, admiring a candy apple red 1957 Chevy. You inspect its cream-colored tuck-and-roll upholstery. That's visual.

You run your hand lovingly across the seat and around the red plastic steering wheel (kinesthetic) and remember what it was like to sit in your dad's 1957 Chevy (linking).

Thanks to our memory, every human face registers as unique. We perceive differences in "internal features" such as the space between eyes, the shape of the nose, the tilt of the mouth, says Dr. Mark Johnson, of the Medical Research Council in London.

January 28, 1986, 11:39 A.M., south of Daytona Beach, Florida: Outside his cockpit window, airline captain O. A. Fish saw the vapor cloud left by the Challenger explosion. That highly emotional scene is locked into his and other people's memories forever. It is called a flashbulb memory because the mind captures it like a clear photo.

The owner tells you about the car (that's verbal). He gives you his business card and you study his name, probably repeating it (that's practicing).

Fast-forward a year. You are at another custom car show and there's a powder blue 1957 Chevy. Your mind sends cues to the files: car show, restored 1957 Chevy, tuck-and-roll upholstery.

"I saw a beautiful candy apple red Chevy just a year ago," you say. The cues dig a little deeper into your files. "The owner, I believe, was a man from Atlanta."

Voilà! Your memory at work.

Mood, too, has an effect on memory and later recall. You remember sad events more easily when you are in a blue mood, and you recall happy moments easily when you are in cheerful mood, Jefferson A. Singer, Ph.D., found in a study at Yale University.

One additional element that prompts your memory is interest, according to Dr. Cohen.

"People who are good card players can remember a whole game for you," he says. "I can remember an enormous number of papers on memory research—who said what, and in what year—because you remember things you are expert in."

MEMORY WHIZ

Experts estimate the average brain can hold as many as one quadrillion (that's a 1 followed by 15 0's) separate bits of information in long-term memory.

But because the short-term gateway is narrow—no one is sure why—the average person can memorize only five to seven chunks of *new* information at a time, says Elizabeth Loftus, Ph.D., professor of psychology at the University of Washington.

Memory is flexible enough, though, that we can train it to work more efficiently and to process great quantities of information. In a study at Carnegie-Mellon University, a student learned to memorize

strings of random digits. Although he could learn only 6 digits at a time in his first tries, after a couple of weeks of practice sessions, he could learn more numbers. After 18 months of practice, he could listen to an 84-digit list and repeat it back to the researcher.

The student, who was also a cross-country runner, learned the digits by taking the numbers in groups of three or four and associating them (linking) with racing times.

His other memorizing abilities stayed the same as those of normal people, scientists noted, but he had taught his memory a special skill for numbers.

The *Guinness Book of World Records* records several supermemories. Telephone operator Gou Yanling memorized more than 15,000 telephone numbers in Harbin, China. Hideaki Tomoyori of Yokohama, Japan, recited, from memory, the mathematical value of pi to 40,000 decimal places.

Additionally, retired accountant Stephen Powelson, 70, of Les-Loges-en-Josas, France, memorized more than 14,300 lines of Homer's 15,693-line *Iliad* in classical Greek. His memorization of the 600 pages of text took about ten years. Occasionally, he recites an hour or two of the classic in exhibitions at schools and colleges.

MISSING MEMORABILIA

So, with such memory potential, why does a name or a word we need sometimes seem poised on the tip of our tongue, but still out of reach?

When that happens, it means the cues we are sending are too few to retrieve the data, says psychology professor Robert Bjork, Ph.D., of the University of California, Los Angeles.

One theory among psychologists is that long-term memory is etched into our minds forever. However, "we are very fallible on the retrieval side," Dr. Bjork says. "Most of what is in long-term memory is not recallable."

In other words, we don't know enough to remember.

Sometimes we don't know any cues. Many people can't remember their early childhood, for example, because "you didn't have a language to label your experience when you were an infant," says Michael Epstein, Ph.D., a psychology professor at Rider College in New Jersey. "A child does have a good sense of smell, however, and that can be a good clue to trigger a memory. Sometimes as an adult we will smell something and it will take us back right away."

Think of the wave of nostalgia that washes over you as you hear a song from long ago, or the secure feeling that enrobes you when a hall light shines at night. Those may be emotional responses to a memory you can't quite recall, says Dr. Bjork.

Sometimes we forget because we want to forget, adds Dr. Epstein. "It's not really that you've forgotten; it's that you don't want to remember. We tend to forget what is painful."

Sometimes we don't see things accurately in the first place, according to Dr. Loftus, who has studied eyewitness accounts. Sometimes our memories are colored by time. Sometimes comparing notes with people and speculating on how or why events occurred unconsciously changes our memories.

And occasionally we forget, but we don't know we've forgotten. Our brain remembers fragments of an event, then fills in any gaps with made-up memories.

AMNESIA'S FEARFUL FOG

In the 1945 Alfred Hitchcock film *Spellbound,* Gregory Peck portrayed an accused murderer suffering from amnesia. Peck's on-screen memory loss stemmed from emotional trauma, but most real-life cases of amnesia can be traced to a *physical* shock. The resulting brain damage destroys the ability to remember things that happen after the trauma occurs. Typically, people can't keep track of day-to-day events.

One of the most famous true stories of amnesia is the tale of a man called "H. M." In 1953, while trying to treat H. M.'s epilepsy, a doctor surgically removed the hippocampus from the man's brain. Afterward, H. M. could remember the details of his life until surgery. And he still had a working memory, meaning he could keep up with a conversation. But if you stepped away and then returned, H. M. would have no recollection of meeting you or what you discussed. The vital connection between short- and long-term memory was severed forever.

121

DIGGING FOR DIGITS

Social Security number. Checking account number. Phone number. Driver's license number. Car license plate number. Credit card numbers. House number. ZIP code. Time. Temperature. Date.

Tally it up. It isn't the stars that rule our lives—it's numbers!

So how can you become the sage of statistics? Here are some tips.

Chunk your numbers. Robin L. West, Ph.D., author of *Memory Fitness over Forty* recommends this method. A seven-digit telephone number has seven parts to remember, but you can organize it into three easier-to-remember parts. The first part is the exchange, and the last four digits are dual two-digit numbers.

Here's an example: To learn the number 381-6529, divide it up into 381-65-29. Say it. Three hundred eighty-one, sixty-five, twenty-nine.

Code your numbers. One universally used code, West suggests, assigns a letter to every number. 0 is s or z, 1 is t, 2 is n, 3 is m, 4 is r, 5 is l, 6 is ch or sh, 7 is the hard c, g, or k sound, 8 is f, ph or v, and 9 is b, d, or p.

Now, translate this number: 902-6744. It translates into PSN-ChKRR (You could call the PoiSoN CheCkeR) or DZN-ShKRR (try remembering DoZeN ShaKeR).

Since each sound is assigned a number, you can translate your words back to numbers when you need them.

Find a relationship between the numbers. For instance, 381-6529 contains a 3 followed by two numbers, then a 6 followed by two more numbers, then a 9. All three numbers—3, 6, and 9—can be divided by 3. Notice the number next to the 3 is one less than 9. The number next to the 9 is one less than 3.

Rhyme your numbers. This is a good trick to help you remember appointments and dates. For a 2:00 P.M. dental appointment, try "I'm blue at 2," or "I'm alive after 5" for a 5:00 P.M. dinner with friends. To remember your wedding anniversary on October 9, 1976, try, "I felt fine on October 9. The marriage was fixed in '76."

"You construct your memories using major features as guidelines. Then you fill in the rest with likelihoods," Dr. Epstein says. You don't know your brain is lying, he adds.

TIPS FOR A KEENER MEMORY

Where did you put your car keys? Did you turn off the oven after supper was cooked? What was that new neighbor's name? Why can't you remember anything anymore?

No, it's probably not Alzheimer's disease. And it's not advancing age that has you walking the parking lot searching for your car. It's simple forgetfulness, and it doesn't matter if you are 30 or 90. We're all affected at one time or another.

A lot of forgetfulness can be blamed on inattention, says Dr. Epstein. More than any other recall-boosting technique, paying attention to what we see and do "would make the single biggest difference in our memories. Learn to be attentive."

Try to link names with something familiar to aid recall. Think, "Mr. Baird wears a beard," or "Mrs. Peacock preens like a bird." Picture Mr. Scott puffing into a bagpipe. See Miss Rosen's face surrounded by flower petals. Imagine Mr. Wolfe as the leader of his pack.

Aging does play some role in memory input and retrieval, but it's not as dramatic as most people assume. "Memory just takes more work the older you get," says Lynn Stern, a social worker with the Turner Clinic at the University of Michigan Medical Center and coauthor of *Improving Your Memory: A Guide for Older Adults.* "Loss and grief, physical illness, fatigue, changes in vision and hearing, inactivity, lack of organization—they can all affect memory. The older you get, the more of these things happen at once."

The three ways memory does change as you grow older are these: Recall slows down; distractions interrupt concentration; learning is slower.

"Fortunately, people can improve their memory at any age," Stern says. She and Janet Fogler teach memory classes to "anyone over 60" under a W. K. Kellogg Foundation grant. But her tricks for a keener memory are useful for everyone, she says. Here are some:

THE NAMES GAME

Never forget a face? How about a name? A few tricks will help. Memory expert Robin L. West, Ph.D., author of *Memory Fitness over Forty,* suggests:
- If you receive a guest list prior to a meeting or party, look over the names before you go. You'll be more likely to remember people you meet.
- Listen carefully to each new name. Repeat it. Ask the person to spell it. Use it. "Sara Jones? Nice to meet you, Sara."
- Give people a "name sentence" by finding words within their names. Dr. West, for instance, suggests "The robin is flying west" for her name.

Take a mental snapshot. When you put your keys down, *see* where you have placed them and say aloud, "Here are my keys." *Watch* your hands turn the iron off. Repeat: "The iron is off."

Keep a calendar. Make it a planner and a diary. Write down when you start a new medication, how much you weigh, how far you jog. Note when bills need to be paid and then check them off when you stick them in the mail.

Do things when you think of them. If you put them off, you'll forget. Keep a list of things to do.

Leave yourself a message. Need to do something at home or the office? Call your answering machine and leave yourself a message.

Change your environment. Put shoes to be repaired by the front door. Move the telephone to remind yourself to make a call. Tack a note on the bathroom mirror so you'll see it in the morning.

Physically jog your memory. Tie a string around your finger. Wear a rubber band on your wrist. Wear your watch on the other wrist, your rings on the wrong fingers.

Exercise and eat well-balanced meals. Healthy people tend to have nimble minds.

Continue to learn. Read as much as you can. Get into the habit of learning new information and discussing it with other people.

If you do forget, take a deep breath, laugh, and admit the word or name has just blanked out of your mind. Your laughter will put your lapse into the right perspective.

And remember, "It's not serendipity when you manage to remember something," Stern says. "The more you use your memory, the better it gets."

WHY ACTORS DON'T FORGET THEIR LINES

Want to deliver a speech to the garden club without notes? Or land that role in the community theater's next production?

Use your memory!

Here are some memorizing tips from the drama department at the University of Southern California, where actors like John Ritter (left, in a scene from his "Hooperman" series) learned their craft.

• Read your script over and over *before* you attempt to memorize, says William C. White, Ph.D., associate chairman of academic services for the department.

• Memorize in complete thoughts. Because whole thoughts are easier to digest, recall will be easier.

• Relax and rehearse your role. If it is a talk for your civic club, visualize yourself presenting your ideas to your friends. For the stage, vividly see yourself becoming the character.

• Learn correctly the first time, Dr. White warns. Your initial memorization will be the way you remember your speech. If you don't get it right then, you'll have problems unlearning it later.

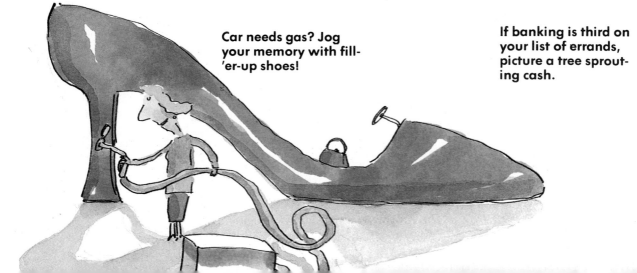

If the hardware store's your tenth and final stop, tuck nails under a giant hen's wings.

MEMORY JOGGERS: THE MNEMONIC MEMORANDUM

Can you remember a Danish pastry covered with pink rubber hose washers? How about giant loaves of bread on 10-foot-tall sticks?

If you can, mnemonic devices—memory cues—will give your memory muscle. Here's how.

There are two famous mnemonic systems—the peg system and the loci method. Both associate what you want to remember with silly, even outrageous, imagery.

If you use the peg system, first you must learn the ten pegs: 1 is a bun, 2 is a shoe, 3 is a tree, 4 is a door, 5 is a hive, 6 is sticks, 7 is heaven, 8 is a gate, 9 is a vine, and 10 is a hen.

Once you learn the pegs, you can use them to memorize a list of from one to ten things you need to do.

Say the first thing you want to remember to buy is a package of rubber washers. Picture 1,000 washers stuck to a huge sticky bun. The more exaggerated your mental picture, the easier (and more fun) it will be to remember. (See the accompanying illustrations.)

The loci method is similar. You combine new information with familiar items. If you want to remember to make a phone call first thing in the morning, picture your telephone earpiece sticking out of the mush in your oatmeal bowl.

Car needs gas? Jog your memory with fill-'er-up shoes!

If banking is third on your list of errands, picture a tree sprouting cash.

SIGHT, SOUND, OR TOUCH—WHICH TURNS YOUR MEMORY ON?

Some people remember their shopping lists like a series of picture postcards. That's visual memory. Some people's feet automatically launch into the latest dance steps whenever the music begins. That's kinesthetic memory. And some people are good at verbal memory. They never forget a name after they've been introduced to someone.

Which is your memory strong point?

Rate yourself with this test. If your answer is "true" or "yes," check the box that follows it. If the answer is "false" or "no," leave the box blank. Then add up the check marks in each of the three vertical columns.

Think about what you had for breakfast this morning.

	Verbal	Visual	Kines-thetic
1. Do you have a vivid visual picture of it?		☐	
2. Did you just reexperience the tastes and smells?			☐
3. Can you list everything you ate?	☐		
4. Can you recall the brand names of the eggs, cereal, coffee, bread, jam, juice?	☐		
5. Can you remember the color of the plate and cup? The tablecloth?		☐	
6. Can you recall where you ate? How you sat? The position of the food on your plate?			☐

Now imagine you are standing in front of the first house you can remember living in as a child.

	Verbal	Visual	Kines-thetic
7. Do you see the color clearly? Do you have a strong image of how many windows there are? The kind of steps? How many steps?		☐	
8. Do you remember the address and phone number?	☐		
9. Go up to the door. Can you remember whether the doorknob is on the left or right? Do you step up after you have opened the door? Is there a closet on the left or right inside?			☐

Now answer these general questions.

	Verbal	Visual	Kines-thetic
10. I am usually very aware of the furniture arrangement in a room.			☐
11. If friends painted their living room a new color I would definitely notice.		☐	
12. I know whether the numbers on my watch are Arabic or Roman numerals.		☐	
13. I know my Social Security number.	☐		
14. I'm good at sports and/or dancing.			☐
15. I respond to the colors around me.		☐	
16. I always got good grades in English.	☐		
17. I didn't have much trouble learning to ride a bike.			☐
18. I love to do crossword puzzles.	☐		

If your scores are about the same in each category, you are good at all three ways of encoding and filing each new memory. If you want to reinforce a new memory, use all three methods. If you're playing cards and want to remember the two of diamonds using kinesthetic memory, for instance, hold the card second from the left in your hand. Prompt your visual memory by looking at the card. Then, fix the verbal memory by saying "two of diamonds."

If you scored best in visual memory, reinforce your verbal or kinesthetic memories with a visual image. Write out names, addresses, and phone numbers and look at them. Imprint that image with a memory picture. See new acquaintances with their names written on their chests. If you learn a physical skill, watch yourself doing it. See how your hands move as you stroke the piano keys. Notice the positions of your body as you dance. Scan your surroundings—the shapes of the trees and the colors of the signs—as you walk to a new bus stop.

If your score is highest in verbal memory, you can help yourself remember things if you name them. When you meet new people, for instance, say their names and add a verbal description. "JoAnn Baker is so thin she doesn't look like she *goes and bakes* very often." Also, make mental lists to back up your visual and kinesthetic memories. If you want to remember where your car is parked in the shopping center lot, tell yourself the name of the store it is nearest and repeat the aisle letter or number.

Is your score best in kinesthetic memory? You probably never misplace your car keys, but you might have problems remembering written instructions or what you were supposed to pick up at the drugstore on your way home. Your best bet is to add a kinesthetic memory to other information so you can remember more easily. Shake hands when you meet a person and notice the texture of the person's hand while you repeat the name. Is the skin soft or calloused? Is the grip strong or light? Learn a new telephone number by dialing it a couple of times. Feel the rhythm as you punch the number onto the keypad.

Need more kinesthetic tips?

If you must learn something new, your best bet is to study in surroundings that will help you remember the material. If you need to study a drivers' manual, sit in your car. Learning how to operate a computer? Don't just read the manual, practice the instructions as you read.

If you are good at two kinds of memory, use both when you need to reinforce information that comes through your weakest skill. If you are poor at kinesthetic memory, visualize your walk from your new bus stop to your office or record the directions on a Walkman tape. If you are poor at verbal memory, make mental pictures and use your body to reinforce words. If your memory is not good at visualizing, tell yourself a story about whatever you are trying to memorize or make your project sensual by touching what you are trying to remember.

Play on your strengths and you'll make your memory work for you.

SPATIAL MEMORY RECALL

How many of the shapes from page 116 can you remember and correctly identify? Correct recall isn't easy because this answer display includes similar and distracting shapes to reduce the chances of successful guesswork.

MUSIC

By drum or guitar, by flute or violin, by cymbals or kazoo, music sends a powerful message. It can inspire or depress. It can calm or scare. It can even heal.

"It's absolutely as valuable as money," says Cheryl Maranto, Ph.D., associate professor of music therapy at Temple University.

Stockbrokers and bankers may disagree with Dr. Maranto, but chances are that they too use—not merely enjoy—music in their own lives. And so do even the most primitive of tribes. They may only clap sticks together or chant in rhythm. But who's to say that's not as valuable to them as a near-perfect symphony is to a trained ear?

Music can be very healthful because it helps alleviate the contemporary plague called stress, says Julian Thayer, Ph.D., assistant professor of psychology at Pennsylvania State University. But before music can do anything else, your brain must process those incoming sounds.

You may be surprised to learn that the brain doesn't handle music the same way it does language. While the left hemisphere of the brain is dominant in processing language, the right hemisphere is typically in charge of processing music.

MORE THAN ONE MELODY

Ever wonder why the sound of Simon and Garfunkel is music to your ears while the arias of *Aida* grate on your nerves? Dr. Shepard has a theory for why many people like only a few kinds of music. "I believe the brain has certain ways of structuring things (internal maps, if you will), and you can probably learn to appreciate only the music that meshes with that structure," he says.

Personal preferences aside, different kinds of music are virtually guaranteed to have predictable effects. In several studies, when people watched a graphic film simulating woodshop accidents set to "horror movie music" (low pitch, high tempo), they had more stressful reactions than when that same film was put to more relaxing music (slow tempo, high pitch).

Music is, in fact, a strong behavior modifier. "Some studies have shown that people with emotional problems will change their behavior positively in order to listen to or perform music," says Dr. Maranto.

And amazingly, music can sometimes reach the seemingly unreachable. "People who are in comas can respond to music," Dr. Maranto says, noting that studies have found coma victims who are exposed to music show increased heart rate and blood pressure, and they open their eyes more frequently.

DECEPTION DOWN BELOW?

Soft, soothing music. Chimes blowing in the wind.

And all you have to do is listen. To become self-confident, to lose weight, to increase your breast size . . .

So say the makers of subliminal tapes, those self-improvement cassettes that supposedly bury powerful suggestions and advice underneath the soundtrack, where they become available to your subconscious.

"Subliminal tapes really have nothing to do with level of consciousness, despite what makers of the tapes often say," explains Tom Bourbon, Ph.D. "You just perceive less and less as you proceed below the threshold. Subliminal is below threshold or subaudible."

So does it really work?

No—and yes. Dr. Bourbon says many subliminal tapes apparently don't have any messages underneath the music, and there is no proof that those that do have messages succeed in communicating those messages to the listener. But he says subliminal tapes may have a placebo effect simply because buyers *believe* they will. "I think the people listening to the tapes deserve more of the credit than the tapes themselves."

MASTERING MUSIC

Talent is important—nobody with a tin ear plays Carnegie Hall. But becoming an accomplished musician takes more than talent, and more than practice, practice, practice.

"One must know how to read music—understand each marking on the page—as well as understand rhythm and have physical coordination, imagination, and a good memory," says Susan Starr, chairperson of the piano department at the University of the Arts in Philadelphia and an internationally known concert pianist.

"Good teachers have students memorize a piece of music in their very first year of training," Starr says. "Memory and imagination are crucial to mastering music and are part of any well-organized teaching plan.

"There are, after all, no real shortcuts to learning music properly," she says.

So music students also learn discipline. And discipline combined with all those other elements that lead to conquering the piano or the tuba, serve music students well in other areas of their lives.

"I think anyone who has had a good music teacher and has been a good student will do well in other fields," Starr says. "They won't have any trouble learning new things."

Advertisers, from supermarkets to car manufacturers, also try to capitalize on music's knack for reaching and stimulating potential buyers. But while all of us can probably hum a few bars from a Toyota commercial, there is debate about whether music actually influences our buying behavior.

Tom Bourbon, Ph.D., professor of psychology at Stephen F. Austin State University, Texas, is one of the skeptics. "I don't know of any reputable study," he says, "that has shown music can influence something as complicated as purchasing behavior."

BEYOND CHARM

Music would be nice to have around even if it were merely distracting. But it is so much more. Pop in a compact disc or a cassette tape and you can reach for one moment in time with Whitney Houston or go back to your favorite white Christmas with Bing Crosby.

Those good feelings, in a sense, give us more power. "Music allows people to key into creative areas of their brains," Dr. Maranto says. "And to find creative solutions."

Still more remarkable is music's ability to heal. Dr. Maranto says music therapy has been especially successful in rehabilitating stroke victims who can no longer speak. "Some of these people [through music therapy] can still sing," she says. "And I think we will soon have data showing that music has positive effects on the immune system. That's the direction we're heading."

Actually, when you consider those primitive tribes and their early use of music in healing rituals, you might say we've come full circle.

THE NEUROLOGIST

Each tear made a tiny splash as it landed on the telephone receiver. Leaning against her kitchen wall for support, Maria Quiroz was taking the phone call that every parent fears. "The coroner called and asked me to come to the hospital because my son, Andrew, had been hurt pretty badly."

Somewhere on a rural country road near Fresno, California, a drunk driver had run a stop sign and plowed into a truck driven by her 19-year-old son, who was only four months away from his high school graduation. In a flash of twisted metal and shattered glass, a promising future had come to a grinding halt.

"When we got to the hospital, the emergency room doctors said he had very little chance of surviving, and if he did he would be just like a vegetable," says Quiroz.

In the violent collision, Andrew had suffered a severe head injury. When his mother first saw him, he was comatose, "covered with bandages, with tubes coming out everywhere. I felt hopeless."

Then a neurologist entered the picture. This specialist's job is to diagnose and treat disorders of the brain, spinal cord, nerves, and muscles. "A psychiatrist treats psychiatric disorders of the mind, while a neurologist treats biological disorders of the brain," explains Kevin Nelson, M.D., a neurologist at the University of Kentucky Chandler Medical Center. Those disorders range from headaches (especially migraines) to multiple sclerosis, seizures, brain tumors, Parkinson's disease, strokes, Lou Gehrig's disease, muscular dystrophy, and head injuries like Andrew's.

FROM FEAR TO HOPE

At the time, though, Andrew's mother knew very little about what a neurologist does. "I thought at first, 'Oh, no, Andrew's going to be crazy or retarded.' I was really scared knowing there was something wrong with my son's brain."

To determine what's wrong with a patient and the extent of the injury, neurologists often use CAT (computerized axial tomography) scans, MRI (magnetic resonance imaging) scans, EEG's (electroencephalograms), arteriograms, spinal taps, myelograms, or evoked potential tests, which record the brain's response to visual, auditory, and other sensory stimuli.

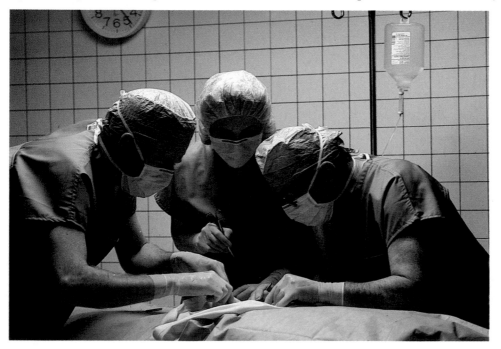

When neurosurgeons open up patients' skulls, their hands are carefully guided by the neurologist's diagnosis. In the case of a brain tumor, its location has been precisely pinpointed, and once it is removed in surgery, the patient may return to the neurologist's care for rehabilitation.

HIS PROSE PLUMBS THE BRAIN'S MYSTERIES

"The entire basement of my house is filled with notes about my patients. I just can't seem to throw them away." Instead, Oliver Sacks, M.D., professor of clinical neurology at New York's Albert Einstein College of Medicine, turns his cache of notes into best-selling books about the brain.

This world-famous neurologist's literary efforts include *Migraine, Awakenings, A Leg to Stand On,* and his phenomenally successful *The Man Who Mistook His Wife for a Hat.*

In his more than 20 years as a neurologist, Dr. Sacks has taken notes on over 20,000 patients, but he sees each one as an individual. "I pay attention to them and explore their problems very deeply."

Unlike those who decide to specialize in neurology while in medical school, Dr. Sacks was destined to be a neurologist from the start. "Both my parents were neurologists, and I remember that all the dinner table conversation about neurological stories and situations was very fascinating to me early on."

It's the future of neurology that fascinates him now. "It's tremendously exciting. Our understanding of brain structure and brain function is becoming more and more detailed almost by the minute. There are some new theories and methods of investigation which will allow us to understand in neurological terms how you become who you are.

While neurology has come a long way, "It's got a long way to go," he adds. "We have only the smallest idea of what the brain's actual potentials are. All of us have far more brainpower available to us than we currently use."

When asked what *he* would do if he suddenly found himself in his patients' shoes, considering what he knows about the brain, Dr. Sacks pauses for a moment and then muses in his slightly British accent, "There's a superstitious part of me that expects it. If it did happen, I would try to lead as full a life as possible. But at the same time, since I'm such an inveterate investigator, I'd bear witness to my disability and try to explore it."

The neurologist who examined Andrew knew the case was a special one. "His injuries were extensive," says Terry Hutchison, M.D., co-medical director of Valley Children's Hospital's Rehabilitation Center in Fresno. "He was eventually sent home from the hospital, but his family was told that he would never get better."

But neither Dr. Hutchison nor Andrew's mother would have any of that. They went to bat for the once-athletic Andrew, and during the course of 20 months of intensive rehabilitative therapy at Valley Children's Hospital, Andy started hitting his own home runs. Step by step, he learned all over again how to sit up, to feed himself, and to speak. "A lot of the recovery he achieved, he achieved on his own," says Dr. Hutchison. "When the natural recovery of the brain began, we were prepared for it and we took advantage of it. We took his initial strengths and used them to help him reach his potential."

They helped him become . . . Andrew. "He's back together as a person again," Dr. Hutchison says. "He's very happy. He has friends. He wants to finish school and become a carpenter. Had we not intervened, he would likely have been permanently, totally disabled."

NEURO-TRANSMITTERS

We are living in the era of global communication. People in Kansas can find out what's happening in Kabul almost instantly. But none of this via-satellite communication would be possible if not for our own cerebral pony express.

Everything we do—from responding to basic feelings of hunger in the pit of our stomach to learning how to build those satellites—is connected to the chemical messengers in our brains: neurotransmitters.

It took days for the pony express to deliver messages, but neurotransmitters can deliver their messages to any nerve, muscle, or organ in your body faster than a thoroughbred can sprint 10 yards—in milliseconds.

In a flash, chemical messages released from one nerve cell travel across a tiny gap, or synapse, to another nerve cell, then another and another. Once the neurotransmitters get to their destination, they either speed up or slow down activity at the target site.

So when you're walking through a crowded shopping mall, balancing packages in both arms, and weaving in and out of the waves of humanity like a running back trying to dodge tacklers, you can thank your neurotransmitters for keeping your movements in harmony—and hopefully, keeping your packages in your arms.

Who are these essential chemical messengers that live inside us? Well, you've probably heard of some of them. Endorphins, for example, are opiate-like substances that are released during physical exertion. They're sometimes referred to as the brain's natural painkillers.

You may also be familiar with dopamine, which is believed to be connected to extroversion and perhaps schizophrenia.

But these are not the only players. Because some researchers like to define neurotransmitters rather narrowly, there is no consensus on the number of neurotransmitters we have. Ten to 16 is the generally accepted range, "but there are probably

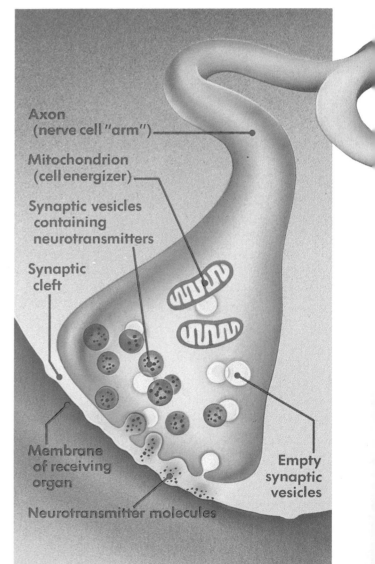

Axon (nerve cell "arm")

Mitochondrion (cell energizer)

Synaptic vesicles containing neurotransmitters

Synaptic cleft

Membrane of receiving organ

Neurotransmitter molecules

Empty synaptic vesicles

Like a factory that never sleeps, the synapse at the end of a nerve cell first manufactures neurotransmitters, then stores them in canisters called vesicles, and finally sends them on their way. The chemical messages travel across the synaptic cleft (a small space between nerve cells). Once on the other side, they bind to a receptor located on the receiving organ. The transmitters then either stimulate or calm their target.

MEET THE MESSENGERS THAT MAKE MIND AND BODY WORK

Scientists say that there are two basic types of neurotransmitters. Excitatory neurotransmitters, such as acetylcholine, *stimulate* the receiving organ; inhibitory neurotransmitters, such as endorphins, *suppress* the receiving organ.

Those simple descriptions may not sound like a big deal. But neurotransmitters affect all that we do—from walking and chewing gum at the same time to performing perfect pirouettes to remembering the names of distant relatives. Or in the case of a neurotransmitter malfunction, stumbling or forgetting your second cousin's name.

Meanwhile, the next time you ram your big toe into a table leg and you're in distress, don't lay all the blame on the table. Give some of it to substance P, a transmitter thought to be at least partially responsible for carrying pain signals. (It's also implicated in migraine headaches.) And once you realize the pain isn't really all that bad, thank those little dynorphins—transmitters that help control pain.

STIMULATORS	FUNCTION	SUPPRESSORS	FUNCTION
Acetylcholine	Activates muscles and affects short-term memory. Also affects body temperature and thirst.	Endorphins (stronger form), enkephalins (weaker form)	Secretion of these opiates reduces pain. Exercise helps release these chemicals, thus, exercise is being used as a tool for pain reduction.
Epinephrine	Also known as adrenaline, it is tied to our "fight-or-flight" survival instinct.	Gamma-aminobutyric acid (GABA)	The primary inhibitory neurotransmitter in the brain. Without GABA, our movements would be difficult to control.
Norepinephrine	Affects ability to focus, feelings of hunger, and long-term memory.		
Dopamine	Too much may cause schizophrenia and too little may cause Parkinson's disease. Slightly higher than normal levels may account for extroversion, while lower than normal levels may contribute to introversion.	Substance P	Considered to be a neuropeptide, it's found in areas of the brain associated with pain.
		Glycine	Leads to inhibition in the spinal cord.
		Dynorphin	This chemical is believed to be a factor in controlling pain.
Phenylethylamine	Believed to be a contributor to happy, even giddy, feelings.	Serotonin	Involved in inducing sleep, dreams, emotions, and sensory perception. Deficiencies may cause insomnia and nonpsychotic depression.

EXTROVERTS HAVE EXTRA

Is the maniac's maniac—comedian Robin Williams—doped up on dopamine, a chemical each of us has in our brain?

Recent research indicates it's possible. Higher levels of dopamine—one of the brain's chemical messengers—were found in patients who completed a psychological test that showed them to be more extroverted than introverted, according to a Stanford University study.

Because the study involved people diagnosed with depression, Roy King, M.D., Ph.D., is not certain how far-reaching the results are.

"But we think the dopamine concentrations reflect something deeper," Dr. King says, "such as a basic personality trait."

Go-o-o-o-o-od morning, dopamine!

neurotransmitters out there that we don't yet know about," says Richard Dubinsky, M.D., a neurologist at the University of Kansas Medical Center.

For now, however, let's look at a few of the neurotransmitters scientists do know about. First up is acetylcholine. "It's the major transmitter from nerves to muscles," says Tim Ebner, M.D., Ph.D., laboratory director of neurosurgery at the University of Minnesota. "When you're lifting weights, acetylcholine is activating the muscles."

And when your pulse quickens before you give a speech or as you enter a big, dark, empty house, epinephrine (adrenaline) is at work.

GABA, or gamma-aminobutyric acid, is the main calming transmitter (scientists call it an inhibitor) and thus should get chief credit for your stability during those slash-and-dash trips through the mall.

Norepinephrine seems to have a lot of jobs to do. But it appears to be a specialist at helping us focus our attention, "to somehow single out one voice in the room at a cocktail party," notes David Morgan, Ph.D., an associate professor of gerontology at the University of Southern California.

NO SIMPLE ANSWERS

Wouldn't it be great to be able to alter your neurotransmitter levels at will? Some researchers have found a correlation between food and levels of certain neurotransmitters (see the box "How Food Affects Your Mood") but there's still a lot to be learned.

Nonetheless, researchers are trying to clear away the ambiguity surrounding the connection between neurotransmitters and behavior. It would be nice if it only took milliseconds, but Dr. Ebner expects such clarity to take many years.

In the meantime, one thing is already clear. "Whether or not you're the life of the party isn't a matter of having too much of a certain neurotransmitter," he says. "Personality is more subtle and complicated than that."

HOW FOOD AFFECTS YOUR MOOD

Low-fat cottage cheese is an upper? Chocolate chip cookies are downers?

Yes, foods are drugs. That is, some foods appear to increase production of chemicals in the brain that stimulate, while others seem to increase production of calming chemicals.

Low-fat cottage cheese, for example, is high in protein. Protein contains an amino acid known as tyrosine, which is the main ingredient in the neurotransmitters dopamine and norepinephrine. Research indicates that when the brain is pro-ducing these two neurotransmitters, "distinct changes in mood and behavior take place," writes Judith J. Wurtman, Ph.D., of Massachusetts Institute of Technology, in her book *Managing Your Mind and Mood through Food*. "In general . . . eating protein food increases alertness and has an energizing effect on your mind."

On the other hand, eating sugary foods, such as chocolate chip cookies, leads to production of the neurotransmitter serotonin. Serotonin has a calming effect and increases concentration.

PROTEINS—THE ENERGIZERS

If your body sometimes feels like a dead battery, proteins might give you the jump-start you need.

To get the most out of proteins, choose foods that have little fat and/or carbohydrates—especially when you want to be in the mental fast lane.

Not only can proteins give you a boost in the morning, but they also can help prevent the after-lunch blues.

The A-team. These foods are excellent choices because they are so low in fat and carbohydrates. Stars of this team are chicken (without the skin), fish, shellfish, veal, and very lean beef.

The B-team. These low-fat vegetable protein sources and low-fat dairy products just missed making first string: dried peas and beans, low-fat cottage cheese, skim or low-fat milk, and soybean-based foods.

The C-team. There's good and bad news here.

These foods are high in protein but also fairly high in fat. Fat, of course, pushes the calorie count up. It also won't do anything to boost your mental energy. Foods on this team include beef (unless very lean), pork and pork products (including sausage and bacon), lamb, lunch meats (excluding those marked low-fat), organ meats such as tongue and liver, hard cheeses, regular yogurt (low-fat yogurt is a B-team food), and whole milk.

CARBOHYDRATES—THE CALMERS

Scientists believe carbs can do a lot for us: they can calm us, help us sleep, and keep us mentally focused. Carbohydrates come in two forms—sugars (also known as simple carbohydrates) and starches (also known as complex carbohydrates). Glucose (a sugar) is the best carbohydrate for getting your brain to make more serotonin—a calming chemical.

Sugars. Almost all sweets made with table sugar, honey, or corn sweetener contain glucose and will thus start the process that leads to the brain making more serotonin. Unfortunately, eating calming foods—cookies, candy, cake, pie, jellies—conflicts with cutting calories.

Fruit, while low in calories, won't help you achieve that calming effect. The body converts fructose (fruit sugar) into glucose too slowly to substantially promote production of serotonin.

Starches. Wheat and corn products, vegetables such as potatoes, and flour products will all help in achieving a calm mood and focused mind. These foods include bread, rolls, bagels, muffins, crackers, pasta, corn, rice, barley, and cereals.

Neutral mood foods. Leafy green and other vitamin-rich, low-calorie vegetables, including lettuce, broccoli, spinach, beets, and carrots fall into this category.

NUTRITION AND YOUR BRAIN

You're about to make the most important decision of your life. You sit down at your desk and begin to sort the papers, forms, and receipts that define your options into neat piles. You sharpen a handful of pencils, pull the calculator out of a drawer, and plop a yellow pad on the desk directly in front of you.

You're ready.

But are you? You just got up from the dinner table and you're feeling a little, well, a little blah. You didn't really overeat, exactly, but you did put away a fair amount.

You started off with a salad and some Thousand Island dressing, worked your way through a small steak, cottage-fried potatoes, cauliflower drizzled with cheese sauce, and finished—although you had started to feel a little uncomfortable—with just a tiny slice of pound cake. No ice cream. And you did try just a smidgeon of your sister-in-law's hot artichoke-mayonnaise-Parmesan cheese dip on one or two crackers before you sat down at the table. All in all, a nice meal. But not excessive, right?

Not right. You may not have eaten as much as you did last Thanksgiving, but you did eat enough of the wrong kinds of foods to put a brake on your brain. In fact, the combination of high fat, high carbohydrates, and lots of calories has just about turned off your ability to think. That's why you feel kind of sleepy. And instead of being in peak mental condition to make an important decision, you're more likely to be ready for a nap.

Right now that meal has already sent your brain several messages along the "hot line" that connects your brain with your gut, explains Carol E. Greenwood, Ph.D., an associate professor of nutrition at the University of Toronto. One is that you've eaten. That message was passed 9 seconds after the first bite of salad hit your stomach. Then came the message that you were filling up. That's why you may have had a little difficulty eating dessert. By the time you got to the pound cake, your brain knew you didn't need it. The discomfort you felt was your brain's silent plea to, please, put down your fork.

And it's too bad you didn't listen. Because food doesn't just send polite messages to your brain, says Dr. Greenwood. It also steps in and affects your brain directly.

A SIP WITH ZIP

Whether they perk it, drip it, or microwave it, for many people the key to morning mental performance is a rich, hot cup of coffee right from the land of Juan Valdez.

Coffee affects your brain within minutes and keeps it clicking along for up to 6 hours, report researchers at the Massachusetts Institute of Technology. And one cup is really all that's needed.

It's the caffeine, of course.

Studies that have measured mental performance after a single morning cup clearly demonstrate that people who drink a caffeinated beverage are likely to think better than those who do not.

It works at the other end of your workday, too. A cup between 3:00 and 4:00 P.M. will pick up your work-weary brain and shift it back into high gear.

IS BREAKFAST IMPORTANT?

For your children, yes. For you, not necessarily. So if the thought of eating bran flakes or a muffin when you're still half asleep appeals to you about as much as walking the dog on a sub-freezing morning, then forget it.

For years, health professionals have advised adults to eat breakfast. They always backed up that advice by citing studies showing that kids who go without breakfast don't perform as well on tests or in other problem-solving situations. But researchers now say the same thing apparently doesn't apply to grown-ups, probably because adults maintain more stable blood-sugar levels overnight.

YOU THINK WITH WHAT YOU EAT

"As the protein from your steak gets into the intestine, for example, enzymes break it down into amino acids, which are then absorbed into your bloodstream," she says. "Now, once the amino acids are in your bloodstream, they can circulate throughout the body.

"Obviously they'll go into tissues like the liver and the muscles. But when those amino acids circulate to the brain and come in contact with the blood/brain barrier, they'll meet carriers on the barrier that are specifically designed to transport them into the brain."

So what goes into your mouth goes into your brain?

Exactly, says Dr. Greenwood. You think with what you eat. Scientists used to believe that the blood/brain barrier was more of a barrier than it actually is. Today they know that it's not really a barrier at all but more like a fine screen or a sieve. It keeps out toxic substances while letting nutrients squeeze through. But not all nutrients can squeeze through the sieve at once. They have to compete with one another for transportation on one of the carriers designed to ferry them through the screen and into the brain.

Think of the carriers on the blood/brain barrier as a fleet of small boats. There are a lot of amino acids trying to catch a ride at the dock, but only a few can fit into a boat at one time. And the amino acids which are most likely to affect your thought processes all need to ride on one special kind of boat. It's made to fit them exactly. So whichever gets aboard first is going to be the one that gets into your brain and affects your thinking. The other amino acids will be left standing on the dock.

AVOIDING A MENTAL MELTDOWN

Two amino acids that significantly affect brain function —and are in direct competition for a seat on the same boat—are tyrosine and tryptophan, says Dr. Greenwood. In the brain, tyrosine is converted into electrically charged chemicals—neurotransmitters—that zip messages from one part of your brain to another. And one of these—norepinephrine—is known to be

BE SURE ABOUT YOUR B VITAMINS

If you're sunk in a funk, exhausted, confused, or forgetful, it may be that your brain isn't getting enough B vitamins.

"The B vitamins are important in mental functioning because they are the catalysts without which many chemical reactions in the brain could not take place," says Priscilla Slagle, M.D.

Here are some additional signs of B depletion.
- You feel more tired, irritable, depressed, emotional, irrational, or anxious than you'd like or than you think is normal.
- You are older and have suddenly developed emotional or mental problems—especially depression—even though you have no prior history of any mental problems.
- You have skin rashes that won't go away.
- You have sores inside your mouth or cracks around the corners of your mouth.
- You have numbness, tingling, or twitching in your legs, or your feet burn.
- You suffer from premenstrual tension or from postpartum depression.

These symptoms may well have causes other than—or in addition to—a B vitamin deficiency. So check with your doctor if you have even one. Meanwhile, ask youself the following questions. A yes answer to any one of these could indicate you're being shortchanged on B vitamins.
- Do you eat a diet high in sugar?
- Have you been under a lot of stress lately?
- Do you have any digestion problems?
- Have you recently had stomach or intestinal surgery?
- Do you take diuretics, antibiotics, birth control pills, cholesterol-lowering drugs, anticonvulsant drugs, or psychoactive (mind-affecting) drugs?
- Do you regularly drink alcohol?
- Do you drink a lot of coffee?
- Do you smoke?
- Do you turn up your nose at liver and whole grains?

crucial to straight thinking and long-term memory.

Tryptophan, on the other hand, isn't known so much for what it does to help you think as for the way it blocks tyrosine. If tryptophan gets on the boat first, tyrosine is left on the dock. It can't get into the brain to help you figure out your income tax or remember long-ago events.

But tryptophan is more than just a spoiler. When tryptophan gets into your brain, it's converted into serotonin, a neurotransmitter that makes you drowsy and impairs your concentration. So not only does it prevent tyrosine from doing its job, it also causes a mental meltdown. If you're planning on taking a nap after you eat, that's fine. If you're planning on making some important decisions, you've got a problem.

THE POWER OF PROTEIN

Fortunately your ability to think and reason doesn't have to depend on the whims of a bunch of amino acids and the neurotransmitters they produce—*you* control the whole process by what you put in your mouth. After all, where do the amino acids come from in the first place? Your food, right?

But what kind of food will boost your brainpower? What kind will slow it down?

The answer coming back loud and clear from research scientists across the country is that protein makes you more alert and carbohydrates slow your thinking down. In a study conducted at the Massachusetts Institute of Technology (MIT), for example, a team of researchers gave 40 men between the ages of 18 and 28 a turkey lunch that included almost 3 ounces of protein. Then they asked them to do some complicated mental tasks. On another day, they gave the men a 4-ounce lunch of wheat starch—almost pure carbohydrate—and again put them through some mental hoops. The result? Mental performance was "significantly impaired" after the carbohydrate meal. It was fine after the protein.

The effects may be especially dramatic for people over 40, says Bonnie Spring, Ph.D., a researcher at the Chicago Medical School. In a study of 184 adults fed either turkey, which is high in protein, or sherbet, which is almost pure carbohydrate, Dr. Spring and her associates found that people over the age of 40 who were fed the sherbet had *double* the difficulty concentrating, remembering, and performing mental tasks than those who had eaten turkey. The adults who were under 40 were far less likely to be affected.

As these studies indicate, it doesn't take much of either protein *or* carbohydrate to have an effect on your thinking. In fact, 3 or 4 ounces of a protein food such as chicken or fish will give your brain enough tyrosine to stimulate the production of norepinephrine, the neurotransmitter that keeps you thinking quickly and accurately, reports Judith L. Wurtman, Ph.D., a nutrition researcher at MIT and author of *Managing Your Mind and Mood through Food*.

On the other hand, 1 to 1½ ounces of a carbohydrate food such as potatoes or pasta will give your brain enough tryptophan to block tyrosine and muddle your thinking.

There is, however, a sneaky way around the effects of carbohydrates on your brain. If you eat *only* protein, or at least eat one-third of the protein component of a meal before you touch a carbohyrate, reports Dr. Wurtman, the tyrosine will reach the blood/brain transportation system first and be ferried into your brain before trytophan can buy a ticket.

If staying on your mental toes after a particular meal is important, then that means starting the meal with a shrimp cocktail or a cup of consommé rather than a salad with lots of dressing. It means no noshing on the bread while you wait for the main course. Or if the main course is your only course, it means eating at least one-third of the meal's protein source —preferably fish, poultry, or lean meat—before a bite of anything else gets near your taste buds. And it means no dessert.

FAT: A LITTLE GOES A LONG WAY

When choosing high-protein foods, it's best to avoid high-fat items like beef, pork, sausage, and hard cheeses. Fat tends to cancel out protein's energizing effect. It slows down the entire digestive process and diverts more blood to the stomach and gut and away from the brain. That slows your circulation. And slower circulation, Dr. Wurtman notes, means slower thinking.

This doesn't mean you should avoid *all* fat, however, as Dr. Greenwood is quick to point out. A small amount of fat—the amount found in low-fat cottage cheese or yogurt, for example—is actually necessary to maintain brain function.

Brain cells are made of up of fats, explains Dr.

POLYUNSATURATES: A SMARTER CHOICE?

Most people know that a lifetime of cheeseburgers and butter brickle ice cream will harden their arteries. But the highly saturated fat in both of these favorites might also harden your brain. At least that's the theory behind some rather startling findings from the University of Toronto.

Carol E. Greenwood, Ph.D., and her colleagues studied the effects of dietary fat on learning. In the laboratory, they took three groups of animals and fed them different diets. One diet was rich in polyunsaturated fats from soybean oil. The second was loaded with saturated fats from lard. And the third—which provided a kind of baseline for comparison— was the animal's regular chow.

Twenty-one days later, Dr. Greenwood and her colleagues tested the animals' ability to learn. They placed each animal in a tub of water with a submerged platform that the animal couldn't see. Then they timed how long it took each animal to find the platform.

The result? Animals on the soybean oil diet learned about *20 percent faster* than those who ate either the lard or the chow. And they were less likely to forget what they learned, as well.

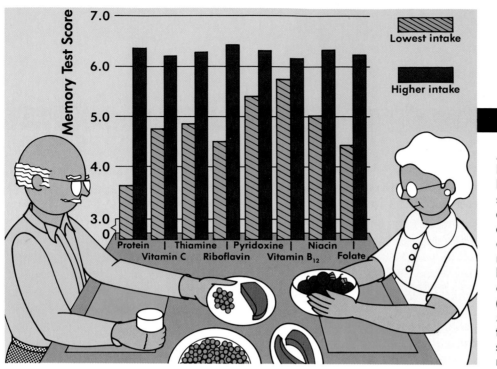

As we age, a well-balanced diet may help keep memories alive. A study of 260 Albuquerque residents over the age of 60 clearly demonstrates the effect of nutrition. Those who had the lowest intakes of various nutrients (scoring in the bottom 5 percent of all those tested) consistently scored lower than the rest on a memory test.

Greenwood. That's why you need some dietary fat. In fact, the fat that you eat can actually alter the physical composition of your brain within 24 days. And that can affect the way you think. No one really understands how, but studies clearly indicate that diets rich in saturated fats—such as the palm and coconut oils frequently added to commercial baked goods—seem to decrease your ability to think, while diets rich in polyunsaturated fats—safflower, sunflower, or soybean oils, for example—tend to increase mental performance.

One special kind of fatty substance called lecithin is especially necessary for normal mental function. Found in egg yolks, soybeans, peanuts, wheat germ, and other foods, lecithin is a rich source of choline. And choline is converted by your brain into the neurotransmitter acetylcholine.

Acetylcholine appears to be responsible for your ability to learn and then remember what you've learned. It's so important that when your brain doesn't have enough, it starts to break down its own membranes to get what it needs. In fact, scientists are now investigating the role a chronic deficiency of acetylcholine may play in the development of senility and even Alzheimer's disease. Both are characterized not only by the inability to remember new things but also by the apparent loss of brain cells.

Is a chronic acetylcholine deficiency responsible for Alzheimer's? The research addressing this question is intriguing but inconclusive. Most studies that examined the effects of a concentrated lecithin supplement on people with this disease have indicated little, if any, effect, says David Levitsky, Ph.D., a professor of nutrition and psychology at Cornell University.

But, as Richard J. Wurtman, M.D., an expert on neuroendocrine regulation at MIT points out, patients in these studies were given lecithin supplements for only a few weeks. The single study in which lecithin supplements were used for a prolonged period of time—six months—revealed that supplementation seemed to account for an improvement in one-third of the group.

Clearly, more research on the long-term affects of lecithin supplementation for older people is necessary. But there is enough evidence of your brain's need for acetylcholine, researchers say, to justify making sure that adequate lecithin is included in a well-balanced diet.

Fortunately, besides being present in high-fat foods like bacon, ham, and calves' liver, significant amounts of choline are also found in oatmeal, rice, and fish.

LIGHT IS RIGHT

Low-fat, high-protein foods like poultry and seafood are good sources of many other brain nutrients as well.

Take copper, for example. Current research indicates that this mineral, like tyrosine, may be a key player in developing the neurotransmitters that help you think straight. But you'd have to eat a whole cup of Brazil nuts—a formidable 919 calories—to reach the suggested daily intake. Four medium-sized oysters, however, will do the same job at a cost of only 37 calories. Clearly, oysters are the better choice. (Navy beans, crab meat, and bananas are some additional sources to consider.)

Zinc, a mineral that helps with the transmission of information-carrying electrical impulses throughout the brain, is also easily obtained from oysters. Tuna, turkey, and lean beef are other good sources.

With minerals as with other brainpower nutrients, it's important to emphasize low-fat, low-calorie sources. In one study, for example, scientists found that people given a mental skills test after they'd eaten a heavy three-course meal totaling 1,000 calories made 40 percent more errors than a group of people who had eaten a light, 300-calorie lunch. Clearly light is right.

What other protein foods should you look at as good sources of brain nutrients? Well, 5 ounces of chicken breast will give your brain enough of the B vitamin niacin to keep turning the foods you eat into

MEMORY SOUP

Wouldn't it be great if you could walk into your kitchen, heat up a bowl of soup, and boost your memory?

That's what folks at the Lipton soup company thought, too. So they developed a plan to add lecithin to their soups.

The lecithin would boost blood levels of choline, the precursor for a brain chemical linked to remembering.

Unfortunately, scientists have yet to prove whether or not adding lecithin to your diet will actually boost your memory. So, at least until they do, Lipton has shelved plans for its, er, souped-up product.

fuel for thought. Two bites of baked mackerel will furnish you with enough vitamin B$_{12}$ to help maintain and repair vital sheathing around brain cells. And three bites of canned Atlantic salmon will provide adequate vitamin D to activate certain enzymes and regulate brain cell activity.

DON'T FORGET YOUR SPINACH

All this emphasis on high-protein animal foods doesn't mean you can ignore your veggies. Vegetables are an important source of other nutrients that are just as necessary to maximum brainpower as protein. Spinach, for example, contains the B vitamin folate, which is used by your brain to make neurotransmitters, as well as brain tissue itself.

Spinach also contains a healthy amount of iron, which—according to James G. Penland, Ph.D., a researcher at the U.S. Department of Agriculture's

THE CEREBRAL SIDE OF FOOD ALLERGIES

The possibilities for treatment are infinitely exciting; the proof equally elusive. But it's just possible that, for some people at least, the last time they felt anxious or depressed it was because their brain had an allergic reaction to lunch.

"There are intriguing little bits of research data that are reported from time to time that make one think something's really going on with this," says John W. Crayton, M.D., a noted researcher in the field of cerebral food allergies at the Hines Veterans Administration Hospital in Illinois.

It's well documented that when certain immune system components attach themselves to blood vessel walls, they produce a local inflammation that changes the permeability of that wall. This mechanism allows your body to send immune system soldiers from the bloodstream to any place in your body they are needed. But that same reaction also takes place in certain susceptible individuals when the body mistakes milk, cola, corn, wheat, or other common allergens for invading enemies and causes an allergic reaction.

"It's possible that this sort of thing happens in the brains of people who ingest a food they're allergic to," Dr. Crayton says. "A reaction like that in the blood vessels of the brain would allow the blood/brain barrier to open up and permit all types of substances to flow in."

Original Offense	Decrease in Antisocial Behavior (%)
Assault	77
Burglary	41
Larceny	7
Runaways	32
Narcotic offenses	44

WRONGFULLY ACCUSED?

Ah, but it seemed so right.

In 1977, an Ohio probation officer testified before Congress that when she prescribed a low-sugar diet for her probationers, they gave up their lives of crime for good. That revelation was followed by a study showing that antisocial behavior in juvenile delinquents dropped dramatically during confinement when soft drinks and other sugary snacks were removed from their diets.

Other researchers have criticized those findings, however, arguing that the sugar/crime theories were based on anecdotal accounts and insufficient evidence. So the sweet link to crime remains controversial. For now, it seems, the jury's still out.

Grand Forks Human Nutrition Research Center—is not only involved making neurotransmitters but is also responsible for getting oxygen to your brain so you can think at all.

Moreover, spinach also contains manganese and magnesium, two minerals that your brain uses to extract energy from other nutrients. Ongoing research suggests that magnesium, which is most likely to be deficient in those with alcoholism, may be one of the key elements your brain needs to function.

SOME SMART REASONS TO CHOOSE FRUIT

But your brain also needs fruits, nuts, and seeds to keep itself learning, thinking, and remembering. A generous handful of sunflower seeds, for example, provides all the thiamine (vitamin B_1) your brain needs to conduct messages from one part of its circuits to another. And half a cantaloupe supplies all the vitamins A and C your brain needs to make certain kinds of neurotransmitters, build brain cells, and absorb iron.

Fruits—particularly prunes, raisins, and dates—are an important source of boron, a trace mineral that is now being investigated by scientists at the Grand Forks research center.

"During one study, there were clear indications that the electrical activity in the brain is significantly influenced by dietary boron," says Dr. Penland. "When people don't have enough boron, the electrical activity in their brain indicates they're less alert than when they're receiving slightly larger amounts."

Why? "The quick answer is that there may be some relationship to neurotransmitters," says Dr. Penland. "But we really don't know."

So how much boron should we consume? That question was the focus of a three-year research project at the Grand Forks research center. It appears that the human daily requirement for boron is somewhere between 1 and 2 milligrams a day—roughly the equivalent of 2 ounces of prunes or a mouthful of raisins.

WHEN FOOD ISN'T ENOUGH

Getting enough boron is going to be an easy job. But some brain nutrients are hard to get from a sensible

DOES FASTING CLEAR THE MIND?

"It seems to happen on about the second or third day. You think you should be tired, but instead you feel very alert and energetic. The mind seems exceptionally clear." That's the way one 34-year-old professional writer described the effects of a brief stint without solid foods.

Many other fasters report the same feeling. It's known as a "fasting high." Theories about why this high occurs are many, "although I don't know of any research confirming that fasting leads to clarified thinking," says Rudolph Ballentine, M.D., a graduate of Duke University's medical school and holistic medical services director at the Himalayan International Institute in Honesdale, Pennsylvania.

Yet that doesn't make him a skeptic. There's a long tradition of fasting in many of the great religions, he says, where the practice is used to increase awareness. "From that point of view, one would expect there's something to it," Dr. Ballen-

tine notes. "But," he adds, "people who enter a fast when they're already nutritionally depleted will only *diminish* their alertness."

diet. You'd have to eat 26¼ ounces of peanut butter, for example, to get enough biotin, an essential nutrient that your brain needs to use fat. There are other sources of biotin, of course, but they generally provide lesser amounts.

Pantothenate, another B vitamin, presents the same problem. Would you rather eat 4 cups of peanut butter, 3 cups of raw peas, or 1½ cups of simmered chicken livers? Probably none of the above. Yet your brain needs adequate pantothenate—every day—to utilize the fats, carbohydrates, and proteins in your food.

That's why even if you incorporate a wide variety of foods into a well-balanced diet, some nutritionists suggest you also take a basic, once-daily type of vitamin and mineral supplement. No megadoses, just an ordinary multiple vitamin/mineral tablet or

capsule. Otherwise, it's just too easy to have a deficiency and not even know.

In a British study, for example, scientists divided 90 12- and 13-year-old schoolchildren into three groups. One group received a multivitamin, one received a similar-looking pill that contained no nutrients, and the third group got nothing extra at all. The children's ability to think and reason was tested at the beginning of the study and again eight months later, at its conclusion.

The result? The students who had taken the multivitamin supplement increased their nonverbal IQ's by nearly ten points. Clearly, the researchers concluded, the students—even though they were well-fed and appeared healthy—must have had vitamin or mineral deficiencies that had significantly impaired their mental performances.

TYROSINE FOR TOUGH SPOTS?

Multivitamin/mineral supplements are a good idea, agrees Priscilla Slagle, M.D., an associate clinical professor at the University of California, Los Angeles. But if you find yourself in a situation where you need intense mental concentration and output for a short period of time—when you're making an important decision, for example—she suggests something extra: a single 500-milligram capsule of L-tyrosine first thing in the morning. Make sure you don't eat for at least 30 minutes, she adds, so the tyrosine has a chance to get to your brain without tryptophan running interference. Then take a B-complex capsule. The result, she says, should turn your brain up to maximum wattage.

Does supplementation with tyrosine really work? A study by Louis Banderet, Ph.D., and his colleagues at the United States Army Research Institute of Environmental Medicine in Natick, Massachusetts, may give us a clue.

Dr. Banderet knew that large amounts of chronic stress—the kind soldiers experience scouting for enemy outposts or standing guard after a battle—tend to depress the levels of neurotransmitters that affect our ability to think. And he wanted to know if supplemental tyrosine could boost them back up and keep battle-weary soldiers on their toes.

Dr. Banderet couldn't simulate the stress of battle in his study, but he could definitely provide stress. In fact, one of the more extreme test conditions simulated being suddenly lifted to a 15,500-foot elevation and being exposed to chilly temperatures without protective clothing.

As subsequently reported to a NATO conference on enhancing troop performance, the soldiers who had received tyrosine performed better at mental tasks—translating messages into a code, charting coordinates on a map, and making complex decisions—than those who did not take the supplements. Moreover, those who took tyrosine had a significant edge in alertness, quick response time, and clear thinking—the same edge that *you* might want when making an important decision.

ARE YOU READY?

So are you ready to make that important decision after eating Thousand Island dressing, steak, fried potatoes, cauliflower with cheese sauce, pound cake, and your sister-in-law's artichoke-mayonnaise-Parmesan cheese dip?

Not on your life. Tomorrow try switching to a low-fat, low-calorie diet that emphasizes lean meat or seafood, vegetables, and fruit. Then see if you don't feel sharper and ready to make your decision.

But for now, maybe you should go to bed.

CAN VITAMINS SLOW PARKINSON'S DISEASE?

New research has shown that high doses of vitamins E and C may retard the progression of Parkinson's disease. And though the findings are preliminary, it seems vitamin therapy could help increase our understanding of how this debilitating disease works.

Researchers at Columbia University in New York administered vitamins E and C to patients not yet receiving L-dopa therapy for Parkinson's disease. Because L-dopa (the current drug treatment of choice for Parkinson's) becomes ineffective in many patients within five to ten years, doctors tend to prescribe it only when symptoms begin interfering with a patient's daily life.

The patients receiving vitamins E and C were able to postpone the start of L-dopa therapy two to three years longer than another group that received no vitamin treatment. These results suggest that Parkinson's may be caused by the oxidation that damage the brain cells needed to produce dopamine, a neurotransmitter essential for muscle control. Vitamins E and C are antioxidants that appear to slow this damage and retard progression of the disease.

PERSONALITY

Imagine two sisters raised in the same home with the same opportunities.

The first girl, Kathy, is only an average student through high school, but in college she works incredibly hard. She becomes a lawyer and then a judge.

The second girl, Denise, is an academic natural, but she gets involved with drugs, is arrested, and spends two years in prison.

How can such differences in achievement be explained? Often in a word: personality.

THE "YOU" IN UNIQUE

Each of us has a personality, although each of us has probably met someone who we thought had none. And though at various times researchers believed personality was entirely genetic or entirely a product of our surroundings, they now are convinced that it's a combination of the two.

"Our understanding of personality and the brain has changed radically over the last two decades," says Eliezer Schwartz, Ph.D., of the Illinois School of Professional Psychology.

THROUGH GUTS . . . GLORY

Genetics seemed to write a script for all that young Scott Hamilton couldn't do in this world. Before Hamilton was in kindergarten, he suddenly stopped growing. Other kids taunted him with shouts of "Peanut, Peanut."

Eventually, Hamilton was diagnosed as having Schwachman's syndrome, a rare disease that obstructs digestion. He couldn't make up for lost time—not in inches and pounds anyway—but, thanks to his strong-willed personality, he was able to take the narrowest opportunity and see it through to an Olympic gold medal for the United States in figure skating.

The skating began unexpectedly when Hamilton, who then still had a feeding tube, decided to try ice skating during a trip to the rink with his sister. He continued to skate, and as time passed, he started growing again.

Hamilton grew to 5'3" tall and 115 pounds. Measuring his determination, however, seems impossible.

"Subconsciously," Hamilton once said, "the whole experience made me want to succeed at something athletic." Add the desire to make fools of nonbelievers who thought he was still a peanut by international standards, and Hamilton was poised to write his own ending on ice.

But the most intriguing questions remain. Why, for example, was Kathy long on common sense, patience, and the will to succeed? And why was her sister, Denise, though apparently blessed with more intelligence, short on self-confidence and long on hostility?

Researchers are working on answers to such questions about specific traits. Two studies—one involving twins and the other involving adopted children—indicate that shyness, for example, is one of our most inheritable traits, says Robert Plomin, Ph.D., a professor of human development at Pennsylvania State University.

Overall, however, these and other studies suggest a weaker genetic influence than was once suspected. His findings, Dr. Plomin says, indicate that usually about 30 percent of our personality is inherited. "A lot of who we are," he says, "isn't genetic."

So what about the other 70 percent? Maybe the female history teacher Kathy looked up to in high school helped motivate her. And maybe Denise was overwhelmed by the example set by her plucky older sister.

"Usually what you find out is that a successful person, an athlete for example, had a mentor or some other person who influenced her," says Dr. Schwartz. "You need to have some talent—be it physical or mental—but whether you use it or not depends more on factors in your environment."

WINNING PERSONALITIES

Can you imagine Denise—years after her parole from prison—as a successful businesswoman and a happy wife and mother? Much stranger things have happened. After all, Denise had considerable intelligence to work with from the beginning.

The people who seem to get the most out of their brainpower, though, also make good use of another personality trait that does seem within each adult's reach—self-reliance.

In a study by the Gallup Organization of 1,500 high-achieving people listed in *Who's Who in America*, 77 percent of those interviewed gave themselves an

EVE'S THREE FACES

She was a vamp, a mousy housewife, and an intelligent woman of poise—but never at the same time. In *The Three Faces of Eve*, Joanne Woodward created an unforgettable triple portrait of a divided personality.

"The most likely cause of multiple personality is physical or sexual abuse as a child," says Robert Mayer, Ph.D., a psychoanalyst at Kean College in New York and author of *Through Divided Minds*.

People who develop multiple personalities never received proper treatment to help them deal with their trauma, Dr. Mayer says. "What was a reasonable defense mechanism as a child becomes pathological as an adult."

"A" rating in self-reliance. Furthermore, two-thirds said they had set clear goals for their lives and careers. And 50 percent gave themselves an "A" in willpower.

Common sense ranked high as an important trait for these superachievers, too. And there's nothing wrong with using common sense to get the most out of your personality: "If you know your strengths and weaknesses," Dr. Plomin says simply, "play for your strengths."

PSYCHIC POWERS

Out of the blue, you find yourself thinking about your zany friend Zelda. You haven't heard from her in months, but something's up. You can just feel it. So you get on the phone.

It sounds crazy, she says, but while departing one of her favorite restaurants after lunch, her motorcycle hit a patch of discarded french fries and slid into the path of a produce truck, which slammed on its brakes and dumped a load of lettuce into the front seat of a convertible, which veered into a roadside display of black velvet paintings of dead rock stars, causing the vendor to further slash his already low, low prices. But don't worry, Zelda says, she wasn't hurt, just awfully shook up ... and amazed that you happened to call, because she was just thinking about calling you.

It's uncanny. No, it's *telepathic,* parapsychologists would say of this apparent extrasensory awareness you had of Zelda's mental state. Maybe you've had other unusual experiences. Perhaps a precognition, a knowledge, or vision of something in advance of its occurrence—like the time you dreamed in vivid detail of a ghastly meal that not only looked and tasted awful but left you food poisoned for three days, too. And a few days later, sitting down for dinner as a guest at your new employer's house, you looked down at your plate and— ugh!—there it was.

GAZE INTO YOUR CRYSTAL BALL

You don't need experience as a gypsy to try reading a crystal ball, claims Katrina Raphaell, author of *Crystal Healing.*

For starters, Raphaell instructs, place your crystal ball between yourself and the person whose reading you are doing. Clear your mind and gaze into the ball's center. "The reflective surface," she says, "will act like a mirror image of that person's inner state." You might see an actual picture of that person's past, present, or future. Or you may feel your consciousness drifting into the ball's center. Be patient. The answers you seek should eventually come clear.

A FIRE IN THE FUTURE

Or how about clairvoyance or clairaudience, seeing or hearing things not perceptible in the ordinary ways? New York psychic Ingo Swann dramatically experienced these at an early age.

"I was 4 years old. I went to bed, then suddenly I saw that my bedroom was consumed by a wall of fire," he says. "I ran into my parents' bedroom screaming, seeing the whole house consumed in flames. I thought what I saw was 'real,' but I knew that it really wasn't. Still, I raised such a fuss that my parents and I spent the rest of the night at my grandmother's house. Later that night, a fire that had been slowly combusting in our attic exploded, engulfing the house in flames. We would never have gotten out alive."

These and other psychic powers, also known as psi, ESP (extrasensory perception), or paranormal abilities, comprise a dormant but valuable "sixth sense" that can clue us in to things we might otherwise be unable to perceive, says Swann, author of *Natural ESP* and other books on psi.

Do you believe in ESP? As many as 60 percent of the American population does, says Swann. Nancy Reagan believed in using the predictive powers of an astrologer to help plan her husband's presidential appointment schedule. Another White House

THE PHYSICS OF MENTAL TELEPATHY

Proving that telepathy and other forms of ESP exist is one challenge for scientists; explaining how they might work is quite another. A number of theories have been postulated.

Electromagnetism. Extrasensory information may be carried from one person to another by some form of electromagnetic wave, much like radio waves.

Bioplasm (or psychoplasm). This "fourth state" of matter, which can be recorded as a kind of surrounding energy field with something called Kirlian photography, may carry ESP information.

Tachyons. A hypothetical particle speeding with a velocity greater than that of light, a tachyon might carry ESP information. In its simultaneous interaction with speedy light particles and slow particles called tardyons, signals may "arrive" on one level before they are "sent" on another and hence seem precognitive.

Psitrons. These unusual particles register probabilities of certain situations in the dimension of time, one theory goes, and also contribute to the alpha rhythms of the brain. An awareness of these registrations may emerge as a precognition of a future event.

Negative energy states. According to this conveniently foggy theory, the energy densities of brain chemicals are high enough to permit manifestations (telepathy, clairvoyance, and precognition) of what are called the nonzero properties of the "perfect vacuum."

---

resident, Abraham Lincoln, reported having precognitive dreams, including one in which he foresaw his assassination.

But among most American scientists, skepticism about paranormal abilities abounds. Even though it was scientists who in the late 1800s formally established the field of parapsychology—a branch of psychology that deals with behavior that cannot be explained in terms of known physical properties.

Researchers still intrigued by paranormal phenomena today conduct studies at renowned institutions like Princeton University and the Foundation for Research on the Nature of Man (formerly the Duke University Parapsychology Laboratory).

MIND OVER MATTER

Brain processes are clearly involved in paranormal abilities, one researcher says. But exactly what they are and how they work, nobody really knows. One theory has it that they have something to do with principles of quantum physics.

"High-energy physicists are now saying what Eastern philosophers have been saying for years: Everything is consciousness," says John Harricharan, a business consultant, author, and practicing psychic. "According to quantum physics, one electron seems to know what another electron is doing, whether it's across the room or across the universe. My brain is not the cause or the source of my powers. It's a transmission instrument."

Harricharan says he's been psychic all his life. (He managed to complete a four-year college degree in only two years, for instance, "not because of extreme brilliance but because at times I knew in advance

BURIED ABILITY

Imagine going someplace you've never been before and taking in the view with wide-eyed fascination. Now imagine getting the same view without ever leaving home, because the only thing taking this trip is your mind.

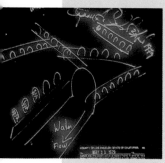

That's how parapsychology researchers conceptualize remote viewing, in which a person, usually in a laboratory, is able to pictorially describe objects and events that are somehow shielded from his or her ordinary perception. In one experiment, remote viewers were able to perceive unknown objects at an underground archaeological site in Egypt.

During the "Alexandria Project," Los Angeles photographer Hella Hammid, an experienced remote viewer, drew a picture *(left)* of the still-buried site as she perceived it. Weeks later, an excavation revealed a remarkably similar sight, an Alexandrian cistern *(above)*.

what would be on the exam.") His individual clients range from movie stars to truckers.

He also works extensively with businesses, from Fortune 500 corporations to small companies. "I can give them valuable information they'll never find on a balance sheet," he says. "An entrepreneur may want to expand into a new area, for instance. I may review his accounts or I may not—I might just get a 'feel' for what's happening. I once told someone, 'You have a partner, don't you?' 'Yes,' he said. 'There are problems with this partnership,' I said. 'How did you know that?' he asked. 'That doesn't matter,' I continued. 'What matters is that he's stealing you blind and forming a competitive business.' My client had suspected as much, and it was all later confirmed."

"There appear to be different types of psychic perceptions," says Swann, who has served as a psychic guinea pig in thousands of experiments and has plowed through just about all the research ever recorded. "Sometimes they're crystal clear and come to you powerfully and involuntarily," he says, along the lines of his dramatic experience as a 4-year-old. On the opposite end of the spectrum is "the kind of gut feeling you get that tells you something is about to take place.

"Psychic skills are actually quite widespread and are anything but paranormal," Swann insists. "After all, anything the mind can produce has to be normal. What we call paranormal must be following laws that exist—we just haven't discovered them yet."

Some of us may be more psychically attuned than others, Harricharan suggests. "There are natural-born clairvoyants and telepaths just as there are natural-born piano players," he says. "It's a talent. With practice, you develop it."

Just about anyone can develop the talent to one degree or another—and would do well to do so, Swann claims. "Our lower functions give us the power to think and solve problems. But our psychic powers allow us to hook up to the past and the future. To the degree that you can predict your own future, you will be successful in life."

LEARN TO BE PSYCHIC IN YOUR SPARE TIME

Do you believe in the existence of psychic powers? Your chances of developing such powers yourself are greatly increased if you do, says Ingo Swann, who outlines a program for such development in his book *Natural ESP.*

Swann says his own abilities have been enhanced by years of participation in psychic experiments. Just about anybody—yourself included—can get better with practice, he says. Swann recommends you begin experiments in remote viewing, or perceiving objects that are hidden or at a distance. Specifically:

● Find an interested friend to work with. Ask him or her to start with objects that are easy to recognize, such as a spoon or a jar. (You can work with more complex objects later as you advance.)

● Conduct your experiment in a quiet room. Avoid excessive talking or bothersome little noises that might distract your attention. Sit at a well-lighted table with a pen and a piece of paper.

● Ask your friend to place the object or objects on a table in another room, in a closed box, or behind a barrier you can't see through.

● Be as calm as possible. An attitude of detachment is most conducive to allowing your abilities to naturally emerge. When you feel ready, produce a drawing of the object as you sense it. Work quickly. Prolonging the experiment interferes with your awareness. Then put your pen down and ask to see the object. Circle those features in your drawing that correspond to the actual object. Do only one or two experiments at a time, and take a break for a day or two between sessions.

● As you become more advanced, try other experiments, like this one in precognition: Choose a date and time in the future and draw the place where you sense you will be then. Carry the drawing with you and compare it with where you actually are when that moment arrives. Don't be surprised if things look strangely familiar.

REASONING

I t's love that makes the world go round—but it's surely reason that keeps it from spinning off its axis.

A world without reason might have bankers and bishops running about in chicken costumes. Two plus two would equal five (except on holidays). Humming "Twinkle Twinkle, Little Star" might warrant the death penalty.

Life without reason would likely resemble a mad tea party such as the one little Alice stumbled upon while adventuring through Wonderland . . .

> The table was a large one, but the three were all crowded together at one corner of it. "No room! No room!" they cried out when they saw Alice coming.
>
> "There's plenty of room!" said Alice indignantly, and she sat down in a large armchair at one end of the table.
>
> "Have some wine?" the March hare said in an encouraging tone.
>
> Alice looked all round the table, but there was nothing on it but tea. "I don't see any wine," she remarked.
>
> "There isn't any," said the March Hare. . . .

The ability to reason—the power to comprehend, draw conclusions, or think in an orderly, rational way—is surely the glue that holds civilization together. It allows for government, mathematics, architecture, music, laws, technology, even simple conversation and afternoon tea parties.

Yet even history's best-known reasoners (such as mathematician and logician Charles Lutwidge Dodgson, who, under the name Lewis Carroll, wrote *Alice's Adventures in Wonderland*) could never quite put their finger on exactly what constitutes good reasoning.

Reason is easier to define in the negative, says Amos Tversky, Ph.D., a professor of psychology at

ELEMENTARY, MY DEAR WATSON

Sherlock Holmes. He was, according to his good friend Dr. Watson, "the most perfect reasoning and observing machine that the world has ever seen."

He was also, of course, the best-known character of British writer Sir Arthur Conan Doyle. There was not a crime in turn-of-the-century England that Holmes could not solve.

In the short story "A Scandal in Bohemia," Holmes *(above, standing)* and Watson discuss their case. They have just read an odd letter in which they are promised a visit that night by a gentleman wearing a mask. And little else.

"This is indeed a mystery," says Watson, whose own powers of reason always left much to be desired. "What do you imagine that it means?" The master detective's response may explain the essence of good reasoning: "I have no data yet. It is a capital mistake to theorize before one has data. Insensibly one begins to twist facts to suit theories, instead of theories to suit facts."

All pigs like corn.

Porky is a pig.

Therefore, Porky like corn.

Stanford University. That is, it's much easier to spot unreasonable thinking, or an unreasonable argument, than it is to spot a reasonable one. (The death penalty for humming a silly song is clearly unreasonable.)

THE REASONING PROCESS

Reasoning comes in three forms, theorizes Robert Sternberg, Ph.D., professor of psychology and education at Yale University, and author of several books, including *Intelligence Applied.* "According to my theory, reasoning goes through at least one, and usually three processes," he says.

First, we employ *selective encoding.* That is, we decide what information is relevant to solving a certain problem. Say you have $10,000 to invest, but you aren't sure where to invest it. The first thing you might do is consider all the pertinent factors, says Dr. Sternberg. For instance, you might ponder interest rates, leading economic indicators, and the stock market pattern over the past year.

The second process is called *selective comparison.* Here we weigh all the factors gathered during the selective encoding process to decide which are the most important. In our previous example, this would involve developing a tentative investment portfolio, choosing bonds based on falling interest rates, and stocks based on rising market trends.

The third process is *selective combination.* This step involves drawing on past knowledge. In our example, this might mean reviewing investments you've made in the past. You might ask yourself, "How well did I do in stocks the last time I invested in the market?" or "How could I have let myself get so badly burned in precious metals last year?"

For very different kinds of decisions, the three reasoning steps would still be much the same, says Dr. Sternberg. Choosing a mate, for example, would first involve deciding what information is relevant, such as personality, appearance, and education. Next, you would weigh these. Third, you would make a selective comparison. ("Well, he's sort of cute, and he's rich, but he reminds me too much of my first husband.")

WHEN LOGIC GOES ASTRAY

As with anything else, there is good reasoning and bad reasoning. You often recognize bad reasoning when you hear it. But can you always say *why* it's bad?

Illustrated here are two syllogisms, arguments in which two propositions are given (and assumed true), and a third proposition is presented as the conclusion. But the conclusion may be valid or invalid.

The problem with syllogisms is that even madness can sometimes sound reasonable. In the example below, you know that Farmer Jones cannot be a pig. But doesn't it seem at first glance that that's exactly what the first two propositions prove? Look again. We learn in lines one and two that Farmer Jones likes corn and so do all pigs. Think of these as subsets of the larger set: everyone (and everything) in the universe that likes corn. This set includes not only farmers and pigs, but many carpenters, horses, and Spanish guitar players as well. Farmer Jones is no more a pig than is a carpenter, a horse, or a Spanish guitar player—they just all happen to like corn.

All pigs like corn.

Farmer Jones likes corn.

Therefore, Farmer Jones is a pig.

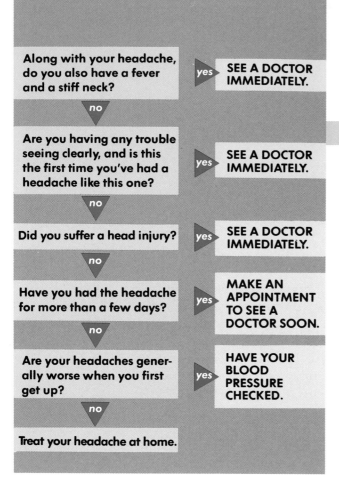

Along with your headache, do you also have a fever and a stiff neck?

yes → SEE A DOCTOR IMMEDIATELY.

no ↓

Are you having any trouble seeing clearly, and is this the first time you've had a headache like this one?

yes → SEE A DOCTOR IMMEDIATELY.

no ↓

Did you suffer a head injury?

yes → SEE A DOCTOR IMMEDIATELY.

no ↓

Have you had the headache for more than a few days?

yes → MAKE AN APPOINTMENT TO SEE A DOCTOR SOON.

no ↓

Are your headaches generally worse when you first get up?

yes → HAVE YOUR BLOOD PRESSURE CHECKED.

no ↓

Treat your headache at home.

AN IMPERFECT ART

The world is full of imperfect reasoners and therefore imperfect reasoning. Common are bad investments, bad marriages, and letters to Ann Landers asking, "Where did I go wrong?"

But the world is also far from a mad tea party. Trains run on time (at least in some countries), people usually make sense when they talk, and two plus two seems to always equal four.

How can we be such good reasoners some of the time, and such poor reasoners at other times? Dr. Tversky has a theory. He says we all fall prey to things called *cognitive illusions*. These illusions, he says, explain how otherwise logical, rational human beings can often act in ways that *seem* unreasonable.

Other people, maybe, but not you? Answer the following question: Are there more words in the English language that have *n* as a second-to-last letter, or are there more words in the English language that end in *-ing*? Quick!

If you're like most people, words that end in *-ing* are easy to think of—walking, talking, reasoning, and so on. But words that have *n* as a second-to-last letter? That's tough. You might reason that there are

Algorithm flowcharts, such as the one illustrated here, are often used by computer programmers to teach machines to "reason." They are graphic representations of linear thinking—logic in action. You can use such a flowchart to help you make complex everyday decisions. The next time you've got a pounding in your head, for instance, and you're not sure why, try this step-by-step guide for coming up with the most logical, and medically prudent, course of action.

lots of words that end in *-ing*, certainly more than there are words that have *n* as a second-to-last letter.

But if you think about it long enough, says Dr. Tversky, you're bound to realize that the group "all words that have *n* as a second to last letter" *includes* "all words that end in *-ing*." Therefore, the *n* group *must* be larger.

SHARPEN YOUR POWERS OF REASON

The study of reason has been a focus of philosophers and educators for many centuries, says Steven Kuhn, Ph.D., associate professor of philosophy at Georgetown University. But understanding the mechanics of reasoning, he asserts, is not at all the same as being a good reasoner.

"It's like speaking the English language," says Dr. Kuhn. "You can speak perfectly good English without knowing the rules of grammar, or you can know all the rules of grammar and be an awful speaker." In other words, signing up for a college course in logic is *not* likely to help you make investments or pick a mate.

What would? Dr. Tversky has a few suggestions.

Respect probability. Many times when reasonable people act in seemingly unreasonable ways, they are simply not taking full account of the rules of probability. Such was the case with our diplomats. A simple rule of probability states that *the probability that both (a) and (b) will happen* (there will be a breakdown in relations *and* there will be a crackdown in Poland) *cannot be greater than the possibility that (a) will happen* (there will be a breakdown in relations).

Beware of words. Imagine you are a doctor. A

new surgical procedure will give your patient a 60 percent chance of survival. Do you try the procedure? Another procedure gives your patient a 40 percent chance of dying. Do you risk this procedure? Studies have shown that where both procedures have the *same* rate of success and failure, doctors can easily be swayed by how the question is asked. It's not just doctors, though. "We are all a lot more vulnerable to language than we think," says Dr. Tversky. He suggests that whenever you see a problem framed in a particular way, frame it in another way, and see how it sounds.

Be your own devil's advocate. On any topic where you've formed an opinion, try to argue the opposition's position to yourself. See how well you can respond. It's a good way to check your logic.

Know your own fallibility. "Most people are grossly overconfident with their impressions and judgments," says Dr. Tversky. He reasons that we could all be better reasoners simply by being a lot more critical. "The first step to wisdom," he says, is realizing how fallible we are.

Be critical of others. Not overtly, of course. But keep in mind that the reasoning of those around you is subject to the same foibles as your own.

This last point is especially pertinent should you find yourself at a tea party with a dormouse, a hatter, and a March hare.

HOW TO WIN A DEBATE

It seems these days that winning a debate means wearing a dark suit and looking unflappable in front of a TV camera.

While these and other techniques usually can't hurt, there is one other essential ingredient to effective debating: keen reasoning, says Don Brownlee, Ph.D., associate professor of speech communication and debate team coach at California State University in Northridge.

The first step to good debating, he says, is to assess the audience. Your task—whether you're a politician or a salesman—is to enter your audience's world, to know what really matters to them, and to draw on common experiences. Then appeal to *their* sense of reason.

"You can't argue outside of someone's realm of experience," says Dr. Brownlee. "I could put together a very good argument in Mandarin Chinese and it wouldn't mean much to an American audience." Instead, stop and think. If you're addressing members of the National Rifle Association, for example, tell a little tale about how your dad taught you to shoot a deer. But tell the same tale to a group of animal rights activists and you'd be better off if it *were* in Mandarin Chinese!

YOUR SENSES AND YOUR BRAIN

Joe Bonham lies in his hospital bed. The war has left him without limbs, eyes, ears, nose, or mouth. All he knows of this world is pain when his wounds are cleaned and his bandages changed, and relief when he's bathed. Not knowing day from night, he can't tell whether he's awake and thinking or asleep and dreaming. In his mind, however, he lives. Mem-

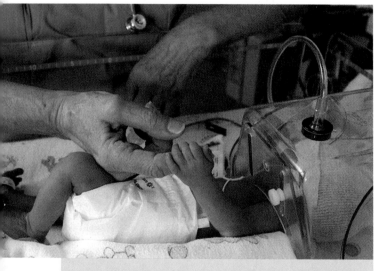

TOUCH TRIGGERS GROWTH

Premature infants who are massaged gain 47 percent more weight per day than preemies who aren't massaged, according to a University of Miami Medical School study. After their discharge, they maintain their weight advantage while doing better on tests of mental and motor skills. "The mechanism is completely unknown to us," says study chief Tiffany Field, Ph.D., professor of pediatrics, psychology, and psychiatry. But very preliminary findings indicate the level of growth hormone in nonmassaged babies drops while the level in massaged babies remains normal. Once parents bring their preemies home, Dr. Field recommends continuing with a daily massage, using baby oil and a gentle but firm stroke. Too light a touch can be tickling and irritating.

ories of hallucinatory clarity bring back the sights of his hometown, a carnival, his girlfriend's gentle touch, the taste of his favorite hamburger with lots of onion and sweet mustard, his mother singing in the kitchen, the smell of rain and perfume and burning wood.

The harrowing story of Joe Bonham, as told by novelist Dalton Trumbo in *Johnny Got His Gun*, drives home an important point: Our senses literally create our reality. Joe Bonham's reality is much different than that perceived by those of us with more fully functioning senses. "It's a sensory world we live in, a constant barrage of sensation," says Washington, D.C., neurologist Richard Cytowic, M.D.

While your eyes, ears, nose, tongue, and skin are continually picking up all those signals from the world, it's your brain that makes them real. When you hear a sound, for example, it's in your brain. So science can now provide the answer to the ancient conundrum: If a tree falls in the forest and there is no human or animal around to hear it, does it make a sound? "If you define sound in the sense of actually stimulating the auditory parts of your brain, the answer is no," says Robert Turner, Ph.D., associate professor of otolaryngology and director of the Auditory and Speech Clinic at the University of California, San Francisco, School of Medicine. "I can electrically stimulate your auditory nerve and you'll think there's sound out there although there isn't. In this way sound, vision, touch, taste, and smell are all illusions. We know only what our brain tells us." No brain, no sound.

NEW INSIGHTS INTO SIGHT

Research into the senses is changing the way science regards the brain. No longer, for example, is it seen as an amazing computer. The brain may function, says Dr. Turner, as a "parallel distributed network." A computer is great for number crunching and word processing, he says. "But there's no room for error. One missing comma or number and the whole program won't work. Every step has to be there."

The brain, however, processes information (visual or otherwise) in parallel. Parallel layers of neurons, which are all interconnected, recognize patterns not just individual steps on a ladder. "This makes the brain very good in dealing with errors and generalizations," Dr. Turner says. Vision researcher Lance Optican, Ph.D., a biomedical engineer and chief of the Neural Modeling Section of the National Eye Institute, puts it this way: "Solving problems with a serial computer is like draining a bathtub with a spoon. The old theories said that the brain could bail faster because it had more spoons. The new theories argue that the brain uses better methods, like pulling the plug."

The latest research has also thrown out the old "grandmother cell" theory, says Dr. Optican. This theory held that your brain had a separate, specialized group of cells for each sensory act—like recognizing your grandmother, for instance. "So when these cells lit up, they would report the presence or absence of your grandmother," he says. And that's all they could do. It's well-known that each of the motor neurons that control your muscles can fire impulses governing strength, speed, and direction. "But we thought that since the vision neurons didn't have to control muscles, they could be stupider, and do only one thing," he says, like recognize a line, or an edge, or a color, or a contour. New findings, however, show vision neurons (and other sensory neurons as well) are as multi-talented as motor neurons.

New research also proves the retina does more than merely relay signals to the occipital lobe of the brain, Dr. Optican says. "The retina is actually a piece of the brain that comes out into the eye in the embryo and forms a little window on the world," he says. Made of six layers of neurons, the retina handles the first stage of vision processing. From the retina, the already partly processed signal is sent down the optic nerve to a relay station, which switches it to the track that takes it to the primary visual area in the occipital lobe. From there, the message spreads forward again, about halfway to the front of the brain, diffusing to at least 24 secondary visual areas in the limbic system.

Philosopher John Locke told of the blind man who comprehended the color scarlet as "like the sound of a trumpet." Children regularly link violet and blue with low frequencies like these emitted by a cello or saxophone, green and yellow with the high frequencies of a clarinet.

VITAL VIBRATIONS

Vision is the most developed sense and requires the most brain cells, but hearing is probably the most complex sense, Dr. Turner says. The mechanical transformation of sound vibrations into electrical impulses involves membranes, tiny bones, hydraulic fluid, cells with tiny hairlike appendages, and the nerve fibers they're attached to. Each fiber has a limited range for intensity and frequency; the fibers join forces to enable the ear to respond to wide ranges of loudness and pitch. Fibers feed this information to the brain for analysis and perception.

Hearing and understanding sound is is more complex than tuning into a glorified microphone on either side of your head. "Speech is a very complex acoustic wave form," Dr. Turner says.

SEEING VISIONS

People the world over have founded religions and civilizations based on hallucinations and visions. This Mexican mural, for example, shows a mother goddess with a highly stylized morning glory behind her. The Aztecs used the seeds of this species, which they called green snake plant, to induce trances and visions. "A hallucination is a stimulation of sensory centers in our brains," explains Albert Hofmann, Ph.D., the Swiss chemist who synthesized LSD. "It's an experience of something that isn't there. But the elements are things you've seen in real life. It may be a monster with three eyes, but you've seen eyes in real life. Your brain is a kind of internal videocassette recorder, on which you've recorded impressions of the world. In a hallucination—or a dream—your brain mixes them up, edits them onto one tape, and plays it back. Hallucinations are akin to dreams which have burst into waking life."

"In vision, what you're looking at is more or less stable in time. But in speech, you're hearing a signal that's changing 20 or 30 times per second, and your brain has to identify each of those changes and make sense of them. On top of that, it has to allow for individual speaker's unique variations in acoustics and accent and dialect."

Hearing perception may be more vital than our visual sense. "Someone who's born blind has a lot of practical problems to deal with, but can evolve perfectly normal speech and language," Dr. Turner says. "Someone born deaf and not helped will grow up unable to communicate and with limitations on the ability to think."

AN APPETITE FOR LIFE

Sight and hearing may be vital, yet your perception would also suffer without taste and smell. "They don't play as obvious a role in human perception as they do in animals," says neurophysiologist Bruce Bryant, Ph.D., an assistant member of the Monell Chemical Senses Center, a research institute affiliated with the University of Pennsylvania. "But it turns out that smell and taste are a big part of your life. You may not celebrate them like you do hearing and seeing and touch. But when smell and taste disappear, life can turn very gray."

Some tastes—the basic sweet, sour, salty, bitter—are "hard-wired into us," Dr. Bryant says. Nerve bundles run from the tongue back to the taste centers in the brain stem. One kind of bundle relays information about temperature, pain, and texture, while the other conveys pure taste. The brain stem combines the signals with olfactory information to produce the perception of flavor. That's why warm beer has a different taste than cold.

"Taste and smell are strongly interconnected," Dr. Bryant says. "All of what we call the taste of roast beef, except the saltiness, is actually smell." In the nose, there are many types of receptors for different odorous substances. When the membrane of nasal receptors picks up these substances, it generates nerve impulses that feed through nerve fibers directly into the olfactory bulb and then on to higher brain centers. The brain looks at the entire pattern and decides what the quality of the odor is. The olfactory system is, evolutionarily speaking, one of the most primitive areas in the human brain. This may explain why these senses are our most powerful sensory evokers of memory.

THE PATH OF PAIN

Our biggest sensory organ is the skin, connected by an incredibly complex maze of nerve fibers to the brain. As quickly as a signal can move from your foot to your brain, it's *too* long when you're standing on hot sand at the beach. So your nervous system short-circuits the signal at the spinal cord, enabling you to hop onto your towel, saving "ouch!!" for a fraction of a second later. Ultimately, touch sensations—including pressure, pain, heat, and cold—reach the sensory cortex in the parietal lobe at the top of your head. From there the signals are dispersed to the limbic system.

The limbic system seems to be the throne of perception. "Everything feeds into the limbic system, in multiple pathways, both directly from the senses and in reentry pathways from the frontal lobes," Dr. Cytowic says. "Brain surgeons discovered that when the limbic system is stimulated during an operation, the patient will often relive past experiences in all of their sensory richness."

In any event, your brain translates sensory signals into a personal reality as unique as your fingerprints. That's why Joe Bonham can still hear and see and smell and taste and touch. And that's why you can use your brain to enrich your perception of the world.

Even sealed off in a flotation tank, you still see flashes of light from spontaneous retinal cell firing, you still feel the water, you hear your body noises. "It's impossible to totally deprive the senses of input," says University of British Columbia psychologist Peter Suedfeld, Ph.D.

17 WAYS
TO SHARPEN YOUR SENSES

Just as physical exercise makes your muscles stronger and improves your body's ability to do the tasks you set for it, so exercising your brain can sharpen your sensory perception to improve your awareness. Although your brain registers all the signals your senses receive, most of the signals never reach your conscious awareness. That's partly for self-protection—weeding out the unnecessary. But perception can also be dulled by the sensory equivalent of couch potatoism. The goal of the exercises presented here is to expand your awareness by heightening your conscious perceptions.

SEE IT ALL

There's more to vision than seeing. Your eyes may be 20-20, but if all you do is watch TV, your visual perception will be limited because parts of your brain's vision centers are underused, thus underdeveloped. Here are a few ways to exercise those neurons.

Start scanning. When you walk down the street, look all around you. Shift your focus from object to object. Look not only at people's faces, but at their bodies. Observe the sky between buildings, trees close to you and down the block, and the store across the street. Gaze into the deep pit of a construction site.

Check the sidelines. Although you look straight ahead most of the time, even then your eyes are picking up visual signals from the periphery. To challenge your brain's peripheral vision pathways even more, sit in a chair and look at a point on the wall level with your eyes. *Without moving your eyes,* concentrate on the blurry impressions coming in from the sides. Blink to relieve eyestrain, and don't spend longer than 15 minutes per session.

Go for detail. Even in an asphalt jungle, there are splotches of color and texture. Seek them out. Buildings have unique masonry detailing, trees have unique bark patterns, each person has a unique face.

Follow motions. Increase your perception of motion by trying to read the license plates of moving cars, the labels of spinning records, or focus on the hoofstrikes of race horses.

TUNE UP YOUR EARS

"Our hearing sensitivity is reduced in a noisy world," says California audiologist Stephen Roberts, Ph.D. "It's not that our hearing is worse biologically, but there's so much extraneous noise that needs to be screened out." Unfortunately, shutting out noise also shuts out things you *should* perceive. These exercises will enable you to tune in or out at will, while keeping your perceptual pathways clear.

Listen between the lines. There's more to speech than words. Listen for tone, tempo, rhythm, timbre, volume.

Hear the world. Just for a minute each day, stop and listen to all the various sounds that surround you and that you normally screen out. One sound tells you a car is approaching and receding. A barking dog, a singing bird, a hissing vent, the rumble of the subway, the click and slap of footfalls, the roar of a jet, your officemate sniffling through an allergy—all tell you what's going on around you.

How low can you go? To increase your low-volume hearing powers and give yourself a rest from noise, turn your TV or radio down to no more than one-quarter the normal volume. When you're accustomed to the new level, turn it down a little more to the point where you have to listen really hard to hear. When strain builds, turn it back up to the one-quarter level. In a couple of weeks you'll find you can hear it fine at that level.

TASTE THE DIFFERENCE

Professional tasting has a long and harrowing history. Tasters' heightened perception of spoiled or poisoned food often saved the lives of monarchs while dooming their own. Today tasters are exalted in the wine cellars and find a good living in the kitchens of microwave dinner makers. But how often do *you* exercise your taste? Do you settle for sweet-

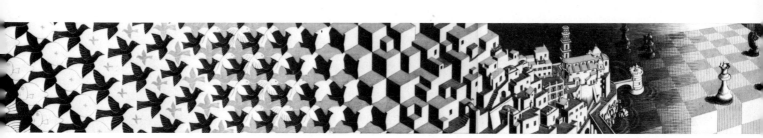

sour-salty-bitter? Your brain is able to perceive a lot more flavor than that, and these exercises will help you open the door to good taste.

Concentrate. Take a small bite of food and focus on the taste. Eat it slowly, making sure it gets to all parts of your tongue. Savor it with your eyes closed to give it your undivided attention. You'll be amazed at all the different taste sensations.

Vary your diet. Eat the same thing all the time and your taste perception gets bored and insensitive. So try alternating bites of the different foods on your plate. Between courses, eat a couple of spoonfuls of light sorbet or sherbet to clean out and perk up your taste pathways.

Investigate the recipe. Let your taste perception be your private eye as you try to detect each ingredient in the food you order at a restaurant.

SMELL THE ROSES

Is your smell perception so bad you need a smoke alarm to tell you your toast is burning? Often we don't use our noses, or the brain cells they're connected to, nearly as much as we should. And those neuron pathways deteriorate from loneliness. Don't blame it on age—a perfumer's perception gets better as he ages because every day it gets the sniffing equivalent of a Jane Fonda workout. With these exercises, you can train and awaken your own sense of smell. Do them in the late morning or late afternoon, when your olfactory powers are at their peak.

Get a whiff of your surroundings. Each day spend a minute concentrating on the smells around you. A new book has a distinctive aroma, for example, while an old book may smell musty. Smell your hands for traces of what they've been handling. Is that Aunt Sally's perfume preceding her up the stairs? What does a rhododendron smell like? Kitchens are good places to smell: Is that your spouse's special spaghetti sauce recipe bubbling away?

Paint a fragrant picture. The places you live, work, or visit have their own smells. When you're at one of those places, try composing a portrait of smells. Then try describing the portrait to another

person in a way that would enable her to instantly recognize the place if she were to visit there.

Single out smells. With a partner to guide you, walk blindfolded through a garden and practice identifying plants and flowers by their smell. You can also try this with your spice rack or at a perfume counter.

A TACTILE TOUCH-UP

Your entire body is an organ of touch, and a relatively big part of your brain is devoted to perception of touch. But too often we rely on our other senses to tell us about an object and leave out the wide world of touch. A blind person's sense of touch is stronger than a sighted person's simply because of the sensory exercise it gets. So do these exercises with your eyes closed or blindfolded.

What's it feel like? Pick up any object and spend a minute feeling it with each hand for clues about its nature. Is your TV remote control just a lump of plastic? Or does it have edges and ridges, planes and curves, odd shaped buttons and varying textures? Is it smooth, satiny, rough, slippery?

Let your hands do the looking. Walk slowly around a familiar room, touching things as you go. Try to figure out what each object is. Then do the same in a room not so familiar.

Find the keyhole. Try to fit a key into a keyhole. You'll fumble around at first, but you'll soon be surprised at how your perception of touch can guide you.

Count your coins. Put a dozen coins of various denominations in your pocket without knowing how much they add up to. Then grasp one of the coins between your fingers and guess which denomination it is. Pull it out, put it on a table, and do the same with the other coins while keeping a mental tabulation. Now look to see how right you were.

SLEEP

Some do it in $200-a-night hotel rooms in Manhattan, others in carpeted bedrooms in quiet suburbs, still others on public park benches beneath a fluttering blanket of old newspapers. Recognizing no distinctions of class, race, or sex, the powerful biological urge sooner or later overcomes us all. We succumb like the earthly creatures that we are, crawling into a comfortable spot, closing our eyes, growing still. Our breathing deepens and the beating of our heart slackens. Our blood pressure sinks and body temperature dips. Our muscles become limp. We are gone to this world, alone and vulnerable. We are sound asleep.

People have been sleeping since the beginning of time and have probably wondered for equally as long how sleep works and what it means. But only recently has sleep become a subject of careful scientific investigation. It hasn't been easy. Such inquiry requires the cooperation of people who are unable to report to researchers how they feel or what they're thinking about when it's happening since, after all, when it's happening, *they're asleep.* The advent of laboratory monitoring equipment—in particular the EEG (electroencephalogram), which measures brain waves, the EOG (electro-oculogram), which records electric currents from the movements of the eyes, and the EMG (electromyogram), which records muscle tension levels—has helped awaken scientists to many of the mysteries of sleep.

Sleep occurs in cycles, explains Swiss sleep expert Alexander Borbely, author of the book *Secrets of Sleep.* Each cycle consists of several stages. You enter the first stage when you lie down and close your eyes. In transition from waking to sleeping for several minutes, your brain waves grow larger and slower, your eyes begin to roll slowly, and your muscle tension significantly decreases. Moving on to stage two, your brain waves become even larger and slower and your eye and muscle movements continue to lessen. This progression continues into stages three and four, when you enter a state of deep sleep that lasts about 20 minutes.

Then, a sudden change: Your eyes begin to flutter rapidly beneath your eyelids. Your brain waves

LOSING SLEEP CAN BE TORTURE

Can you lose your mind over lost sleep? If the loss is severe enough, yes. Actor Laurence Harvey, in the film *The Manchurian Candidate,* played a prisoner of war transformed into a cold-hearted assassin by Chinese captors who were able to brainwash him after forcefully depriving him of sleep.

The effects of sleep loss worsen the more you lose. Staying up all night to finish a project, for instance, can reduce your judgment and ability to make decisions. Spend two consecutive nights awake and you'll probably feel tense and unmotivated. More than that and you may have hallucinations or become paranoid.

quicken, reasserting the pattern of stage one. But aside from an occasional twitch, your muscles have become completely relaxed. You have entered REM (rapid eye movement) sleep, which lasts from 10 to 40 minutes. During this period, certain higher centers of your brain are very active, with individual brain cells busily firing away. Scientists for the most part believe that it is during REM sleep that you do most of your dreaming, or at least dream most vividly. People awakened during REM sleep report dreams that are much more detailed than those recalled after nonREM sleep.

After a period of REM sleep, the sleep cycle repeats itself. This time you'll skip transitional stage one but again ease your way through stages two, three, and four, then conclude with more REM sleep. As the night wears on, the length of your deep sleep periods decreases but REM sleep increases. You will probably run through four or five cycles in the course of a good night's sleep.

TO SLEEP, PERCHANCE TO SURVIVE

Anything we spend a good third of our lives doing *must* be somehow beneficial to body, mind, and spirit, but scientists still don't understand exactly how. At the very least, surmises Dr. Borbely, perhaps sleep evolved to help us survive nighttime dangers in our environment—like cold and darkness, not to mention sharp-eyed, sharp-clawed predators.

"The purpose of sleep is one of the big 'why' questions to which we certainly don't have the definitive answer," says Arthur Spielman, Ph.D., associate professor of psychology and director of the sleep disorders center at City College of New York. "However, it's quite clear that sleep is necessary to maintain alertness, performance capacity, and good mood the next day."

Not to mention maintaining life itself. Studies of laboratory animals, says Dr. Spielman, have shown that depriving them of sleep for two or three weeks leads to death. Several processes of recovery and regeneration, all of them coordinated by the brain,

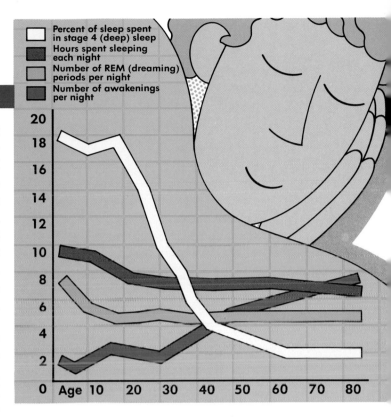

☐	Percent of sleep spent in stage 4 (deep) sleep
■	Hours spent sleeping each night
▨	Number of REM (dreaming) periods per night
▨	Number of awakenings per night

Our sleep patterns change over the years. We sleep as much as 17 hours a day during infancy, but we're down to about 6½ or 7 hours by age 65. Kids wake up less often during the night than adults and have more periods of REM (dream) sleep. Our stage four (deep) sleep changes, too. As kids, about 20 percent of our sleep time is in stage four. As we age, we spend considerably less time in very deep sleep but a larger percentage in REM sleep.

seem to take place during sleep. For example, levels of the "stress hormone" cortisol drop during sleep, while levels of hormones that promote tissue growth and healing rise. One's overall ability to grow may be linked to hormones that are released during the deep sleep stage, Dr. Spielman says. Evidence suggests that children who have sleep disorders that interfere with deep sleep don't follow the normal growth pattern, he says, and their growth may be stunted.

THE SANDMAN . . . AND OTHER THEORIES

Aristotle theorized that sleep results when fumes from food a person has eaten rise to the head, causing drowsiness. A British scientist in the 18th century suggested that work and motion drain "animal spirits" from the body, interfering with the free movement of fluids from the brain to organs and muscles, eventually resulting in sleep.

Scientists today are pursuing a number of more modern explanations, among them:

Rhythmical. Sleep is a biological rhythm, says Margaret Moline, Ph.D., associate professor of physiology in psychiatry at New York Hospital–Cornell Medical Center. An inner clock (or clocks) in your brain signals you with a sense of drowsiness when it thinks you ought to take a snooze, generally twice daily—first in the middle of the afternoon, and then before your regular bedtime (an hour that varies from person to person). But your brain's sleepytime signal doesn't actually control your behavior with the same ease with which it can control your temperature or other daily fluctuations, Dr. Moline points out. "We are often able to override it consciously," she says, as when we decide to stay up for a late movie. Which makes sleep a difficult rhythm to scientifically track, she adds.

Electrical. Scientists have discovered that electrical stimulation of the front of the reticular formation (an extensive network of nerve cells in the brain stem) will instantaneously awaken an animal. Conversely, stimulation of the back of the recticular formation will put an animal to sleep.

Chemical. Some scientists believe sleep may be regulated through the interaction of brain chemicals called monoamines—the neurotransmitters serotonin, noradrenaline, dopamine, and acetylcholine. Others have experimentally linked sleep to a variety of other substances, including factor S (S for sleep) found in cerebrospinal fluid.

A MINIMUM REQUIREMENT?

Though you can't just turn sleep on and off at will, there are ways of ensuring that you get all the sleep your brain and body need. But just how much sleep *do* you need? No universal rule exists, says one sleep

PREVENTIVE NAPPING

Taking a nap can help you counteract some of the effects of losing sleep—especially if you nap *before* you get too tired, according to a study conducted at the Institute of Pennsylvania Hospital.

Researchers kept a group of healthy adults awake for 56 hours except for one 2-hour nap, the timing of which varied from person to person. Those who napped 6 or 18 hours into the experiment—before

they lost too much sleep—performed best on a series of tests. The later the person's nap, the worse the person's performance.

The bottom line: If you're anticipating a long night flight or an all-night work session, plan a preventive nap prior to the big event.

scientist, "In this, as in size of feet, there are big individual differences." Some people can get by on as little as 5 hours of sleep a day, while others require as many as 10. Most people sleep from 7 to 9 hours a day.

You've noticed, though, that you don't always sleep the same number of hours per night. External circumstances can cut into your sleep time, whether it's something you're worrying about, a project you want to finish, or a party that doesn't end till dawn. "You can decrease the amount of time you sleep," says Dr. Spielman, "but there's a price to pay. The composition of your sleep changes, the proportion of nonREM to REM sleep increases. And you'll probably notice some decrease in performance capacity, mood, or alertness the next day."

ACHIEVING SOLID SLUMBER

"Consolidated" sleep is preferable to sleep that is "fragmented," many sleep experts say. In other words, a solid block of sleep is better for you than brief nighttime sleep supplemented by daytime naps. However, Dr. Spielman points out, there are plenty of countries, such as Spain, where people habitually take an afternoon siesta and do just fine. "It's only when somebody has a sleep problem that we assume that napping might be contributing to it," he says.

Insomnia—having a hard time getting to sleep, waking up often or sleeping restlessly, or waking up too early in the morning—is a serious and chronic problem for millions of people. Its causes are many. "As a group, insomniacs seem to feel more stress than good sleepers," notes Dr. Spielman. But just having a cold or the flu can keep you awake, as can taking certain medications.

Sleeping pills, by the way, offer no long-term solution. True, they may help you sleep, says Dr. Spielman, but they actually change the physical form of your sleep. Studies have shown that some medications change brain wave patterns, he says, interfering with deep sleep. Also, repeated use of sleeping pills may produce a kind of daytime hangover, and can become addictively habit forming.

DEEP WATERS = DEEP SLEEP

More than just a relaxing ritual, a warm bath actually fosters deeper sleep—apparently by warming the brain, a pair of scientists in England have discovered.

Up to their chests in steamy bubble baths (the bubbles act as an insulator to keep the water warm), volunteers showed average increases in body temperature of 2°F after 30 minutes. After they were tucked into bed, night-long EEG monitoring showed a greater quantity of the slow brain waves that characterize deep sleep. The subjects were also able to fall asleep more quickly than they could previously.

Try this sleep-enhancing soak no more than 2 hours before bedtime. More time than that between bath and bed lessens the effects, the researchers found.

A number of more natural approaches can contribute to solid slumber, according to the Association of Sleep Disorders Centers and other experts.
- Exercise regularly. The best times are in the morning or late afternoon but never right before bed. (Sex at bedtime, though, can enhance sleep.)
- Cut evening caffeine and alcohol. Caffeine has a stimulating effect on your nervous system. Alcohol, on the other hand, is a sedative but wears off after several hours and may wake you up in the middle of the night.

BREAKING YOUR DREAM'S SECRET CODE

That guardian angel you dreamed about last night represented a spiritual leader who regulates the processes of your psyche. A dream child suggests a new attitude toward life, while a bomb refers to danger or something shocking. At least that's what some dream interpreters would claim.

But interpreting your dreams is not really that simple, says psychoanalyst Robert Langs, M.D. Author of the book *Decoding Your Dreams,* Dr. Langs says that the meaning of our dreams is unique to every one of us.

"Paying attention to your dreams is like having a private counselor inside of you," Dr. Langs says. The problem is, the counselor often appears in disguise and speaks in code.

A daily routine outlined by Dr. Langs can help you recognize the real meaning behind your disguised dreams. For starters, take time alone in a quiet room, preferably first thing in the morning, to review your dream. (Not everyone, by the way, has a knack for remembering dreams. There's nothing wrong with you if you don't, Dr. Langs says.)

A Party with a Problem

First, think about your dream's cast of characters and setting. Let's say you dreamed of being alone at home getting ready to go to a party.

Next, look at the obvious themes that situation suggests, such as how well you were coping, and what needs and conflicts you were experiencing. You may have been looking forward to having fun at the party, for instance, but you couldn't decide what to wear. By the time you worked your way through every item in the closet, you were sweaty, panicky...and late for the party. You were absolutely certain that none of your clothes looked right. Now ask yourself how these things might touch on past events—like a difficult childhood with an overcritical parent, for instance.

Most important, says Dr. Langs, is finding your dream's "triggers," situations in your current life that might have prompted the dream—recent feelings of depression, for instance. Finally, spend a few minutes "free associating," allowing whatever comes to your mind to do so whether or not it seems connected to your dream. This stream of thought may give you insight into your dream's true meaning: If you find yourself thinking about how you spend just about every weekend cleaning your house, you may suddenly realize that constantly worrying about appearances makes you depressed and prevents you from freely enjoying life.

Interpreting your dreams takes effort, but it's well worth it, Dr. Langs says.

HARNESS YOUR DREAMPOWER

There's a lot more to dreaming than lying back and seeing what happens, say some dream experts who believe we can actively put our dreams to work for us.

"Dreams can be effectively used to improve our daily lives," says Harry Fiss, Ph.D., director of psychology at the University of Connecticut Health Center. Dr. Fiss conducted "dream immersion" research with psychiatric patients who had reached an impasse in their treatment. Each patient was asked to think about his or her biggest problem and to try to dream about it that night. The patients were awakened during REM periods to tape-record recollections of their dreams, and the recordings were played back to them throughout the next day. After a week, says Dr. Fiss, the patients made dramatic breakthroughs in self-awareness and symptom reduction.

One extremely passive and dependent patient, for instance, dreamed that he killed a lion in a lion hunt. "The next day," says Dr. Fiss, "he really was like a lion, being very assertive and taking care of things most uncharacteristically."

Anyone can put his dreams to work by following a simple process, says psychologist Gayle Delaney, Ph.D., author of the book *Living Your Dreams*.

Begin by "incubating" the problem you want to work on, writing it out in one sentence on a piece of paper. Turn out the light and repeat the sentence again and again as you fall asleep.

"This is so easy—so boring, actually—that it puts you to sleep very quickly," Dr. Delaney says.

When you wake up in the middle of the night or in the morning, write down whatever is on your mind, whether it's a dream or not. Don't be surprised if you get your answer immediately, Dr. Delaney says. "One woman asked, 'Where is my relationship with George going?' In her dream, George asked her to join him on a voyage. 'What's the name of the ship?' the woman asked him. 'The *Titanic*,' he answered."

● Beware of bright lights. Light triggers your brain to wake you in the morning. And at night, bright light may keep you awake, says Dr. Moline. "If a person happens to expose herself to bright light at bedtime, she may shift her rhythms inadvertently."

● Don't worry. Make an effort to be happy and leave your troubles behind. And certainly don't worry about whether or not you'll be able to sleep.

LEARN WHILE YOU SLEEP

There appears to be no single "center" of sleep in the brain, says Dr. Borbely. But one thing is for certain: The brain is as active while we sleep as it is while we're awake. "Our brain does not sleep when we do," he says.

That's why the hours you spend sleeping may be a key time for expanding the powers of your mind, say some researchers. Sleep appears to play an active role in helping us learn and cope with problems, they say.

You might be able to better remember something you recently learned—like all those facts and figures you need to memorize for a meeting tomorrow—if you go to sleep a couple of hours after you learn them. If you stay awake, your recall begins to sharply decline.

"It appears that the work of processing and storing new information into long-term memory continues during sleep," says researcher Rosalind Cartwright, Ph.D., author of the book *Night Life*. This seems to happen even more efficiently if you sleep long enough to get a period of REM—or dream—sleep. (Some sleep experts believe, in fact, that the whole purpose of dreams is to integrate new experiences with understandings of the world from as far back as childhood. Others, claim that dreams are simply caused by chemical activities in the brain.)

REM sleep may also help take some of the emotional stress out of your life. In one study, subjects were shown a stress-producing movie and then allowed to sleep. Some were awakened before REM dream periods, while others were allowed REM sleep. Later, when shown the movie a second time, those who had REM sleep showed less stress reaction to the movie than those who were REM-deprived.

Keep your eyes peeled for more fascinating findings in this field—that is, when you're not closing them tight, fast asleep.

WISDOM

Suppose two women came to you, each claiming the same infant as her own. Would you be as wise as King Solomon?

Today, a judge in the same position might order a blood test rather than suggest cutting the infant in half. "But certainly a large measure of wisdom—today as in biblical times—is the ability to solve tough problems," says Gerald S. Held, a Justice of the Supreme Court of the State of New York.

What other qualities make up wisdom? This has been a burning question for generations of philosophers. The Greek sage Aristotle stoked the debate with the contention that wisdom was knowledge about the highest and most fundamental of things, such as the nature of the universe and ethical matters.

Even before Aristotle, ancient Jewish thought held wisdom to be "knowledge beyond knowledge . . . understanding," says Rabbi Yitzchak Rosenbaum, teacher of rabbinical studies at New York's Rabbi Isaac Elchanan Theological Seminary. Adding his own thoughts on the matter, wisdom, he says, is a combination of "intelligence, a broad education, and strong common sense."

But according to another source, wisdom is whatever can fit onto two or three lines of print and doesn't give you indigestion after a Chinese meal. So says Yong Lee, a Massachusetts businessman who provides fortunes to fortune cookie bakeries nationwide.

Certainly wisdom, like beauty, is largely in the eye (or cookie) of the beholder. But by almost anyone's definition, the wise seem to share at least a few traits.

SIGNS OF A SAGE

The wise are those to whom others turn instinctively for advice, says Donald Montagna, a leader of the Ethical Society in Washington, D.C., a religious and educational fellowship that sees ethics as its core. People are drawn to the wise, he says, for their cleverness and their honesty. The wise really have to be honest, for "if someone lives by lies and deceit, he gets to where he can no longer tell falsehood from truth," says Montagna.

The wise also tend to be serene, says Rabbi Rosenbaum. He tells of the legend of Zuche, a wise but terribly poor rabbi, whose wife was forever nagging and yelling at him. One day a student came to

SOME WORDS FROM THE WISE

It isn't necessary to blow out the other person's light to let your own shine.

—CONFUCIUS

The optimist proclaims that we live in the best of all possible worlds; and the pessimist fears this is true.

—JAMES BRANCH CABELL

Many wealthy people are little more than the janitors of their possessions.

—FRANK LLOYD WRIGHT

Experience is a good school. But the fees are high.

—HEINRICH HEINE

Nearly all men can stand adversity, but if you want to test a man's character, give him power.

—ABRAHAM LINCOLN

No one can make you feel inferior without your consent.

—ELEANOR ROOSEVELT

You cannot shake hands with a closed fist.

—INDIRA GANDHI

A friend is one who knows all about you and still likes you.

—MARK TWAIN

Beware of little expenses: A small leak will sink a great ship.

—BENJAMIN FRANKLIN

Television has proved that people will look at anything rather than each other.

—ANN LANDERS

Distrust all men in whom the impulse to punish is powerful.

—FRIEDRICH NIETZSCHE

More than just an impressive face on a five-cent coin, Thomas Jefferson was a scientist, philosopher, architect, inventor, geographer, and, of course, President of the United States. He was also the epitome of wisdom. "Enlighten the people generally, and tyranny and oppressions of body and mind will vanish like evil spirits at the dawn of day," he wrote. To that end, he penned the Declaration of Independence, championed the Bill of Rights, and worked unceasingly to establish his democratic ideals.

Zuche and asked "How does a person develop tolerance for the difficult things in life?" Zuche responded: "*I* should tell you? My life is terrific!"

And the wise are compassionate, says Sensei Daido Loori, a Zen Buddhist teacher and spiritual director at the Zen Mountain Monastery in Mount Tremper, New York. They feel a sense of unity with their fellow men."Compassion," he says, "is the activity of wisdom on Earth." In Buddhism, Master Loori adds, wisdom may be defined as "the realization of union with all of the universe."

How does one realize union with the universe? Is wisdom within *your* grasp? The experts unanimously agree that, yes, wisdom is yours for the *earning*.

THE ROAD TO WISDOM

"Having wise parents who provided an environment conducive to exploration and learning certainly is helpful. But if you didn't have that environment, it's never too late to create one for yourself," advises Justice Held.

Most modern education is overly specialized, often relying on memorization and regurgitation of facts. But wisdom comes from a variety of learning experiences.

"Meditation is at the bottom of wisdom," says Master Loori. "Meditation creates a quieting of the mind . . . a point of stillness. It's out of this point that wisdom comes."

Confucius believed that wisdom started with humility. "The person who knows everything has a lot to learn," said the ancient Chinese prophet.

Along similar lines, the wise person knows that he has something to learn from everyone, and never stops learning, says Rabbi Rosenbaum. The road to wisdom, he says, can be traveled by "keeping your eyes open, your ears open—and often—your mouth shut."

And should two women come to you claiming the same infant? *Do not* suggest cutting the baby in half, says Justice Held. After all, had Solomon's bluff been called, it's highly unlikely he would have gone down in history as a model of wisdom.

SOURCES & CREDITS

SOURCE NOTES

Aging and Your Brain

page 12

"Puzzle Power" created by Stanley Newman

Alertness

page 15

"Asleep at the Wheel," adapted from "Acute Effects of Meals on Perceptual and Cognitive Efficiency," by Angus Craig, D. Phil., *Nutrition Reviews/Supplement,* May 1986, p. 163.

Creativity

page 30

"Creative Games," from *Creative Growth Games,* by Eugene Raudsepp and George P. Hough, Jr. (New York: Putnam Publishing Group, 1977), pp. 22, 28, 106, 107, 113. (Reprinted with permission of the publisher.)

page 32

"How Creative Are You?," from *Creating Excellence,* by Craig R. Hickman and Michael A. Silva (New York: Penguin Books, 1984), p.

109. (Copyright 1984 by Craig R. Hickman and Michael A. Silva. Reprinted by arrangement with New American Library, a division of Penguin Books USA, Inc., New York, NY.)

Diseases of the Brain

page 46

"Aspirin Reverses Stroke Mind Damage," from *Medical World News,* March 28, 1988, vol. 29, no. 6, p. 16.

page 47

"Better Diagnosis, Better Treatment," from "A New Approach to Stroke Management," by John Rothrock, M.D., Barbara T. Taft, R.N., P.A.-C., and Patrick D. Lyden, M.D., University of California, San Diego, California, in *American Family Physician,* October 1987, p. 195.

Gender and Your Brain

page 55

Graph adapted from "Mean SAT Scores for College Bound Seniors: 1967–1987" from *1987 Profile of SAT and Achievement Test Takers,*

ANSWERS

CROSSWORD SOLUTION

CREATIVITY GAME ANSWERS

1. The answer to this puzzle illustrates how the unconscious rules we carry with us inhibit our problem-solving ability. Most people cannot exceed the imaginary square-shaped boundary of the dots, though no restrictions on boundaries were ever part of the problem as posed.

2. Many people see this as a problem of reach, asking themselves, "How can I get to the second string?" The secret lies in asking "How can the string and I get together?" Put that way, it may occur to you to tie a key, ring, or other object to one string and set it swinging. Then you can grab it while still holding the other.

REAL COUPLES REVEALED

Did you guess which couples from page 93 were romantically involved and which couples had just met? The middle two couples are real couples; they are romantically involved. The couples at the top and bottom of the page are not; they're total strangers.

Educational Testing Service, College Entrance Examination Board, 1987, p. iii.

Intelligence

page 88

"IQ Is Inflating" adapted from "The Means of Americans: Massive Gains 1932 to 1978" by J.R. Flynn, *Psychological Bulletin,* vol. 95, p. 45. (Copyright 1984 by the American Psychological Association, Inc.)

page 93

"Couples in Intelligence" adapted from *Intelligence Applied: Understanding and Increasing Your Intellectual Skill,* by Robert J. Sternberg, Ph.D. (New York: Harcourt Brace Jovanovich, 1986), pp. 303–15.

Intuition

pages 96–97

"How Intuitive Are You?" from *The Intuitive Edge: Understanding and Developing Intuition,* by Philip Goldberg (Los Angeles: Jeremy P. Tarcher, 1983), pp. 110–13. (Reprinted with permission of the publisher.)

Medications and Your Brain

page 111

"A Bum Steer" statistics from Concensus Conference on Prescription and Nonprescription Drugs, Booklet #3, "Effects on Driving Performance," edited by James F. O'Hanlon

(Princeton Junction, N.J.: Communications Media for Education, Inc., 1985), p. 6.

pages 112–113

"Drugs That Tamper with Your Mind" from *The Essential Guide to Prescription Drugs,* 1988 Edition, by James W. Long, M.D. (New York: Harper & Row, 1988), pp. 927–39. (Reprinted with permission of the publisher.)

Meditation

page 114

"Turn on Some Concentrated Brainpower" from *TM: Discovering Inner Energy and Overcoming Stress,* by Harold H. Bloomfield, M.D., Michael Peter Cain, and Dennis T. Jaffe in collaboration with Robert Bruce Kory (New York: Delacorte Press, 1975), Chart #5.

Memory

page 116

"Test Your Spatial Memory" from *The Rand McNally Atlas of the Body and Mind* (London: Mitchell Beazley Publishers, 1976), p. 131. (Reprinted with permission of the publisher.)

page 126

"Sight, Sound, or Touch— Which Turns Your Memory On?" adapted from *Total Recall,* by Joan Minninger, Ph.D. (Emmaus, Pa.: Rodale Press, 1984), pp. 106–9.

page 127

"Answers" from *The Rand McNally Atlas of the Body and Mind* (London: Mitchell Beazley Publishers, 1976), p. 201. (Reprinted with permission of the publisher.)

Nutrition and Your Brain

page 140

Chart statistics from "Association Between Nutritional Status and Cognitive Functioning in a Healthy Elderly Population," by James S. Goodwin, M.D., Jean M. Goodwin, M.D., M.P.H., and Philip J. Garry, Ph.D., *JAMA,* June 3, 1983, vol. 249, no. 21, p. 2919.

page 143

"Wrongfully Accused" statistics from "Types of Offenses Which Can Be Reduced in an Institutional Setting Using Nutritional Intervention: A Preliminary Empirical Evaluation," by Stephen J. Schoenthaler, Ph.D., and Walter E. Doraz, Ph.D., *The International Journal for Biosocial Research,* 1983, vol. 4, no. 2, p. 78.

Reasoning

page 154

Algorithm flow chart adapted from *Take Care of Yourself: A Consumer's Guide to Medical Care,* 3d ed., by Donald Vickery, M.D., and James Fries, M.D. (Reading, Mass.: Addison Wesley Publishing Company, 1986), p. 263.

Sleep

page 163

Chart adapted from *Electroencephalography (EEG) of Human Sleep: Clinical Applications,* by Robert L. Williams, Ismet Karacan, and Carolyn J. Hursch (New York: John Wiley and Sons, 1974), pp. 75, 77–78, 86.

PHOTOGRAPHY CREDITS

Cover: Angelo Caggiano

Staff Photographers: Angelo Caggiano: pp. 7, right; 9; 53; 67; 103, bottom; 109; 148; 164. Carl Doney: pp. 54; 64. John P. Hamel: pp. 101; 139. Mitchell T. Mandel: pp. 63; 98; 142; 165. Sally Shenk Ullman: pp. 6, left; 24;–25; 26;–27; 28;–29; 89; 117; 136; 137; 156;–57.

Other Photographers: Eric Lars Bakke: pp. 81; 118;–19. Burton Berinsky: p. 155. Brian Brake/Science Source/Photo Researchers, Inc.: p. 50. Mike Brown/ Gamma-Liaison: p. 119, top. Dan Budnik/Woodfin Camp and Associates: p. 11, bottom. Bill Coleman: p. 31. T. D. Friedman/Photo Researchers, Inc.: p. 58. Peter T. Furst: p. 158. John Gichigi/Allsport: p. 52. Ziggy Kaluzny/Gamma-Liaison: p. 11, top. Michael A. Keller/FPG International: p. 130. J. P. Laffont/Sygma: p. 59. Acey Lee: p. 83, top. Christopher Morris/Black

Star: p. 83, bottom. Terry Murphy/Animals Animals: p. 16. Pariseau/Edwards Communication, Inc.: p. 115. Photogram by Diane Petku, Debbie Sfetsios, and Margaret Skrovanek: p. 151. David Redfern/Retna Ltd.: p. 129. Anthony Rodale: p. 82, right. Galen Rowell/ Mountain Light: p. 23. Bonnie Schiffman/Onyx: p. 134. Paul Von Stroheim/ The Stock Shop: p. 65. Anthony Suau/Black Star: p. 82, left. George Tames/ NYT Pictures: pp. 38;–39. Scott Thode/U.S. News & World Report: p. 131. David York/Medichrome: p. 156, left. Tom Zimberoff/ Gamma-Liaison: p. 14. J. Zimmerman/FPG International: p. 49.

Additional Photographs Courtesy of: Academic Press, Inc., from *Nadia: A Case of Extraordinary Drawing Ability in an Autistic Child,* by Lorna Selfe, copyright 1977 by Academic Press, Inc., Ltd. (London), reprinted by permission of the publisher: p. 57, left. The Bettmann Archive: pp. 87, left; 169. Capital Cities ABC, Inc.: p. 124. Dr. Richard Coppola/National Institute of Mental Health: p. 43. Cordon Art, from *The Magic Mirror of M. C. Escher,* by Bruno Ernst, p. 71, copyright 1988 by M. C. Escher Heirs (Cordon Art-Baarn, Holland): pp. 160–61. Culver Pictures: pp. 33; 87, inset, right; 90,

right; 91, left; 162. DDB Needham Worldwide, Creative Director/Writer: David Lewis; Art Directors: Debby DiPrizio and Jim Nawrocki; Producer: Greg Popp: pp. 36;–37. Focus on Sports: p. 146. Four By Five, Inc.: p. 95. Harcourt Brace Jovanovich, Inc., from *Intelligence Applied,* by Robert J. Sternberg and Jerome Kagan, copyright 1986 by Harcourt Brace Jovanovich, Inc. (New York), reprinted by permission of the publisher: p. 93. Scripps Howard: p. 22. Lyn Jones: p. 84. Princess Yasmin Aga Khan: p. 41. The Mobius Society: p. 150. Movie Star News: p. 147. Movie Still Archives: p. 121. National Institute of Mental Health: p. 45. Shady Grove Adventist Hospital: p. 66. The Sharper Image: p. 20. Michele Szoka: p. 103, top and middle. UCSD Medical Center: p. 47. University of Washington, St. Louis, copyright 1989 Discover Publications: p. 6, right; 79. UPI/ Bettmann Newsphotos: pp. 90, left; 91, right. U. S. Postal Inspection Service, Forensic and Technical Services Division: p. 120. Windsor Castle, Royal Library, Her Majesty Queen Elizabeth II: p. 57, top right.

Photographic Stylists: Barbara Fritz: pp. 136; 137. Renee R. Keith: pp. 24;–29; 64. Pamela Simpson: pp. 89; 117; 156;–57. Troy Schnyder: pp. 63; 151; 164; 165.

ILLUSTRATION CREDITS

Jean- François Allaux: pp. 77; 144. Karen Barbour: pp. 70: 71. Laura Cornell: pp. 34; 125; 153; 159. Robert Dominguez: p. 107 (illustration reprinted from *Drawing on the Right Side of the Brain,* by Betty Edwards [Los Angeles: J. P. Tarcher, Inc., 1979] p. 107, reprinted with permission of the publisher). Mellisa Edmonds: pp. 32; 74; 75 (illustration adapted from *Principles of Anatomy and Physiology,* 4th ed., by Gerald Tortora and Nicholas P. Anagnostakos [New York: Harper & Row, 1984], p. 239, copyright 1984 by Biological Sciences Textbooks, Inc., Anatomy and Physiology Textbooks, Inc., and Elia Sparta, Inc.); 157. Leslie Flis: pp. 15; 46; 55; 88; 111; 140; 143; 163. Carol Gillot: pp. 60;–61; 100; 149. Narda Lebo: pp. 17; 48; 73; 76; 94; 132;–33. George Masi: pp. 96; 104; 122;–23. Susan Rosenberger: pp. 6;–7; 18;–19; 141. Jason Simonds: p. 35. Kurt Vargo: pp. 7, left; 21; 166. Wallop: pp. 68;–69; 99.

Special Thanks to:
Barclay Booksellers, Emmaus, Pa.; Danskin; Everything Goes Furniture, Allentown, Pa.; Gateway Institute, St. Luke's Hospital, Bethlehem, Pa.; Dr. Denis Gorges; Kahle's Music, Emmaus, Pa.; Recreations

Maternity, Columbus, Ohio; Sherwood's Furniture, Emmaus, Pa.; West End Music, Allentown, Pa.

INDEX

Note: Page references in **boldface** indicate tables.

Disorientation, drugs causing, **112**
Dopamine, 132, **133,** 134, 135
    Parkinson's disease and, 43, 44, 145
    schizophrenia and, 45
    sleep and, 164
Drawing, brain hemispheres and, 107
Dreams, 166, 167
Drugs. *See* Medications
Dynorphins, 50, 133, **133**

E

Education, creativity and, 35
EEG (electroencephalogram) 162, 165
Einstein's brain, 56
Elderly. *See* Aging
Electroencephalogram. *See* EEG
Electromagnetism, 149
Electromyogram, 162
Electro-oculogram, 162
Elephant behavior, 16
Emotions
    facial expressions and, 82–83
    limbic system and, 76–77, 82
    problem solving by, 25–26
Endorphins, 50–51, 132, 133, **133**
Enkephalins, 50, **133**
Epilepsy, 42–43, 80, 105–6
Epinephrine. *See* Adrenaline
ESP, 148–51
Euphoria, drugs causing, **113**
Excitement, drugs causing, **113**
Exercise
    aging and, 13
    brain and, 52–53
    endorphins released by, 51
    sleep and, 165
Exploration, problem solving by, 28
Extroversion, dopamine causing, 132, **133,** 134

F

Face, 82–83, 103
Factor S, 164
Facts and figures, problem solving by, 24–25
Family, 66
Fasting, 144

Fat, dietary, 47, 139–40
Fear, concentration and, 22
Folate, 13, 142
Food, mood affected by, 135
Food allergies, 142
Forgetfulness, 122
Friendship, 59, 66
Frontal lobe, 80, 81
Fruit, 143

G

GABA (gamma-aminobutyric acid), **133,** 134
Gender
    brain and, 54–55
    intuition and, 95
Genetics, personality and, 146, 147
Genius, 56–57
Glial cells, 56, 76
Glucose, 135
Glycine, **133**
Gorilla, intelligence of, 16, 17
Growth of premature infants, 156

H

Halcion, 110
Hallucinations, 158
Hamilton, Scott, 146
Hayworth, Rita, 41
Head injury, 48–49
Healing power of brain, 58–71
    mechanism of, 62–64
Health, music and, 128, 129
Hearing, 80, 157–58
    loss of, 13
    ways to sharpen, 160
Heart disease, 13
Hemispheres of cerebrum, 79–80, 102–9
Hemorrhagic stroke, 46, 47
Heuristics, 20–21
Hill, Napoleon, 87
Holmes, Sherlock, 152
Hormones, 54, 163
Hospital rooms, view from, 63
Hunger, 74
Huntington's disease, 13
Hypnosis, 84–85
Hypnotherapist, 85
Hypothalamus, 13, 74

I

Imagery, 67–71
Imagination, 86–87
Immunity, 61, 68
Infants, premature, 156
Information processing, concentration for, 22
Insomnia, 165
Intelligence, 88–93
    artificial, 20–21
    in children, 89
    tests, 88–89, 92
Interest, memory and, 119
Interpersonal intelligence, 91
Intrapersonal intelligence, 91
Intuition, 94–97
    decision making and, 39
    problem solving by, 25–26
    quiz on, 96–97
IQ, 56, 88–89, 144
Iron, 142–43
Irritability, drugs causing, **113**
Ischemic stroke, 46, 47

J

Jet lag, 15

K

Kinesthetic intelligence, 91
Kinesthetic memory, 126, 127
Knowledge, wisdom and, 169

L

Language
    left brain and, 102–3
    reasoning and, 154–55
Laughter, 62, 66
L-dopa, 44, 145
Learning, 98–101, 169
    best environment for, 99
Lecithin, 140, 141
Left brain, 102–3
Levodopa, 44, 145
Limbic system, 76–77, 82, 159
Linguistic intelligence, 90
Lobes, of brain, 80–81
Logical errors, problem solving and, 27–28
Logical intelligence, 90

Rodale Press, Inc., publishes PREVENTION, America's leading health magazine.
For information on how to order your subscription,
write to PREVENTION, Emmaus, PA 18098.